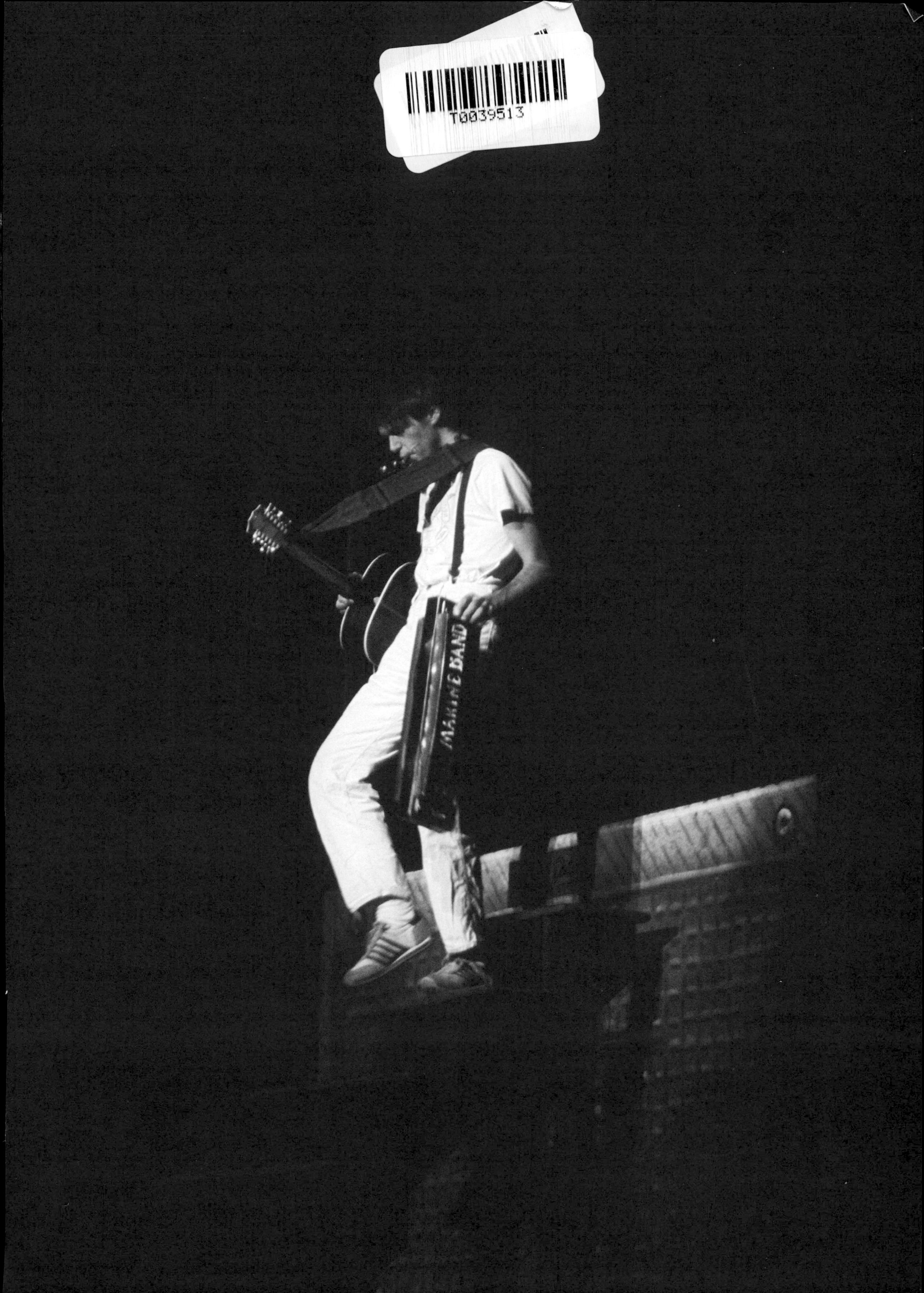
MARINE BAND

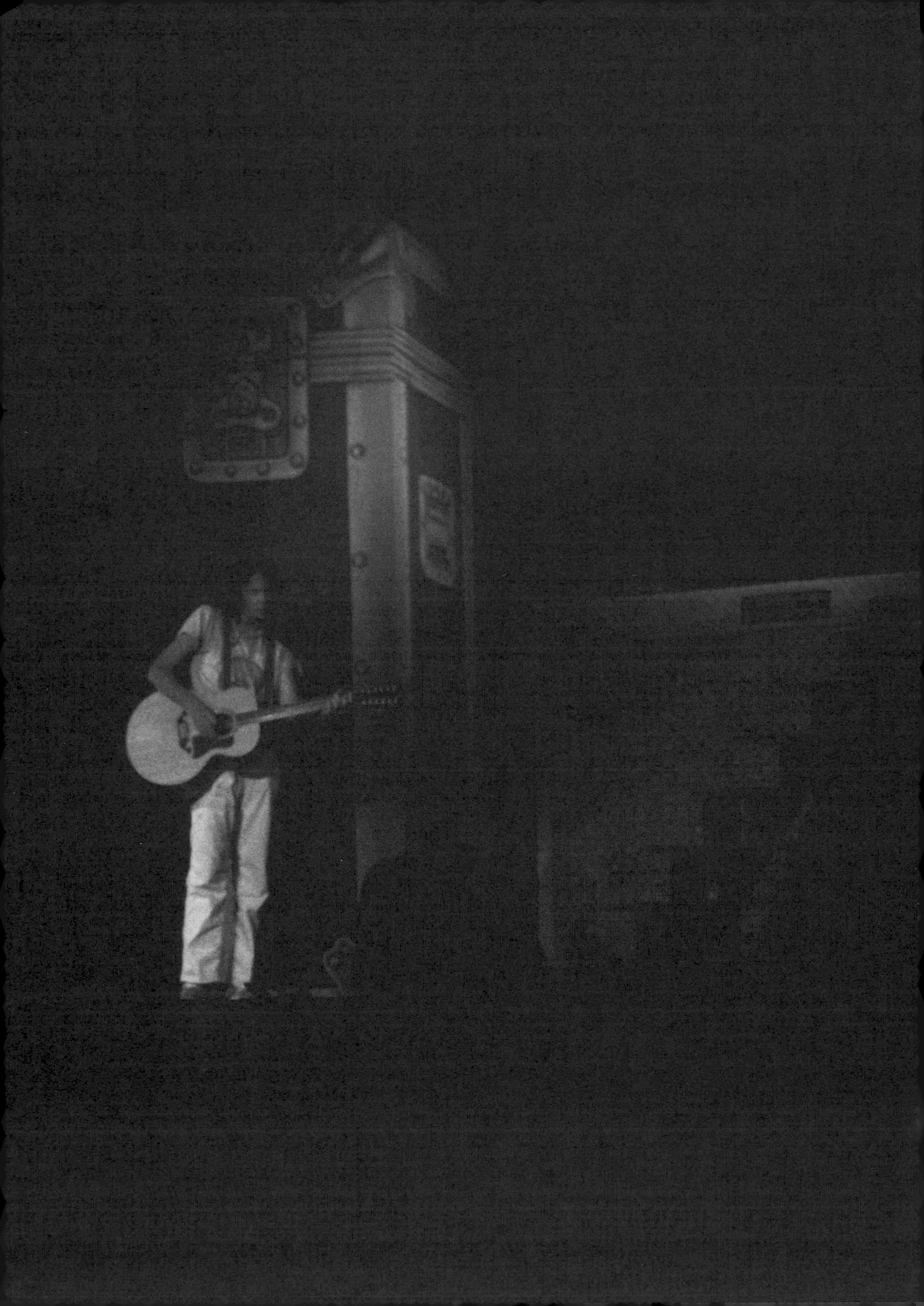

RECORDED VERSIONS GUITAR

AUTHENTIC TRANSCRIPTIONS WITH NOTES AND TABLATURE

NEIL YOUNG & CRAZY HORSE

RUST NEVER SLEEPS

Music transcriptions by Addi Booth

ISBN: 978-1-4234-3122-0

HAL•LEONARD® CORPORATION
7777 W. BLUEMOUND RD. P.O. BOX 13819 MILWAUKEE, WI 53213

In Australia Contact:
Hal Leonard Australia Pty. Ltd.
4 Lentara Court, Cheltenham, Victoria, 3192 Australia
Email: ausadmin@halleonard.com.au

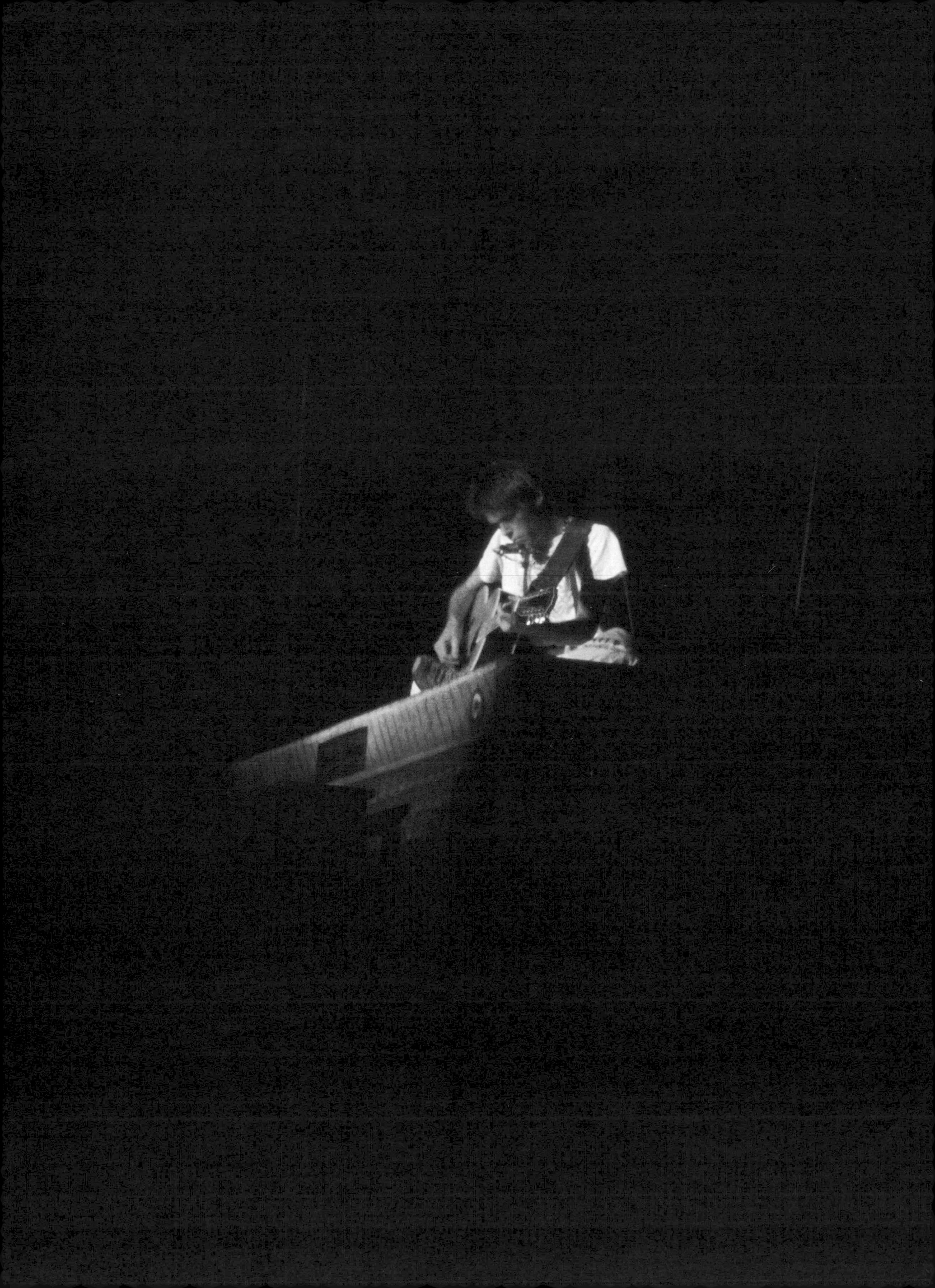

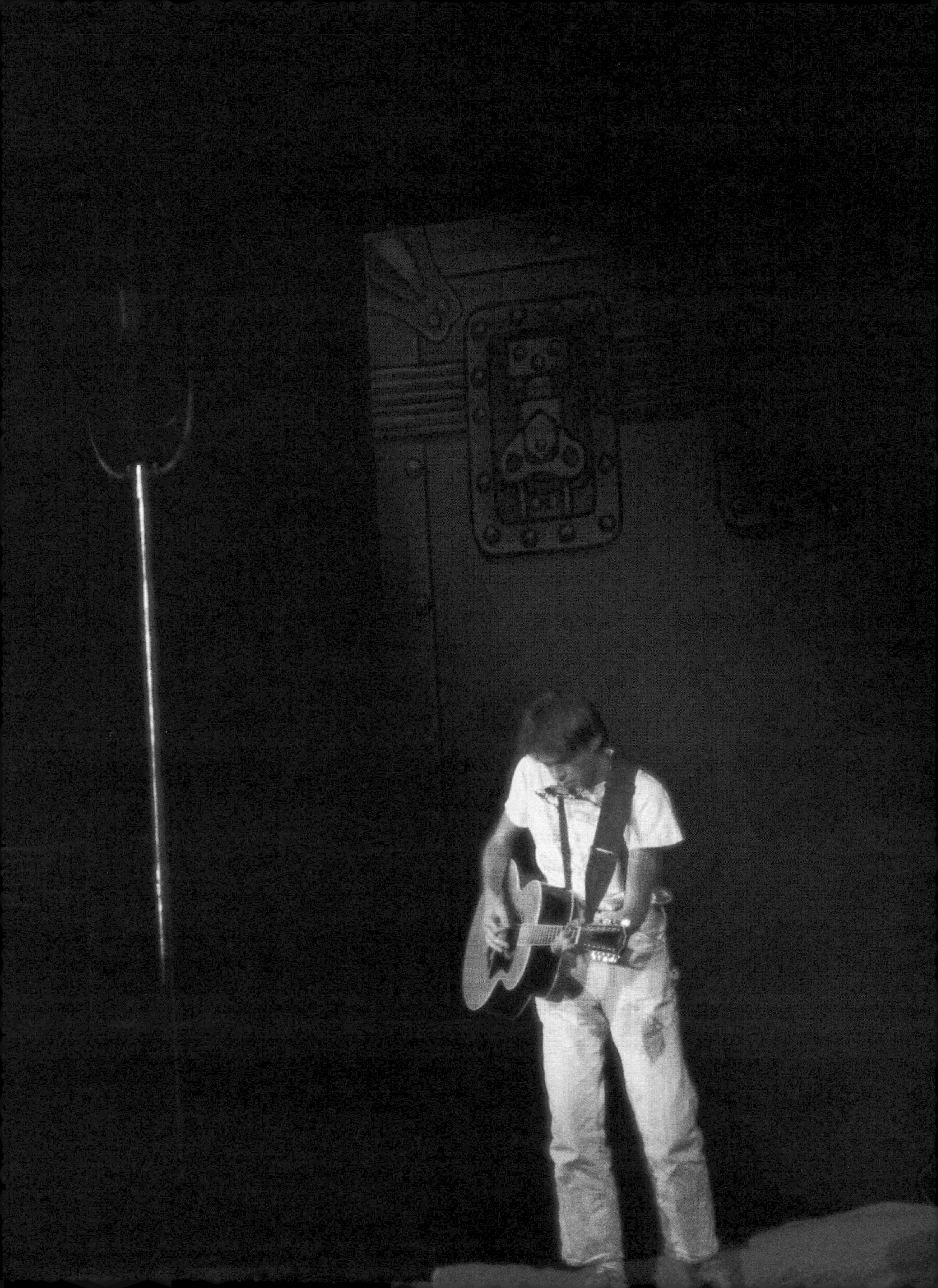

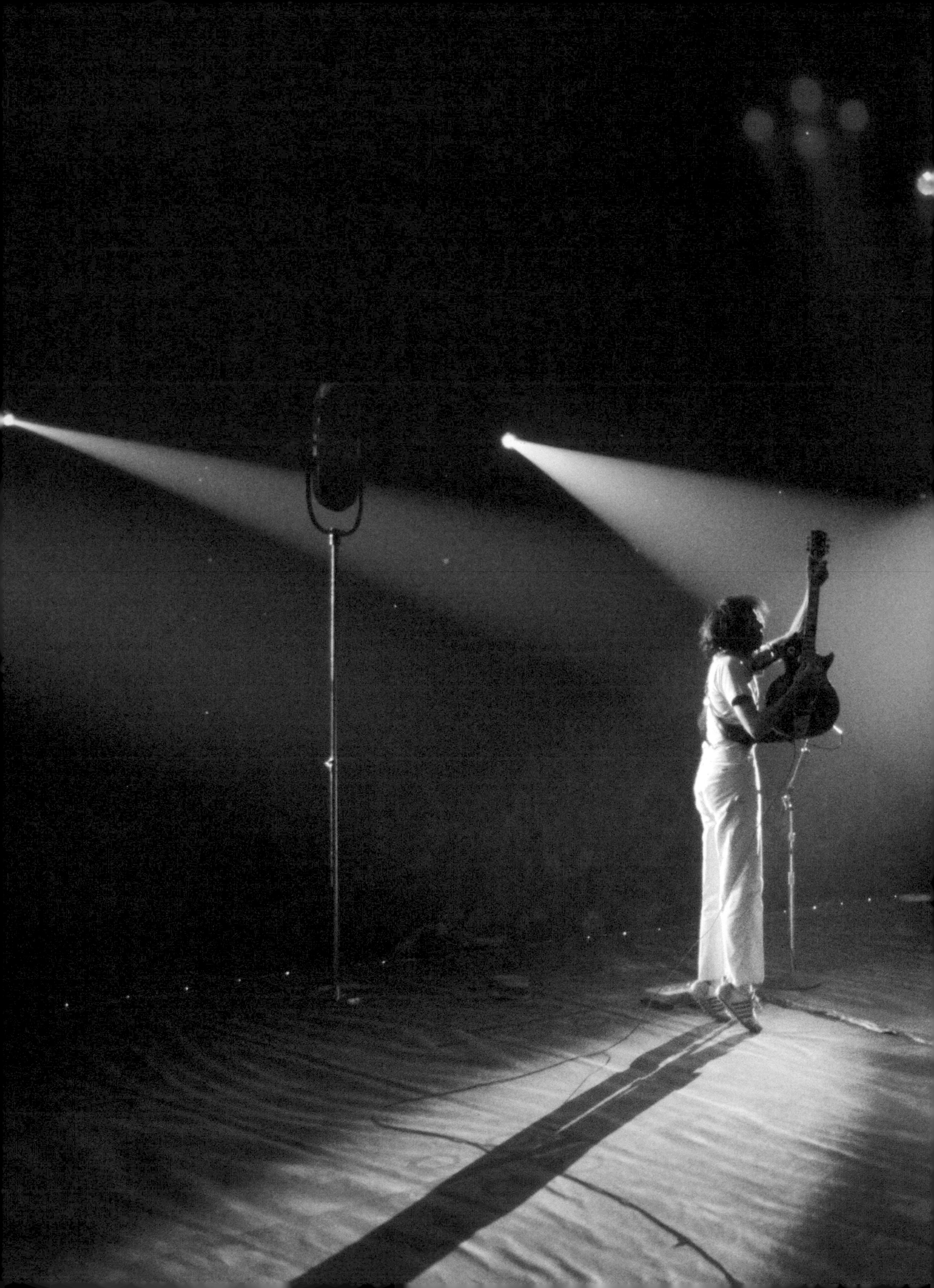

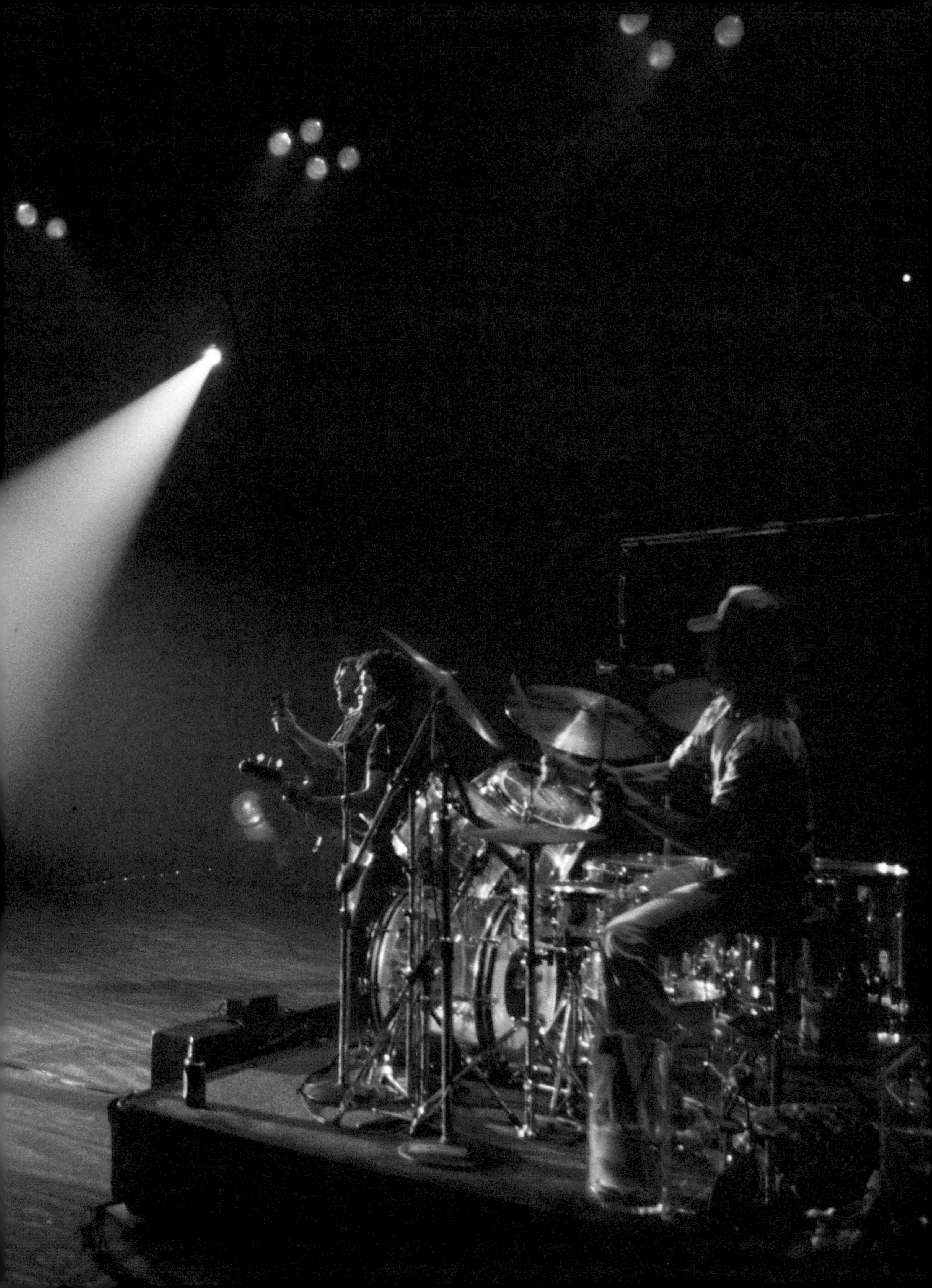

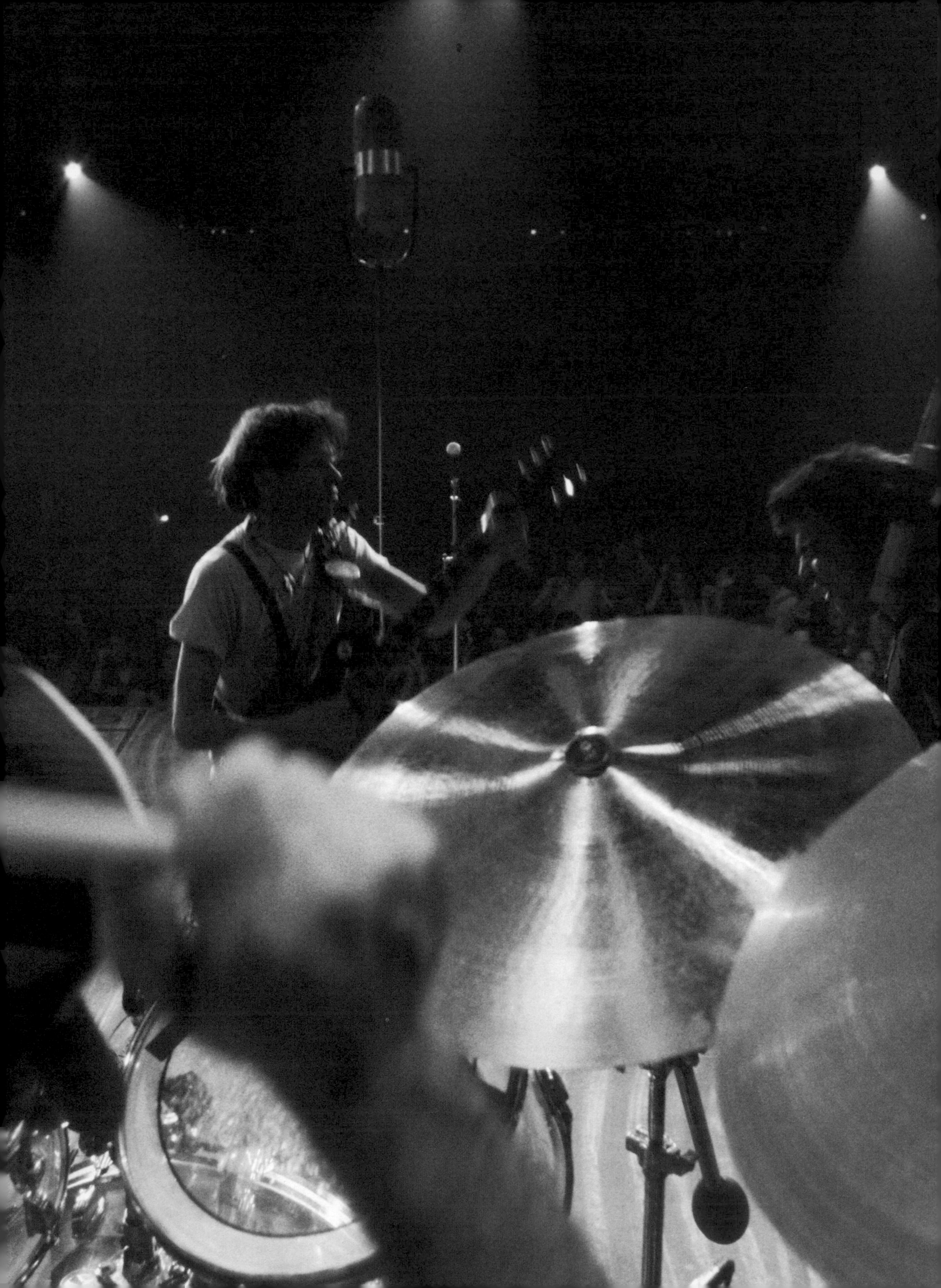

MY MY, HEY HEY
(OUT OF THE BLUE)

Words and Music by Neil Young & Jeff Blackburn

My my, hey hey
Rock and roll is here to stay
It's better to burn out
Than to fade away
My my, hey hey

It's out of the blue and into the black
They give you this, but you pay for that
And once you're gone you can never come back
When you're out of the blue
And into the black

The king is gone but he's not forgotten
This is the story of a Johnny Rotten
It's better to burn out than it is to rust
The king is gone but he's not forgotten

Hey hey, my my
Rock and roll can never die
There's more to the picture
Than meets the eye

My My, Hey Hey
(Out of the Blue)

Words and Music by Neil Young and Jeff Blackburn

Tune down 1 step:
(low to high) D-G-C-F-A-D

Intro

Moderately ♩ = 125

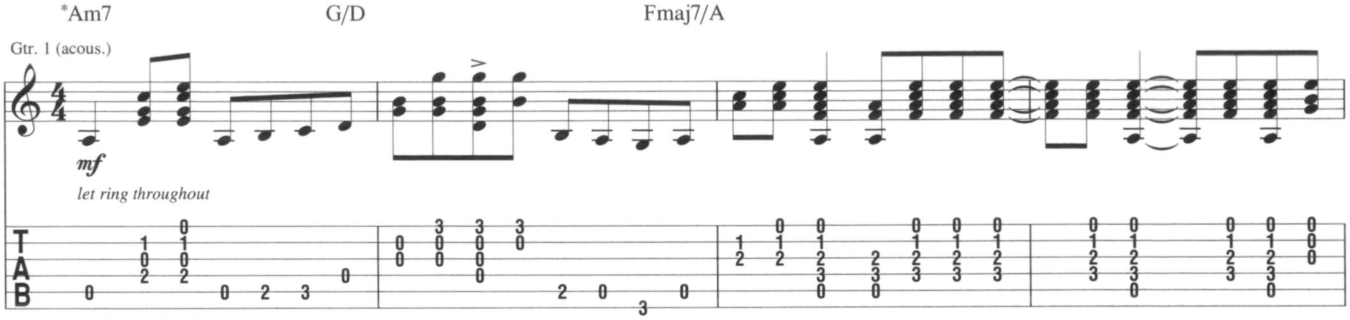

*Chord symbols reflect basic harmony.

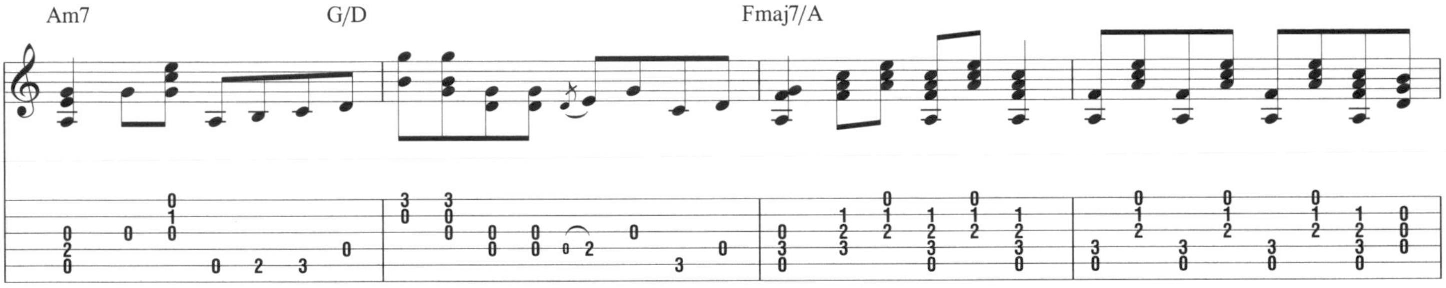

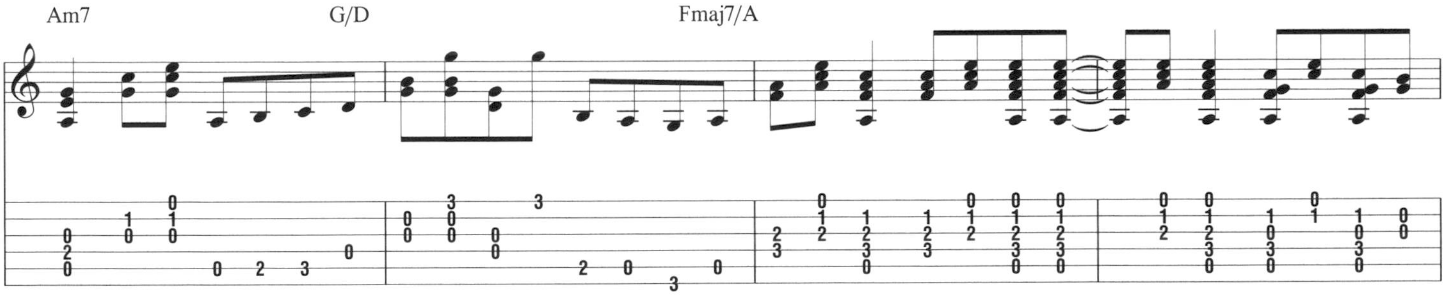

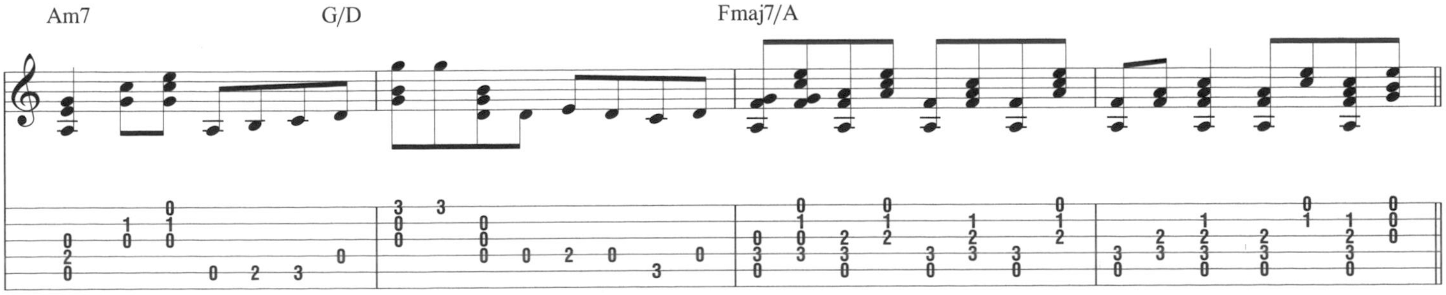

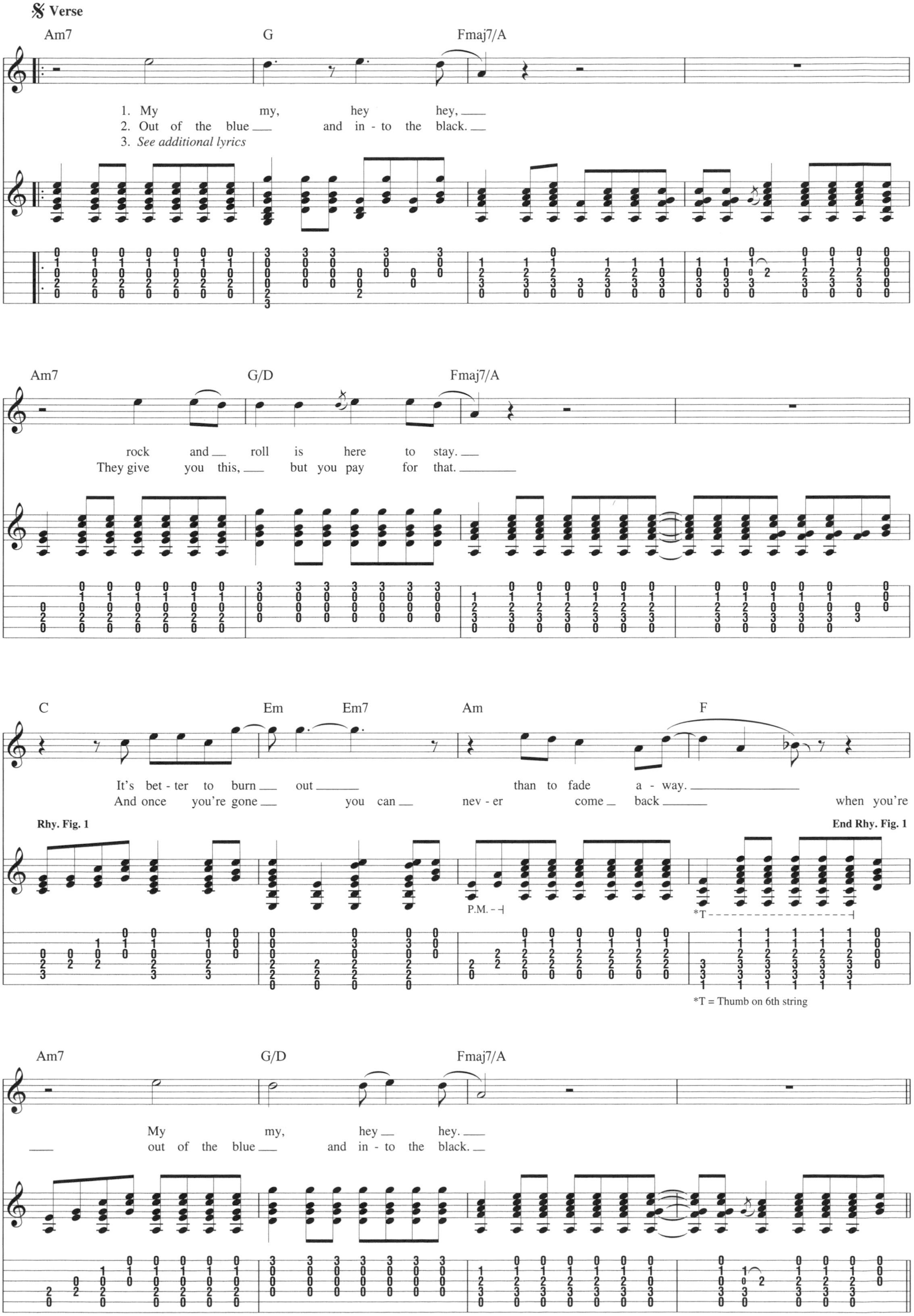
Verse
Am7
G
Fmaj7/A
1. My my, hey hey,
2. Out of the blue and in - to the black.
3. See additional lyrics
Am7
G/D
Fmaj7/A
rock and roll is here to stay.
They give you this, but you pay for that.
C
Em
Em7
Am
F
It's bet - ter to burn out than to fade a - way.
And once you're gone you can nev - er come back when you're
Rhy. Fig. 1
End Rhy. Fig. 1
P.M.
*T
*T = Thumb on 6th string
Am7
G/D
Fmaj7/A
My my, hey hey.
out of the blue and in - to the black.

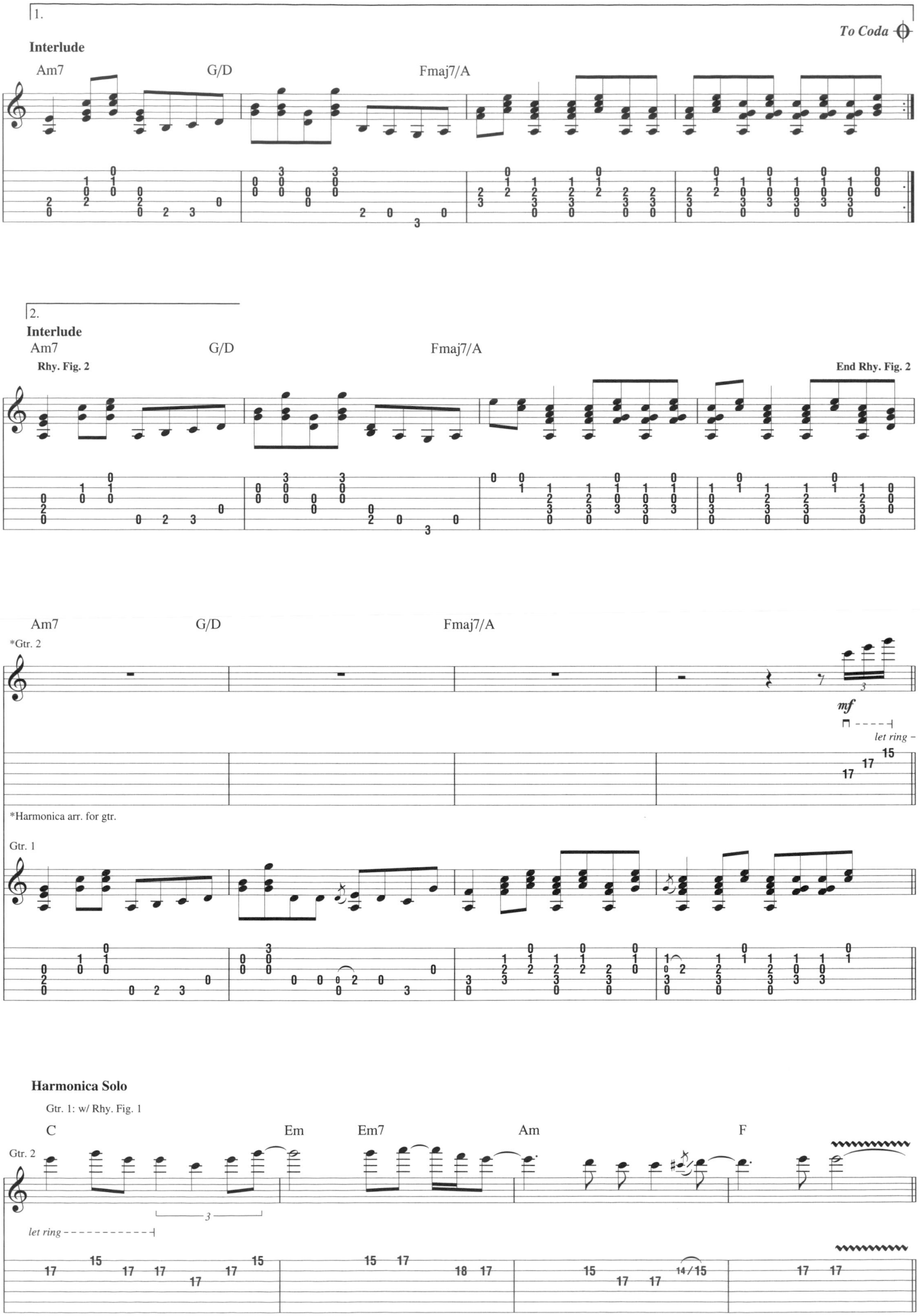
1.
To Coda
Interlude
Am7
G/D
Fmaj7/A
2.
Interlude
Am7
G/D
Fmaj7/A
Rhy. Fig. 2
End Rhy. Fig. 2
Am7
G/D
Fmaj7/A
*Gtr. 2
mf
let ring
*Harmonica arr. for gtr.
Gtr. 1
Harmonica Solo
Gtr. 1: w/ Rhy. Fig. 1
C
Em
Em7
Am
F
Gtr. 2
let ring

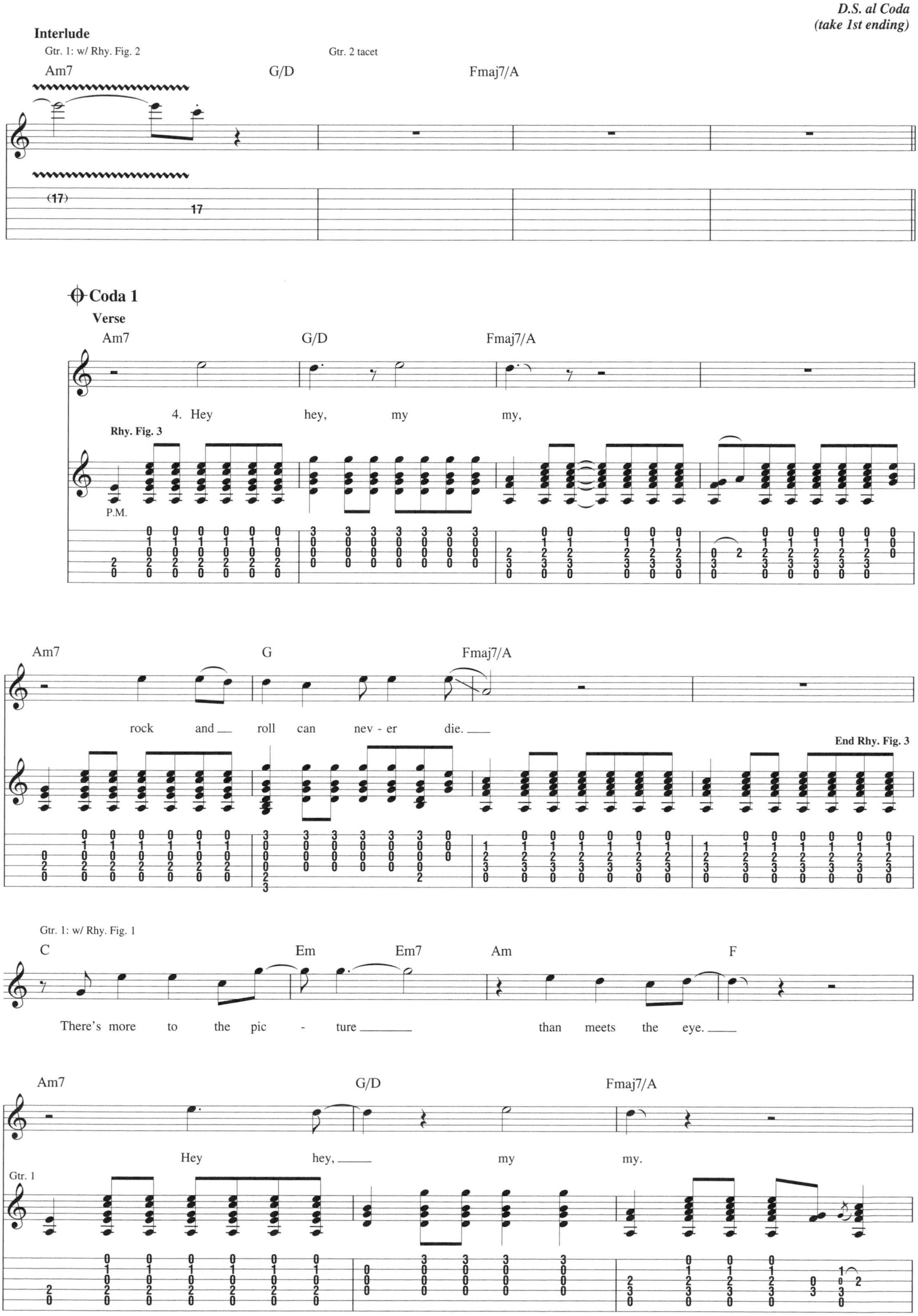
D.S. al Coda
(take 1st ending)
Interlude
Gtr. 1: w/ Rhy. Fig. 2
Gtr. 2 tacet
Am7
G/D
Fmaj7/A
Coda 1
Verse
Am7
G/D
Fmaj7/A
4. Hey hey, my my,
Rhy. Fig. 3
P.M.
Am7
G
Fmaj7/A
rock and roll can nev - er die.
End Rhy. Fig. 3
Gtr. 1: w/ Rhy. Fig. 1
C
Em
Em7
Am
F
There's more to the pic - ture than meets the eye.
Am7
G/D
Fmaj7/A
Hey hey, my my.
Gtr. 1

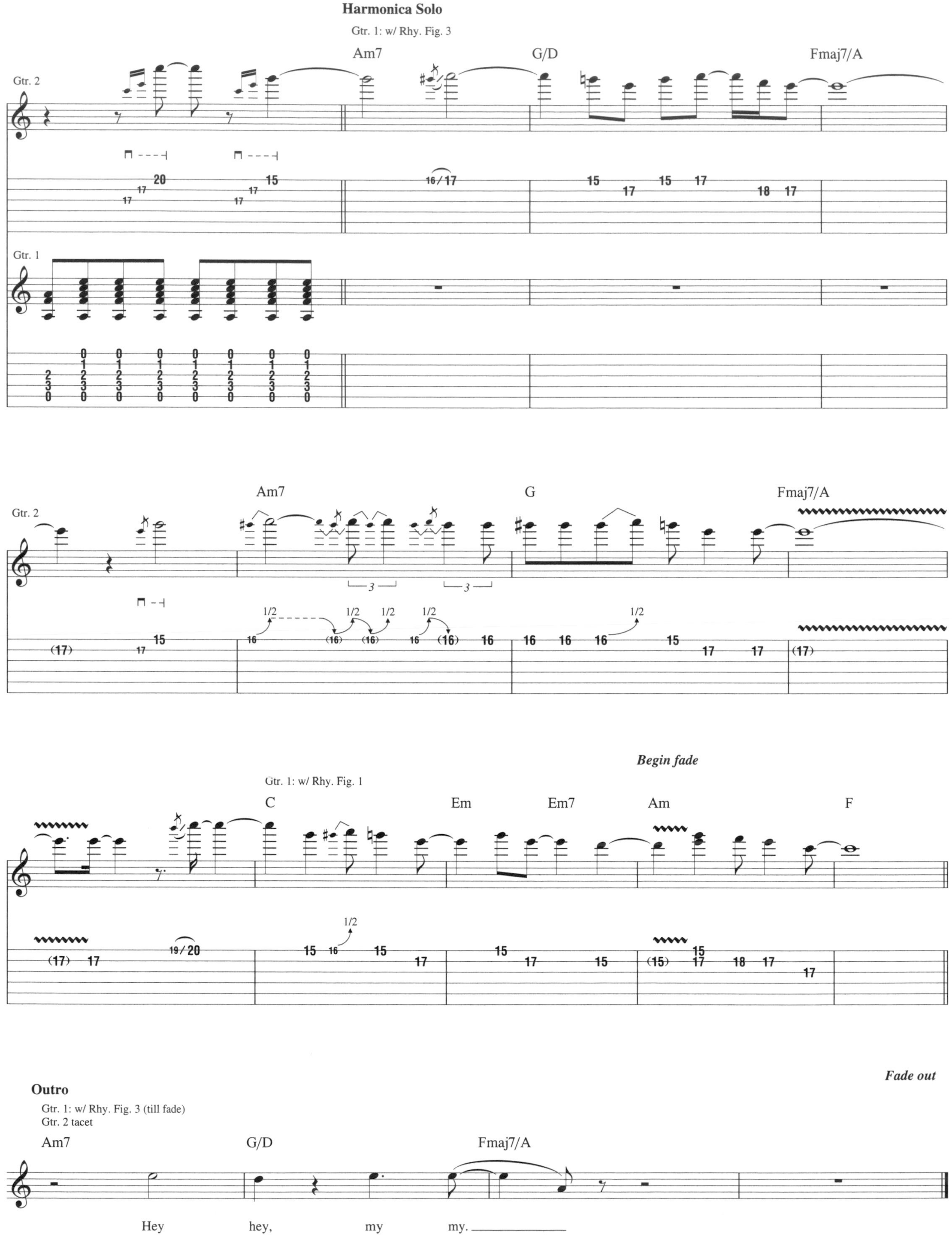

Additional Lyrics

3. The king is gone but he's not forgotten.
This is a story of a Johnny Rotten.
It's better to burn out than it is to rust.
The king is gone but he's not forgotten.

THRASHER

Words and Music by Neil Young

They were hiding behind hay bales,
 they were planting in the full moon
They had given all they had for something new
But the light of day was on them,
 they could see the thrashers coming
And the water shone like diamonds in the dew

And I was just getting up, hit the road before it's light
Trying to catch an hour on the sun
When I saw those thrashers rolling by,
 looking more than two lanes wide
I was feelin' like my day had just begun

Where the eagle glides ascending there's an
 ancient river bending
Down the timeless gorge of changes
 where sleeplessness awaits
I searched out my companions, they were lost
 in crystal canyons
When the aimless blade of science slashed
 the pearly gates.
It was then I knew I'd had enough, burned my
 credit card for fuel
Headed out to where the pavement turns to sand
With a one-way ticket to the land of truth
 and my suitcase in my hand
How I lost my friends I still don't understand

They had the best selection, they were
 poisoned with protection
There was nothing that they needed, they had
 nothing left to find
They were lost in rock formations or became
 park bench mutations
On the sidewalks and in the stations
 they were waiting, waiting.
So I got bored and left them there, they were
 just deadweight to me
It's better on the road without that load
Brought back the time when I was eight or nine
I was watchin' my mama's T.V., it was that great
 Grand Canyon rescue episode.
Where the vulture glides descending on
 an asphalt highway bending
Thru libraries and museums, galaxies and stars
Down the windy halls of friendship to the rose
 clipped by the bullwhip
The motel of lost companions waits with
 heated pool and air-conditioned bar

But me I'm not stopping there, got my own
 row left to hoe
Just another line in the field of time
When the thrashers come, and I'm stuck in the sun
 like dinosaurs in shrines
Then I'll know the time has come to give what's mine

Thrasher

Words and Music by Neil Young

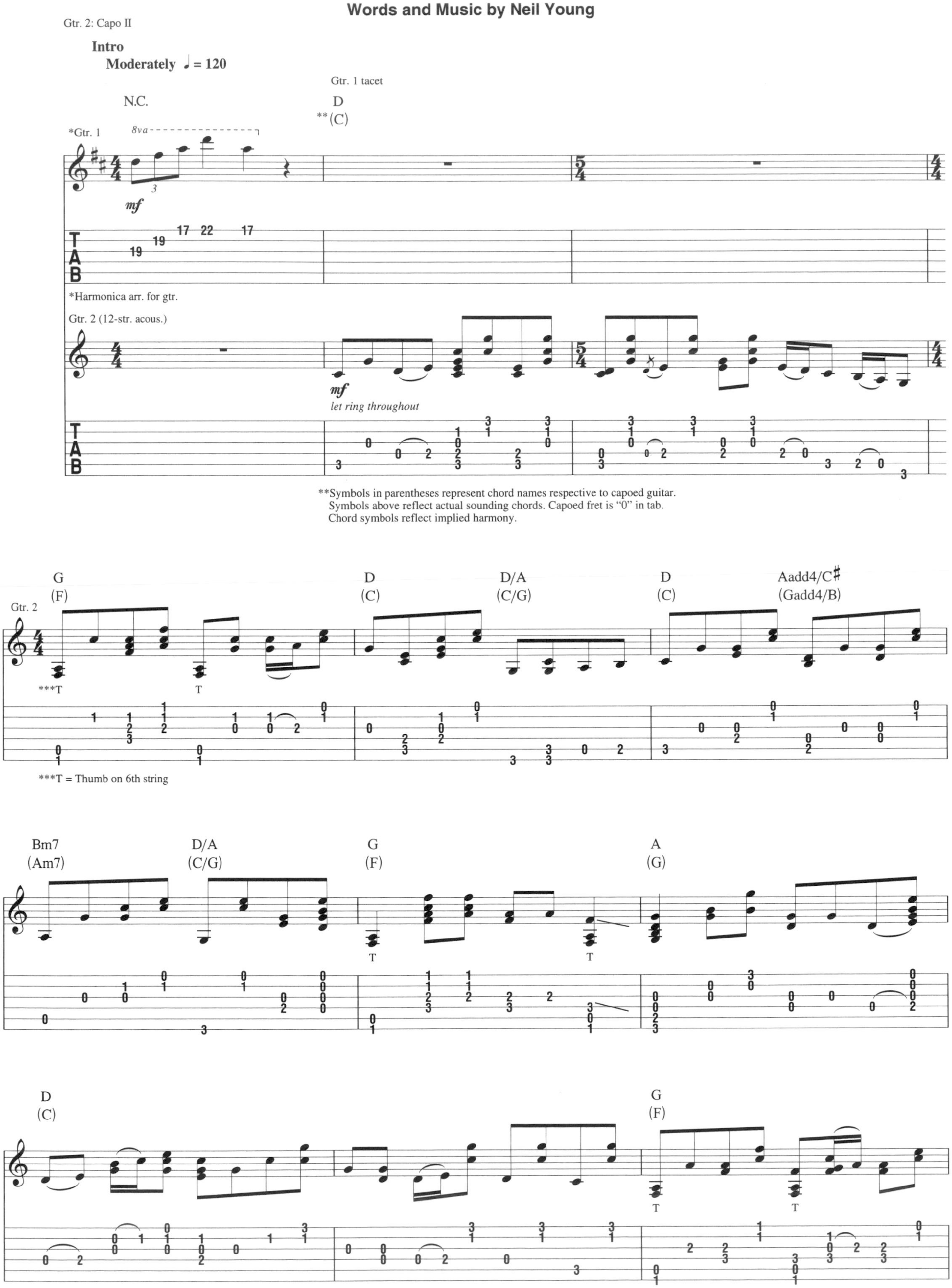

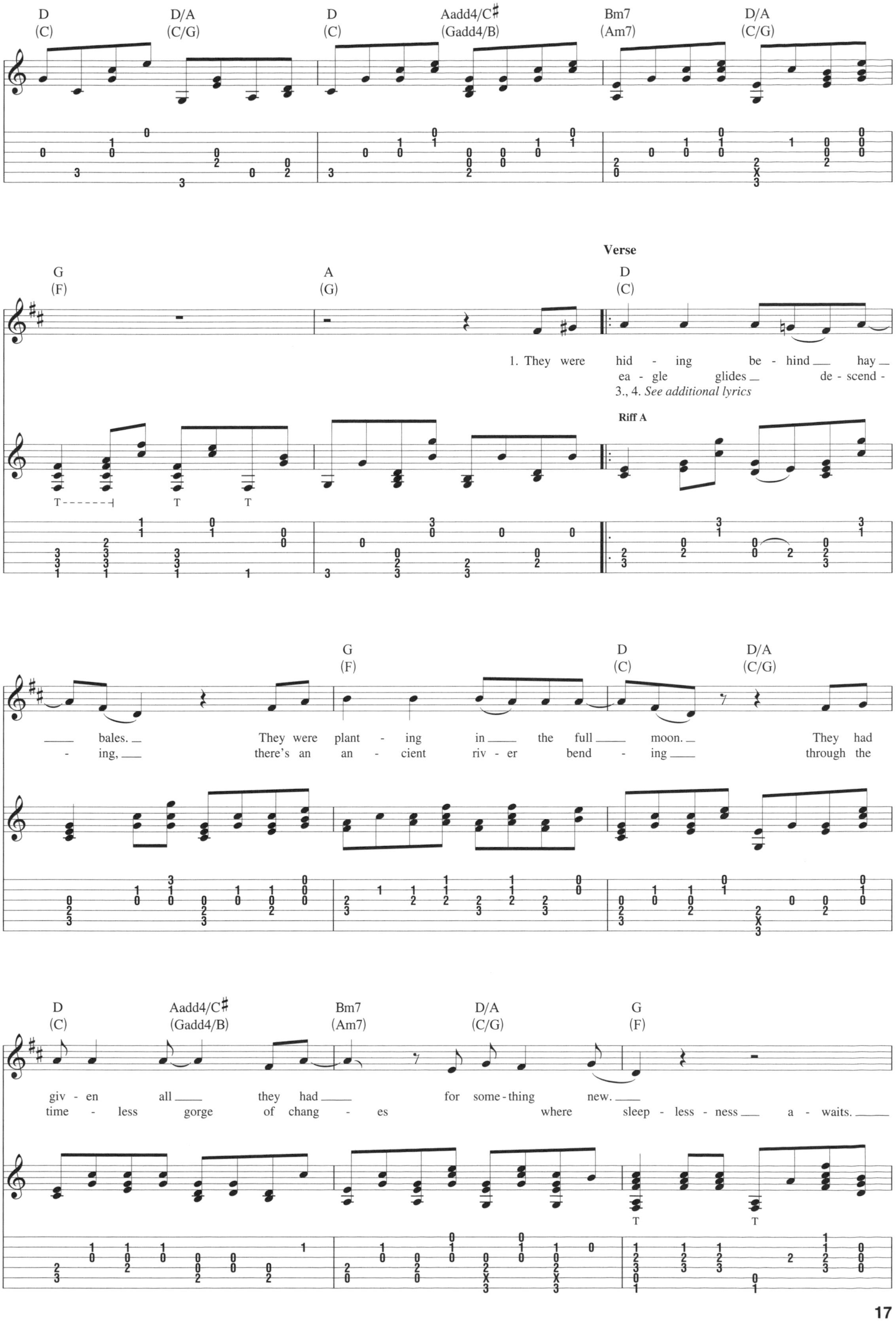
D (C) D/A (C/G) D (C) Aadd4/C♯ (Gadd4/B) Bm7 (Am7) D/A (C/G)
Verse
G (F) A (G) D (C)
1. They were hid - ing be - hind hay
ea - gle glides de - scend -
3., 4. See additional lyrics
Riff A
bales. They were plant - ing in the full moon. They had
- ing, there's an an - cient riv - er bend - ing through the
G (F) D (C) D/A (C/G)
D (C) Aadd4/C♯ (Gadd4/B) Bm7 (Am7) D/A (C/G) G (F)
giv - en all they had for some-thing new.
time - less gorge of chang - es where sleep - less - ness a - waits.

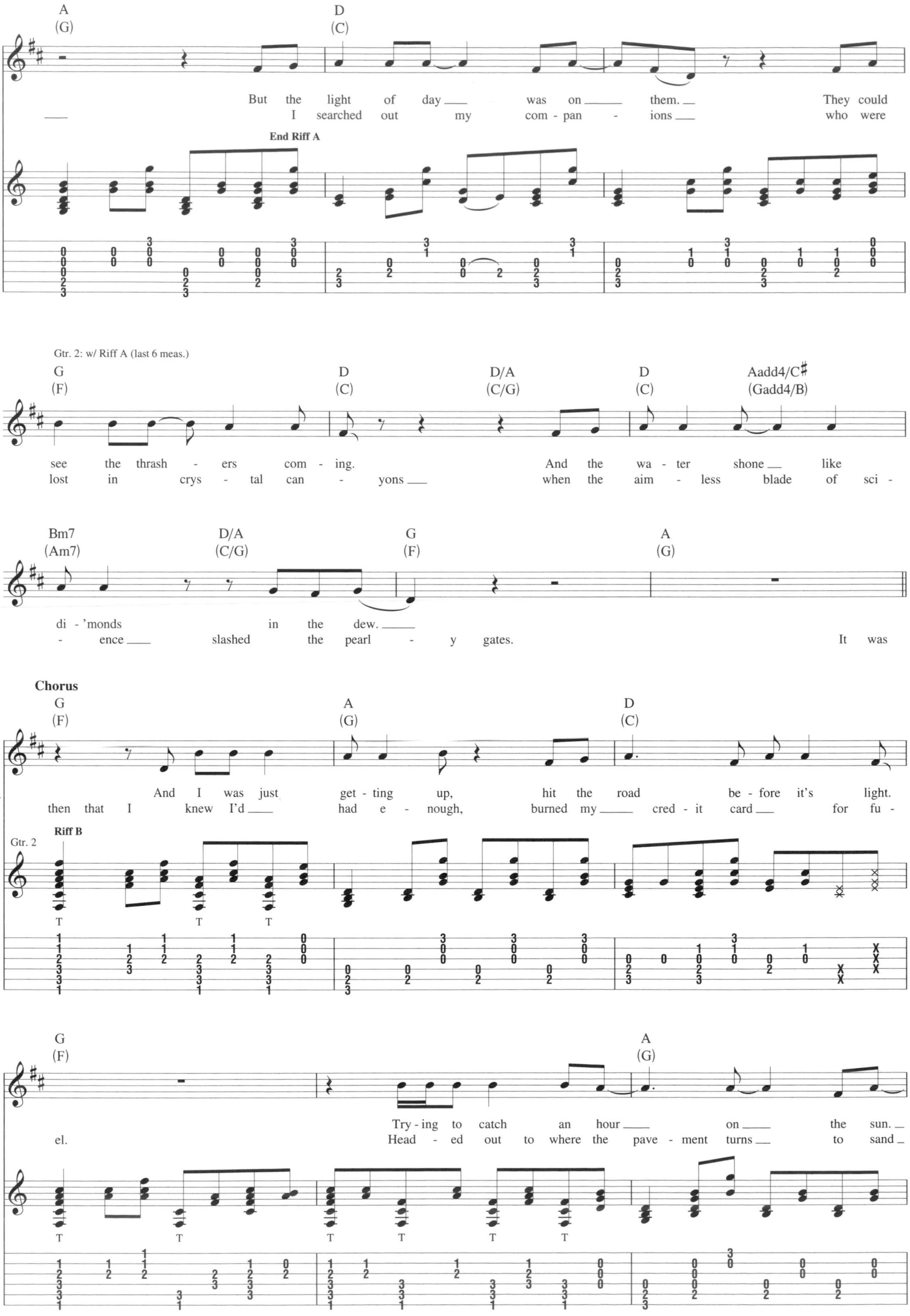
A
(G)
D
(C)
But the light of day was on them. They could
I searched out my com - pan - ions who were
End Riff A
Gtr. 2: w/ Riff A (last 6 meas.)
G
(F)
D
(C)
D/A
(C/G)
D
(C)
Aadd4/C♯
(Gadd4/B)
see the thrash - ers com - ing. And the wa - ter shone like
lost in crys - tal can - yons when the aim - less blade of sci -
Bm7
(Am7)
D/A
(C/G)
G
(F)
A
(G)
di - 'monds in the dew.
- ence slashed the pearl - y gates. It was
Chorus
G
(F)
A
(G)
D
(C)
And I was just get - ting up, hit the road be - fore it's light.
then that I knew I'd had e - nough, burned my cred - it card for fu -
Riff B
Gtr. 2
G
(F)
A
(G)
Try - ing to catch an hour on the sun.
el. Head - ed out to where the pave - ment turns to sand

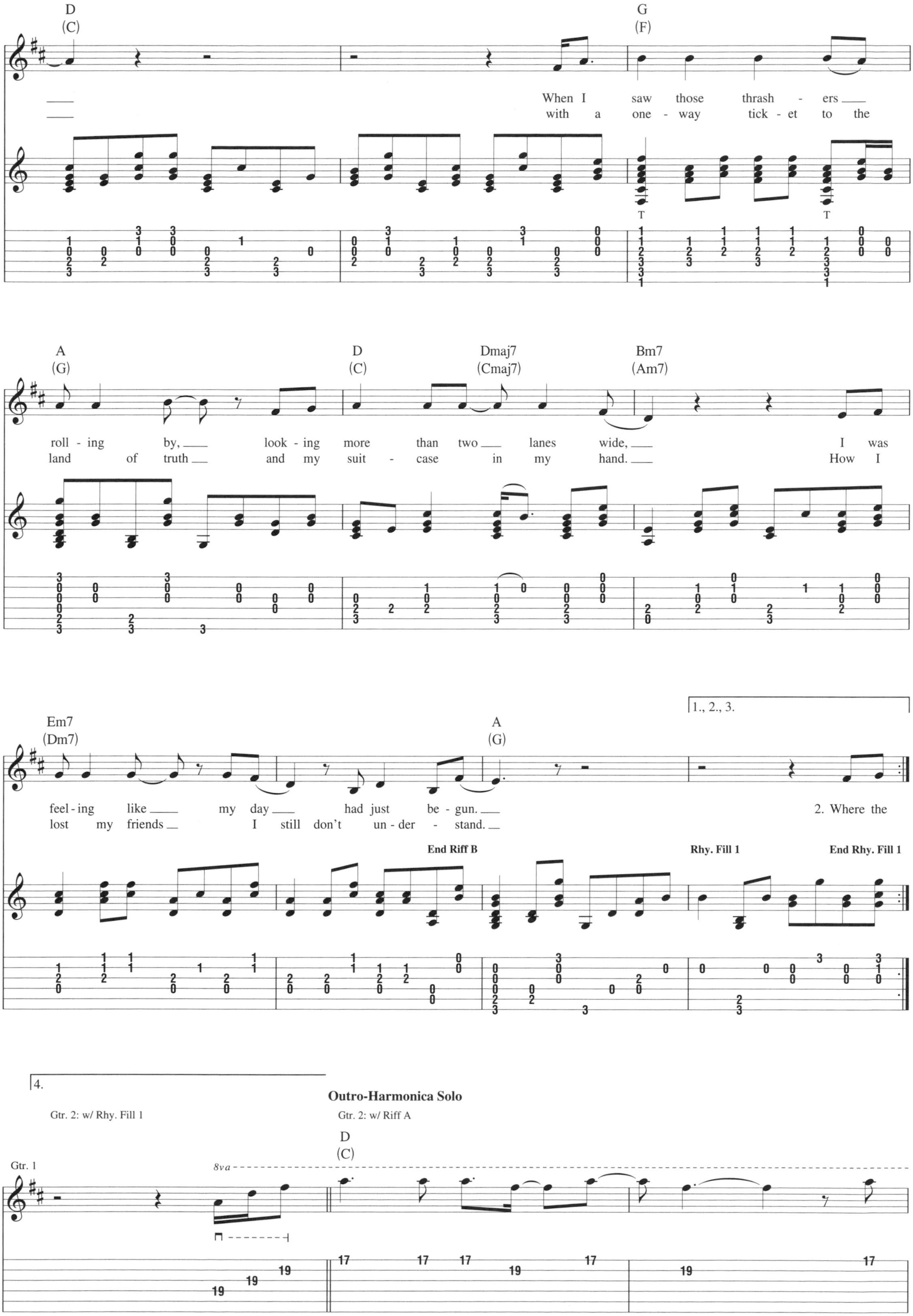
D
(C)
G
(F)
When I saw those thrash - ers
with a one - way tick - et to the
T
T
A
(G)
D
(C)
Dmaj7
(Cmaj7)
Bm7
(Am7)
roll - ing by, look - ing more than two lanes wide, I was
land of truth and my suit - case in my hand. How I
1., 2., 3.
Em7
(Dm7)
A
(G)
feel - ing like my day had just be - gun. 2. Where the
lost my friends I still don't un - der - stand.
End Riff B
Rhy. Fill 1
End Rhy. Fill 1
4.
Outro-Harmonica Solo
Gtr. 2: w/ Rhy. Fill 1
Gtr. 2: w/ Riff A
D
(C)
Gtr. 1
8va

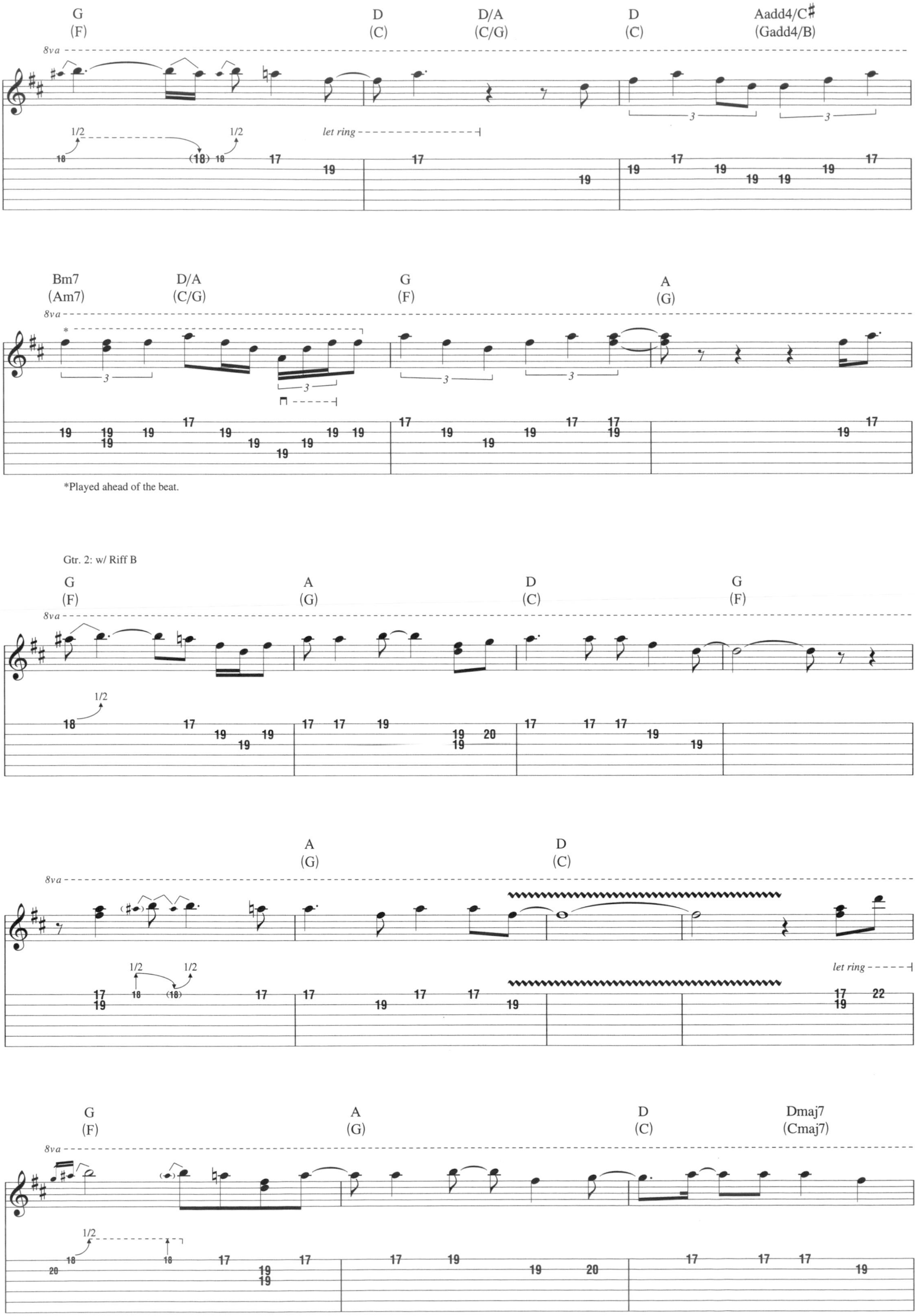
G (F)
D (C)
D/A (C/G)
D (C)
Aadd4/C♯ (Gadd4/B)
8va
let ring
Bm7 (Am7)
D/A (C/G)
G (F)
A (G)
*Played ahead of the beat.
Gtr. 2: w/ Riff B
G (F)
A (G)
D (C)
G (F)
A (G)
D (C)
let ring
G (F)
A (G)
D (C)
Dmaj7 (Cmaj7)

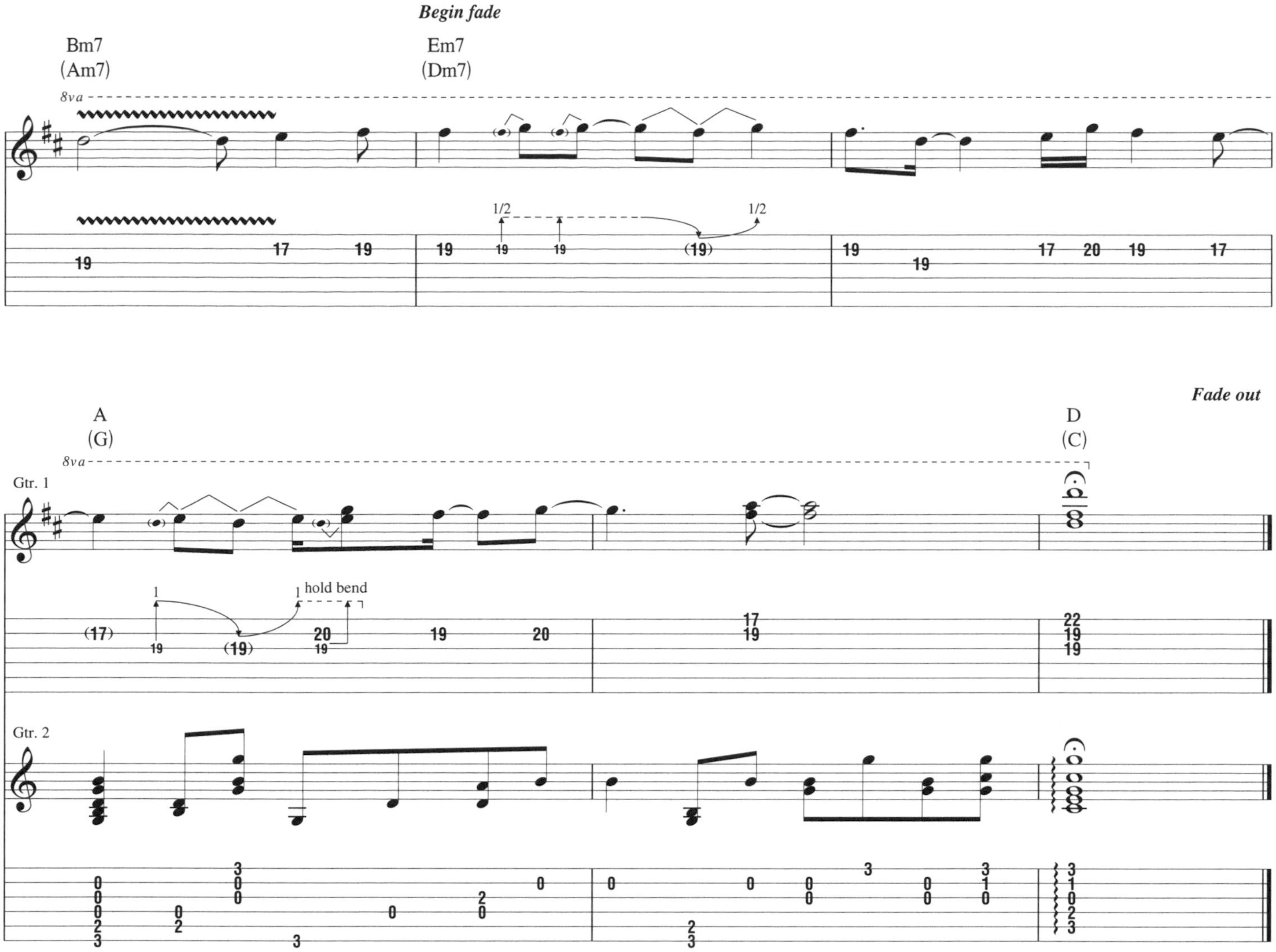

Additional Lyrics

3. They had the best selection.
They were poisoned with protection.
There was nothing that they needed,
Nothing left to find.
They were lost in rock formations
Or became park bench mutations.
On the sidewalks and in the stations
They were waiting, waiting.

Chorus 3. So I got bored and left them there,
They were just dead weight to me.
It's better down the road
Without that load.
Brings back the time when I was eight or nine,
I was watching my mama's T.V.
It was that great Grand Canyon rescue episode.

4. Where the vulture glides descending
On an asphalt highway bending,
Through libraries and museums,
Galaxies and stars,
Down the windy halls of friendship
To the rose clipped by the bullwhip.
The motel of lost companions
Waits with heated pool and bar.

Chorus 4. But me, I'm not stopping there,
Got my own row left to hoe
Just another line in the
Field of time.
When the thrasher comes I'll be stuck in the sun
Like the dinosaurs in shrines,
But I'll know the time has come
To give what's mine.

RIDE MY LLAMA

Words and Music by Neil Young

Remember the Alamo when help was on the way
It's better here and now, I feel that good today
I'd like to take a walk but not around the block
I really got some news
I met a man from Mars
He picked up all my guitars
And played me traveling songs
And when we got on ship
He brought out something for the trip
And said, "It's old but it's good"
Like any other primitive would
Ah, ah, ah, ah

I'm gonna ride my llama from Peru to Texarkana
I wanna ride him good thru my old neighborhood
I'm gonna ride him good in my old neighborhood
I'm gonna ride him good in my old neighborhood

And when we got on ship
He brought out something for the trip
And said, "It's old but it's good"
Like any other primitive would
Ah

Ride My Llama

Words and Music by Neil Young

Double drop D tuning, capo II:
(low to high) D-A-D-G-B-D

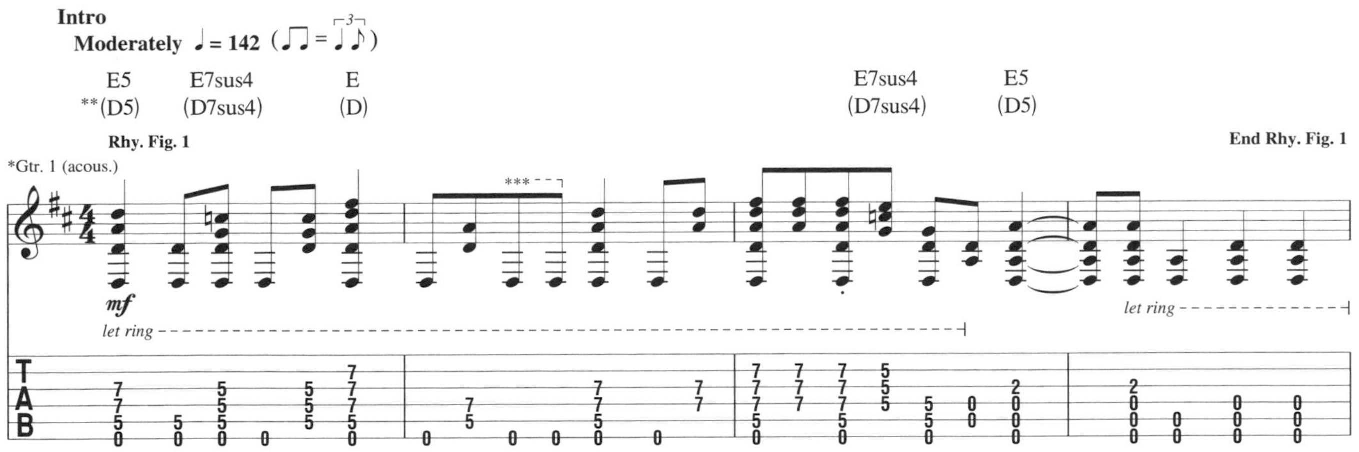

*Two gtrs. arr. for one.

**Symbols in parentheses represent chord names respective to capoed guitar. Symbols above reflect actual sounding chords. Capoed fret is "0" in tab.

***Played as straight eighth-notes.

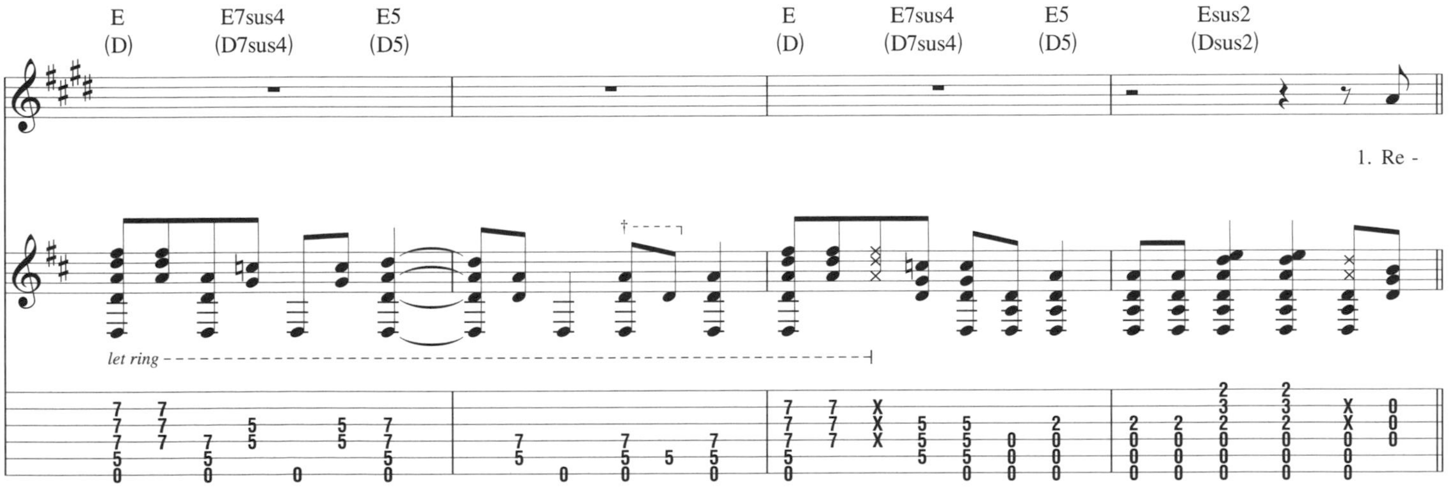

†As before

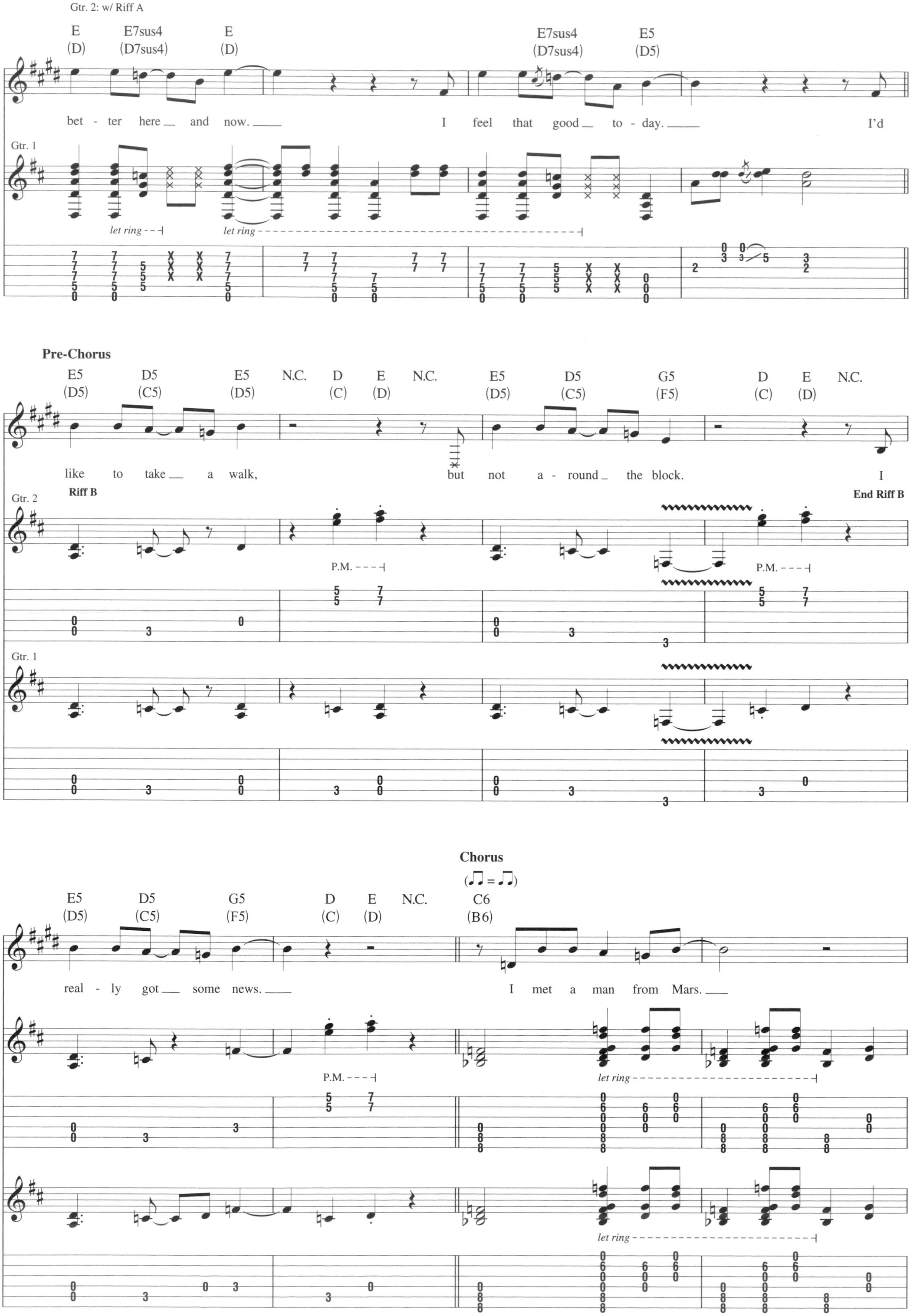
Gtr. 2: w/ Riff A
E (D) E7sus4 (D7sus4) E (D) E7sus4 (D7sus4) E5 (D5)
bet - ter here and now. I feel that good to - day. I'd
Gtr. 1
let ring
let ring
Pre-Chorus
E5 (D5) D5 (C5) E5 (D5) N.C. D (C) E (D) N.C. E5 (D5) D5 (C5) G5 (F5) D (C) E (D) N.C.
like to take a walk, but not a - round the block. I
Riff B
Gtr. 2
End Riff B
P.M.
P.M.
Gtr. 1
Chorus
E5 (D5) D5 (C5) G5 (F5) D (C) E (D) N.C. C6 (B6)
real - ly got some news. I met a man from Mars.
P.M.
let ring
let ring

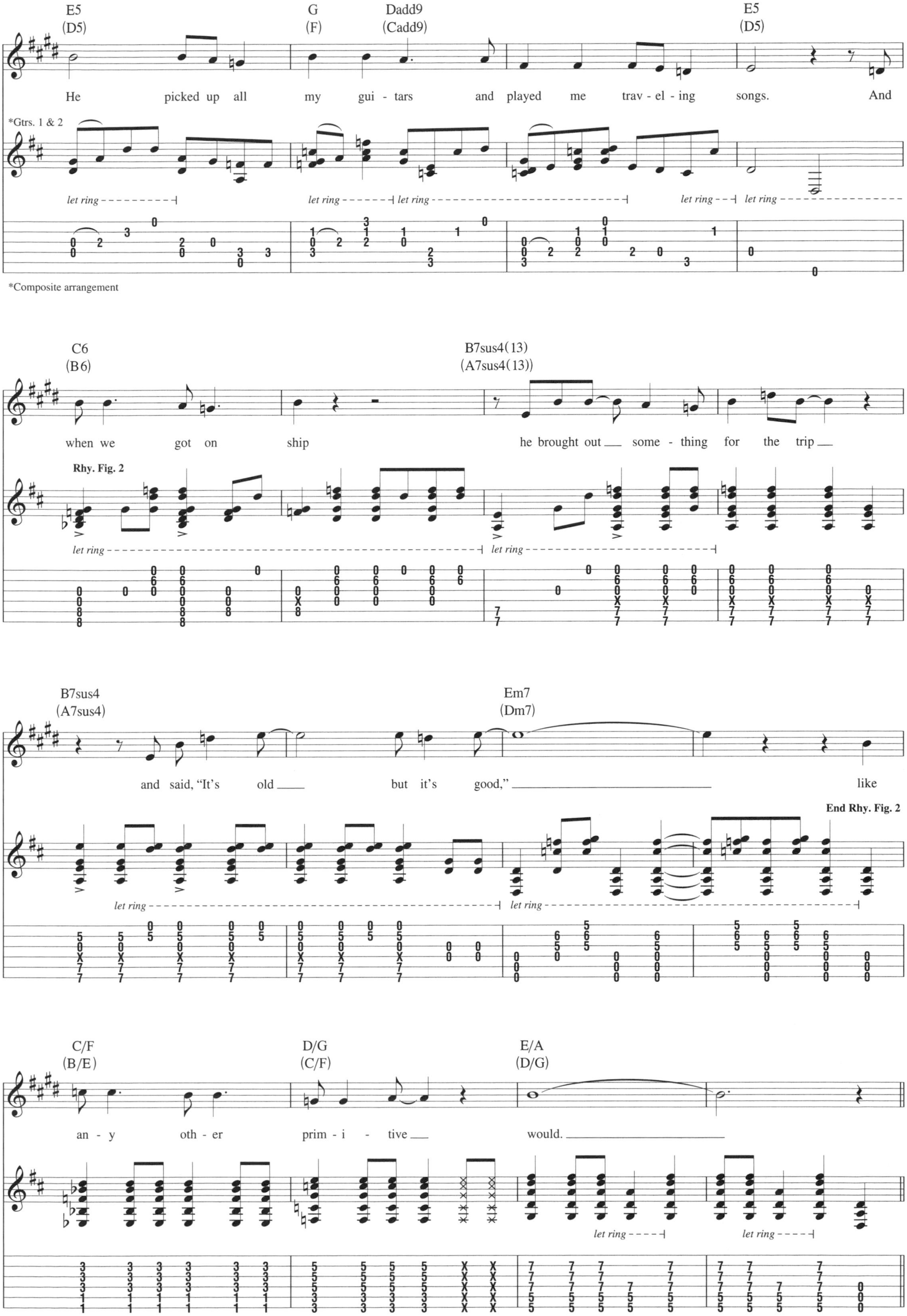
E5 (D5)
G (F)
Dadd9 (Cadd9)
E5 (D5)
He picked up all my gui - tars and played me trav - el - ing songs. And
*Gtrs. 1 & 2
let ring
*Composite arrangement
C6 (B6)
B7sus4(13) (A7sus4(13))
when we got on ship he brought out some - thing for the trip
Rhy. Fig. 2
B7sus4 (A7sus4)
Em7 (Dm7)
and said, "It's old but it's good," like
End Rhy. Fig. 2
C/F (B/E)
D/G (C/F)
E/A (D/G)
an - y oth - er prim - i - tive would.

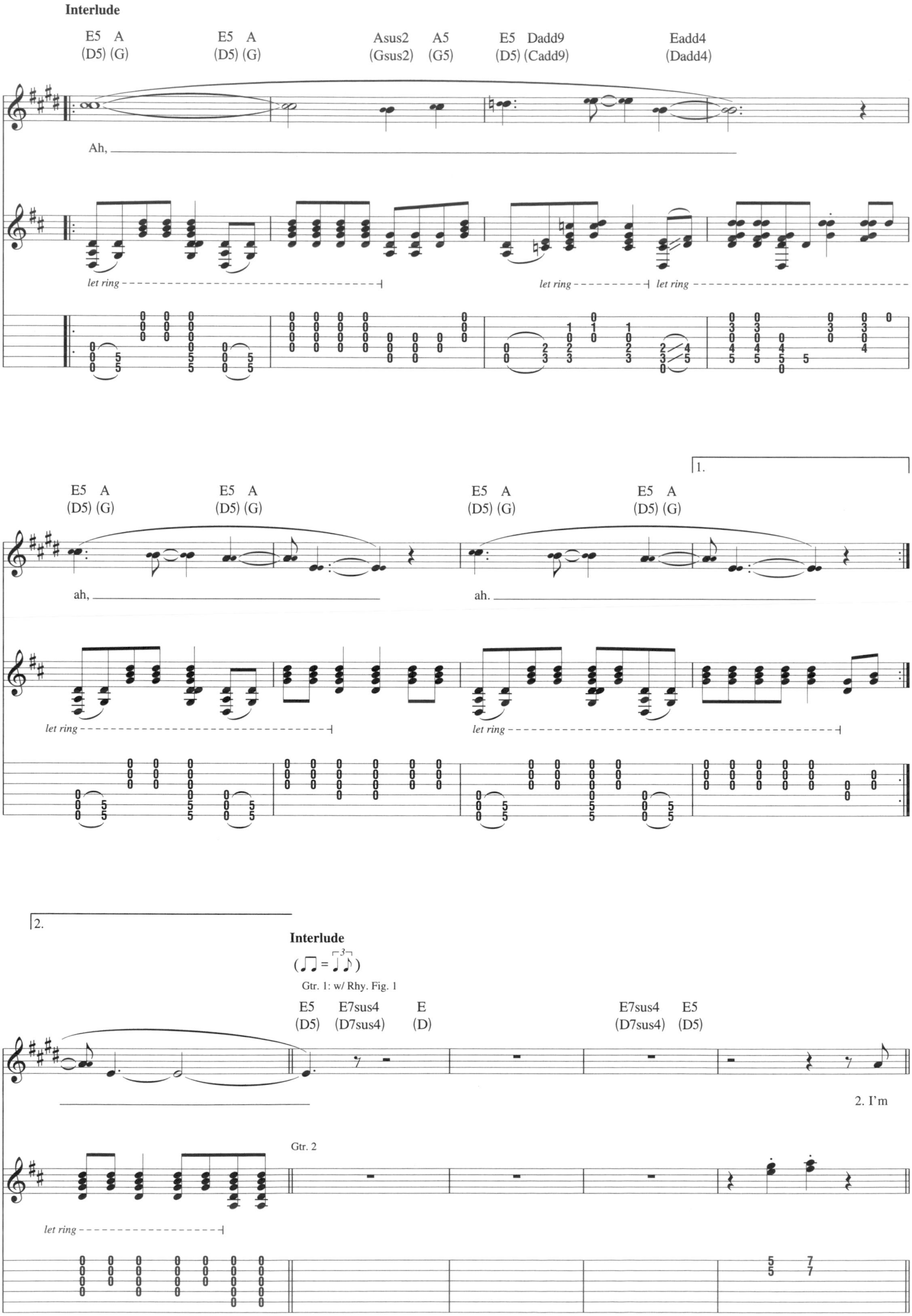
Interlude
E5 A
(D5) (G)
E5 A
(D5) (G)
Asus2 A5
(Gsus2) (G5)
E5 Dadd9
(D5) (Cadd9)
Eadd4
(Dadd4)
Ah,
let ring
let ring
let ring
1.
E5 A
(D5) (G)
E5 A
(D5) (G)
E5 A
(D5) (G)
E5 A
(D5) (G)
ah,
ah.
let ring
let ring
2.
Interlude
Gtr. 1: w/ Rhy. Fig. 1
E5 E7sus4 E
(D5) (D7sus4) (D)
E7sus4 E5
(D7sus4) (D5)
2. I'm
Gtr. 2
let ring

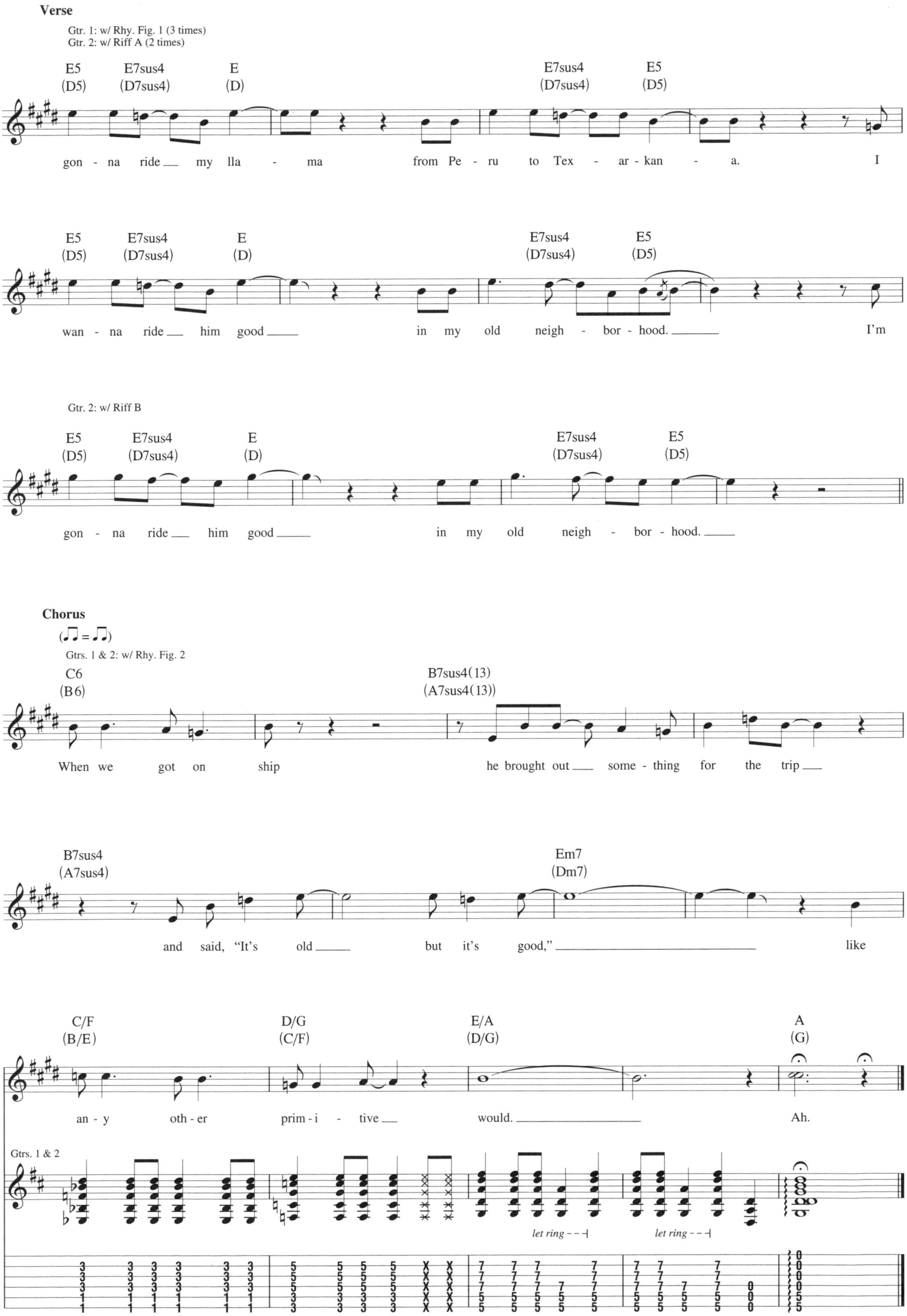
Verse
Gtr. 1: w/ Rhy. Fig. 1 (3 times)
Gtr. 2: w/ Riff A (2 times)
E5 (D5) E7sus4 (D7sus4) E (D) E7sus4 (D7sus4) E5 (D5)
gon - na ride my lla - ma from Pe - ru to Tex - ar - kan - a. I
E5 (D5) E7sus4 (D7sus4) E (D) E7sus4 (D7sus4) E5 (D5)
wan - na ride him good in my old neigh - bor - hood. I'm
Gtr. 2: w/ Riff B
E5 (D5) E7sus4 (D7sus4) E (D) E7sus4 (D7sus4) E5 (D5)
gon - na ride him good in my old neigh - bor - hood.
Chorus
Gtrs. 1 & 2: w/ Rhy. Fig. 2
C6 (B6) B7sus4(13) (A7sus4(13))
When we got on ship he brought out some - thing for the trip
B7sus4 (A7sus4) Em7 (Dm7)
and said, "It's old but it's good," like
C/F (B/E) D/G (C/F) E/A (D/G) A (G)
an - y oth - er prim - i - tive would. Ah.
Gtrs. 1 & 2
let ring
let ring

POCAHONTAS

Words and Music by Neil Young

Aurora borealis
The icy sky at night
Paddles cut the water
In a long and hurried flight
From the white man to the fields of green
And the homeland we've never seen

They killed us in our tepee
And they cut our women down
They might have left some babies
Cryin' on the ground
But the firesticks and the wagons come
And the night falls on the settin' sun

They massacred the buffalo
Kitty corner from the bank
The taxis run across my feet
And my eyes have turned to blanks
In my little box at the top of the stairs
With my Indian rug and a pipe to share.

I wish I was a trapper
I would give thousand pelts
To sleep with Pocahontas
And find out how she felt
In the mornin' on the fields of green
In the homeland we've never seen.

And maybe Marlon Brando
Will be there by the fire
We'll sit and talk of Hollywood
And the good things there for hire
And the Astrodome and the first tepee
Marlon Brando, Pocahontas and me
Marlon Brando, Pocahontas and me
Pocahontas

Pocahontas

Words and Music by Neil Young

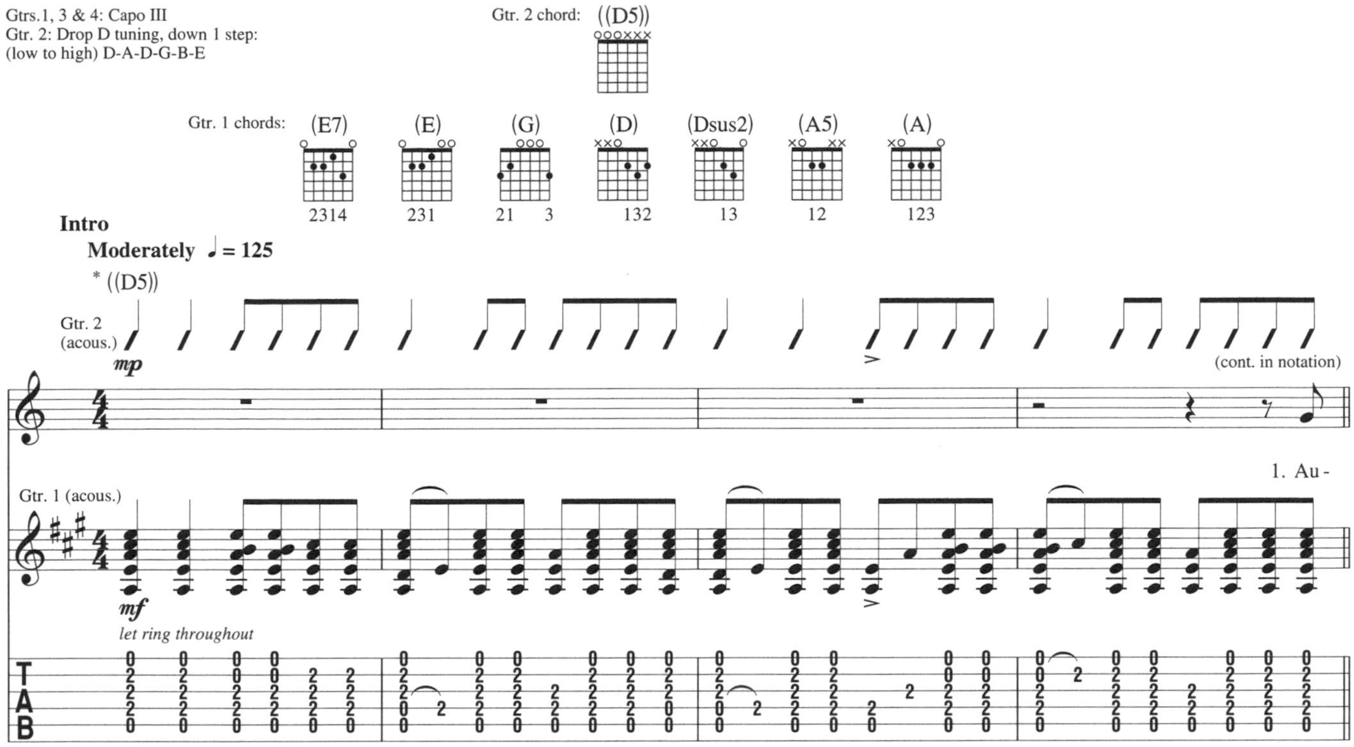

*Symbols in double parentheses represent chord names respective to detuned guitar.

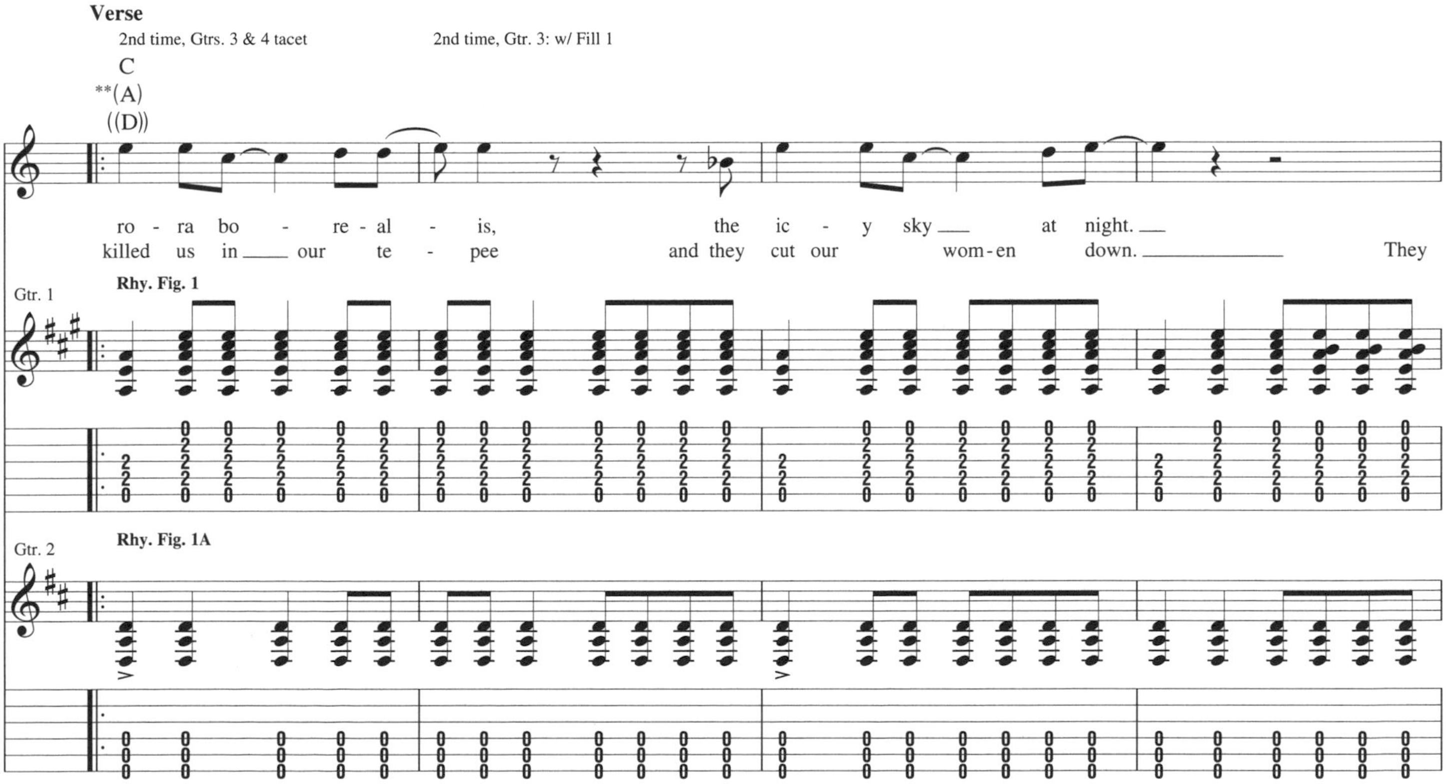

**Symbols in parentheses represent chord names respective to capoed guitar. Symbols above reflect actual sounding chords. Capoed fret is "0" in tab. Chord symbols reflect basic harmony.

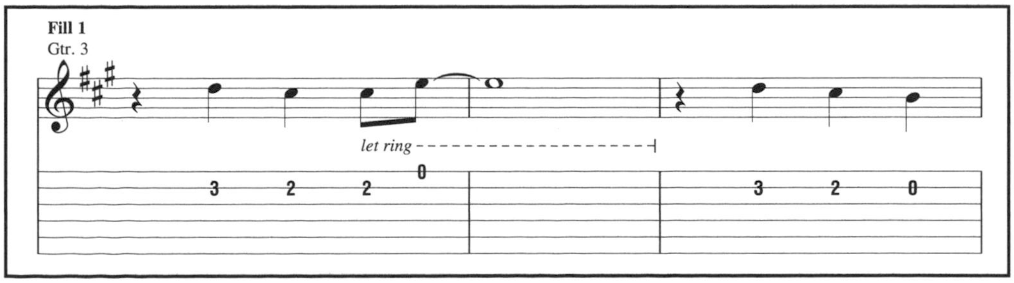

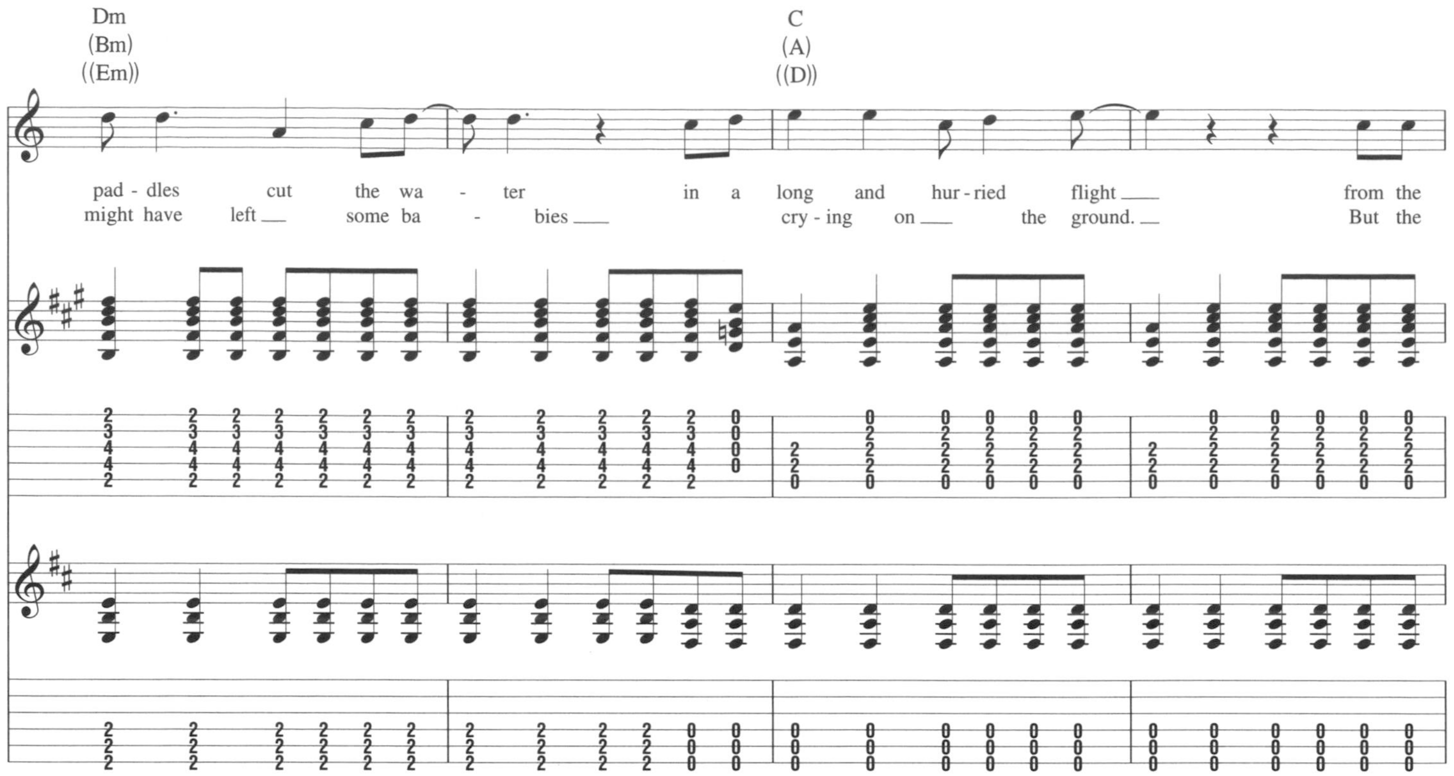
Dm
(Bm)
((Em))
C
(A)
((D))
pad - dles cut the wa - ter in a long and hur - ried flight from the
might have left some ba - bies cry - ing on the ground. But the

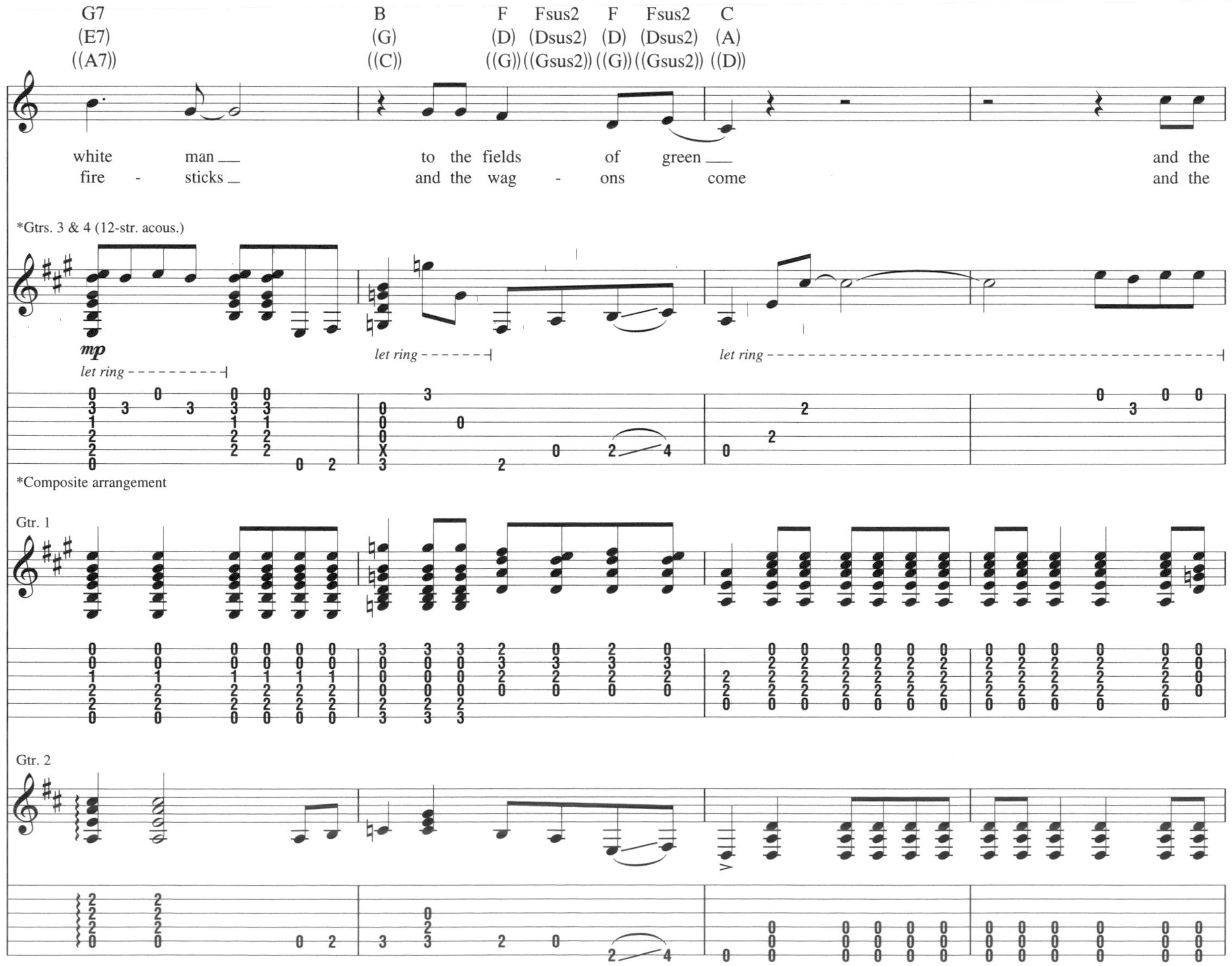
G7
(E7)
((A7))
B
(G)
((C))
F Fsus2 F Fsus2 C
(D) (Dsus2) (D) (Dsus2) (A)
((G)) ((Gsus2)) ((G)) ((Gsus2)) ((D))
white man to the fields of green and the
fire - sticks and the wag - ons come and the
*Gtrs. 3 & 4 (12-str. acous.)
mp
let ring
let ring
let ring
*Composite arrangement
Gtr. 1
Gtr. 2

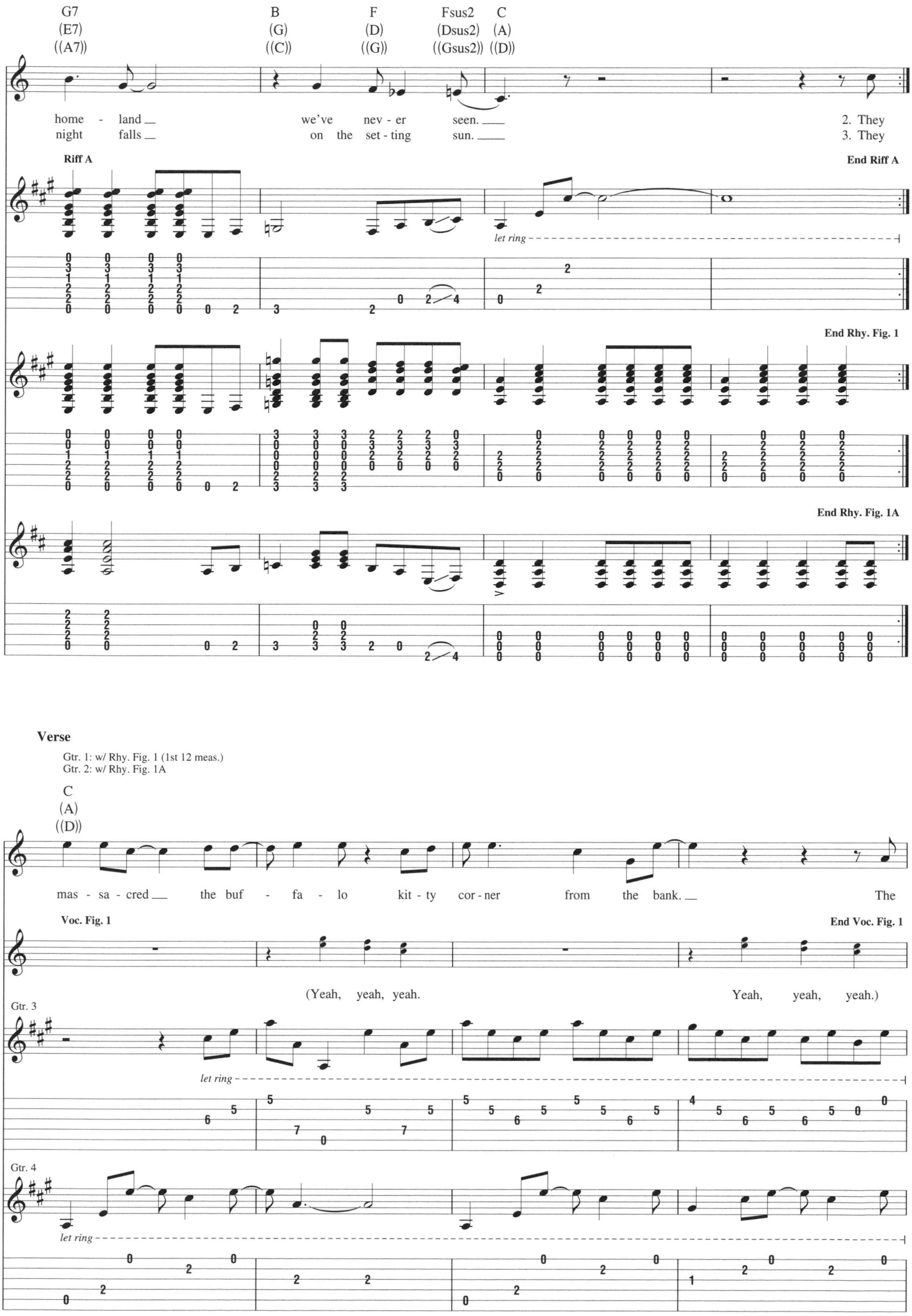
G7
(E7)
((A7))
B
(G)
((C))
F
(D)
((G))
Fsus2
(Dsus2)
((Gsus2))
C
(A)
((D))
home - land we've nev - er seen. 2. They
night falls on the set - ting sun. 3. They
Riff A
End Riff A
let ring
End Rhy. Fig. 1
End Rhy. Fig. 1A
Verse
Gtr. 1: w/ Rhy. Fig. 1 (1st 12 meas.)
Gtr. 2: w/ Rhy. Fig. 1A
C
(A)
((D))
mas - sa - cred the buf - fa - lo kit - ty cor - ner from the bank. The
Voc. Fig. 1
End Voc. Fig. 1
(Yeah, yeah, yeah. Yeah, yeah, yeah.)
Gtr. 3
let ring
Gtr. 4
let ring

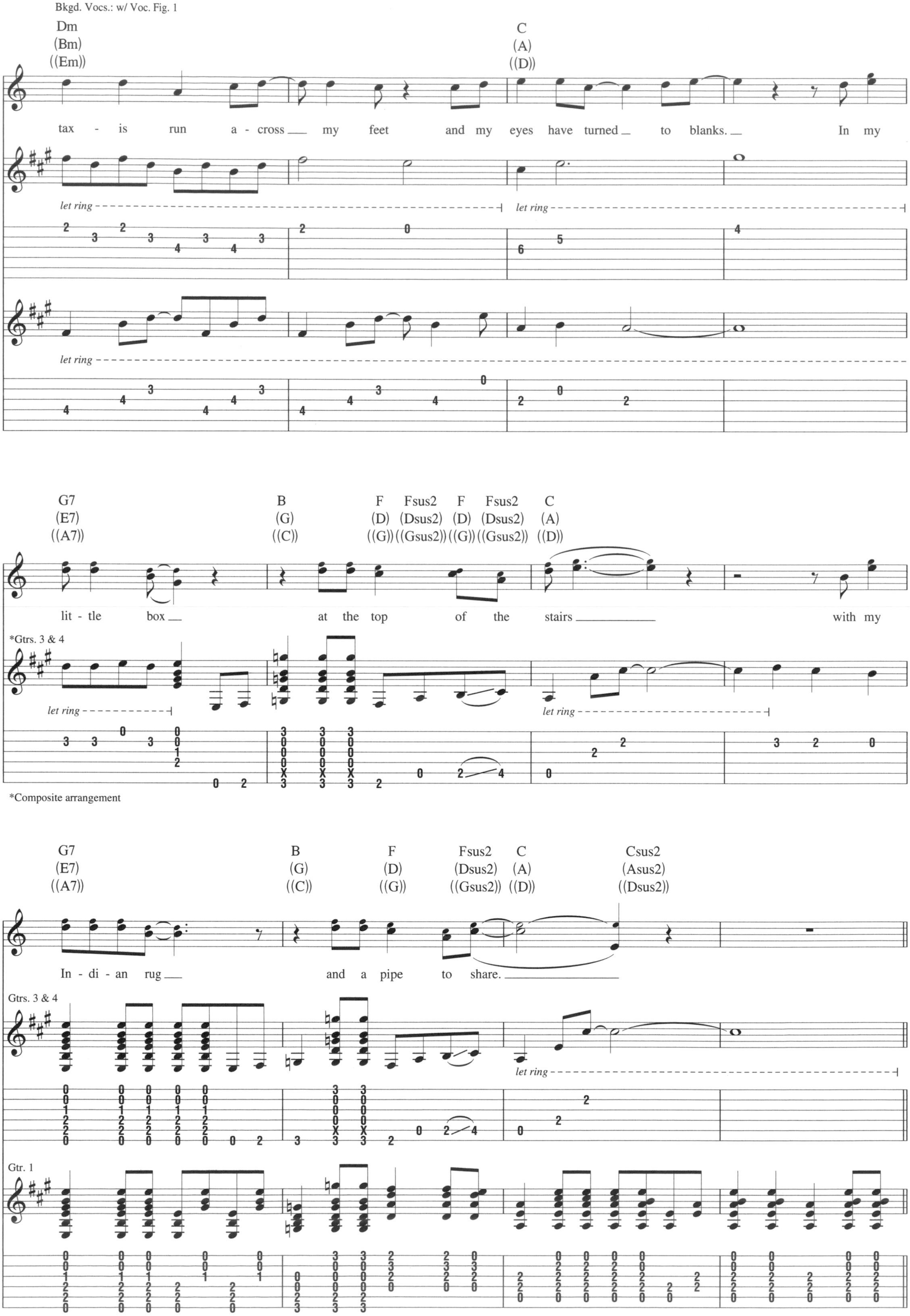
Bkgd. Vocs.: w/ Voc. Fig. 1
Dm (Bm) ((Em))
C (A) ((D))
tax - is run a - cross my feet and my eyes have turned to blanks. In my
let ring
G7 (E7) ((A7))
B (G) ((C))
F (D) ((G))
Fsus2 (Dsus2) ((Gsus2))
F (D) ((G))
Fsus2 (Dsus2) ((Gsus2))
C (A) ((D))
lit - tle box at the top of the stairs with my
*Gtrs. 3 & 4
let ring
*Composite arrangement
G7 (E7) ((A7))
B (G) ((C))
F (D) ((G))
Fsus2 (Dsus2) ((Gsus2))
C (A) ((D))
Csus2 (Asus2) ((Dsus2))
In - di - an rug and a pipe to share.
Gtrs. 3 & 4
let ring
Gtr. 1

Interlude

Gtr. 2: w/ Rhy. Fig. 1A (1st 12 meas.)
Gtrs. 3 & 4 tacet

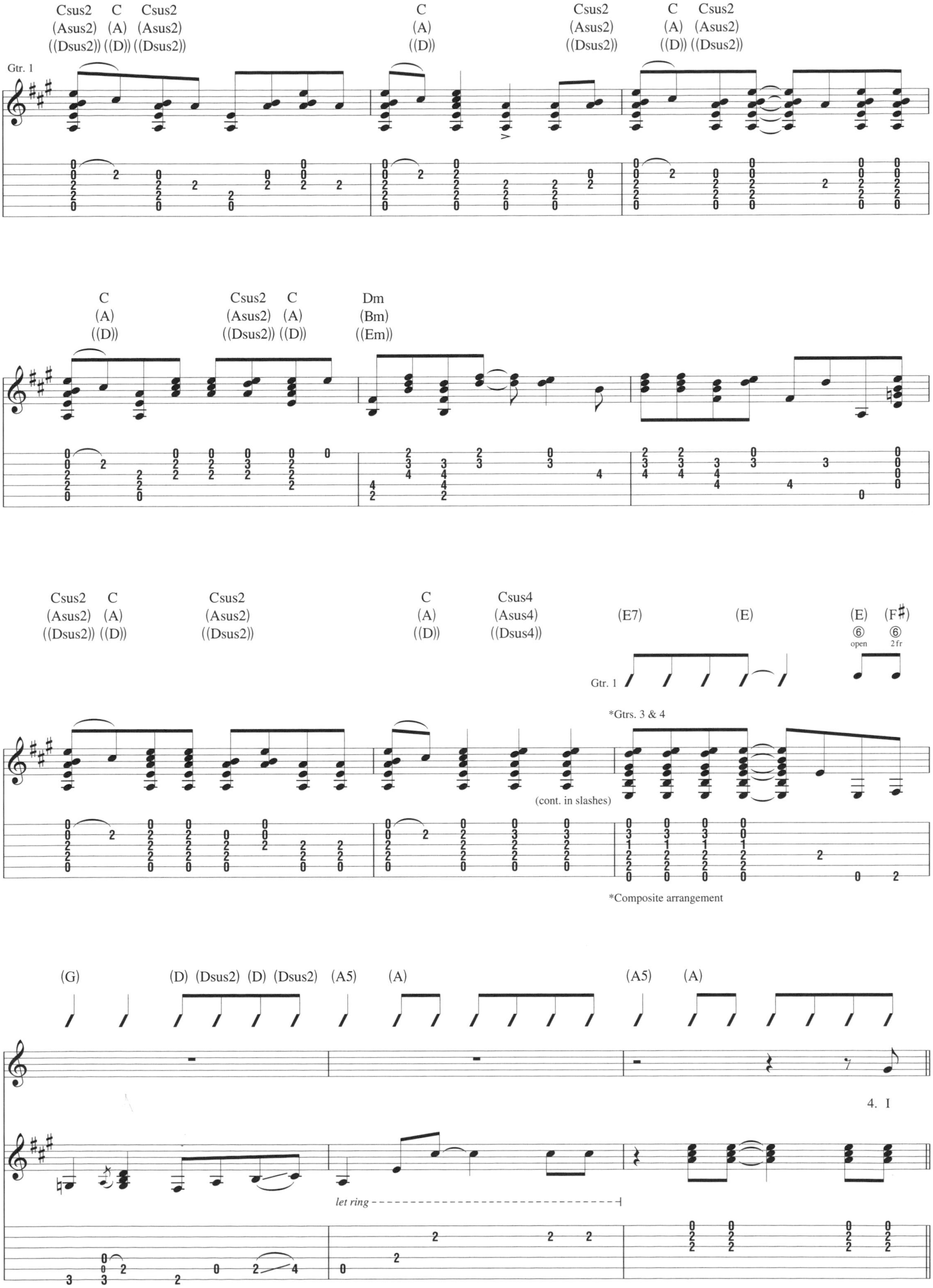

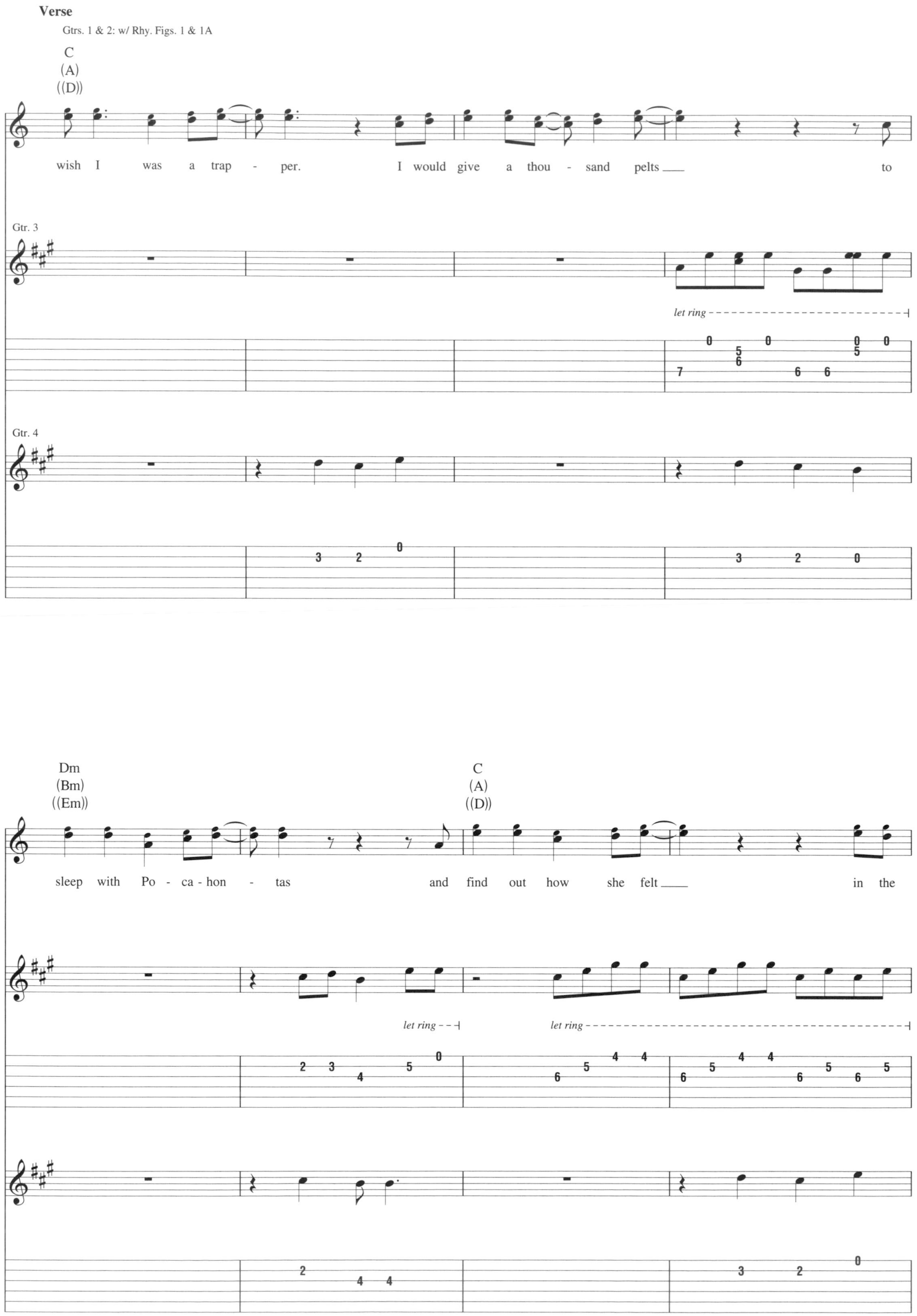
Verse
Gtrs. 1 & 2: w/ Rhy. Figs. 1 & 1A
C
(A)
((D))
wish I was a trap - per. I would give a thou - sand pelts ___ to
Gtr. 3
let ring
Gtr. 4
Dm
(Bm)
((Em))
C
(A)
((D))
sleep with Po - ca - hon - tas and find out how she felt ___ in the
let ring
let ring

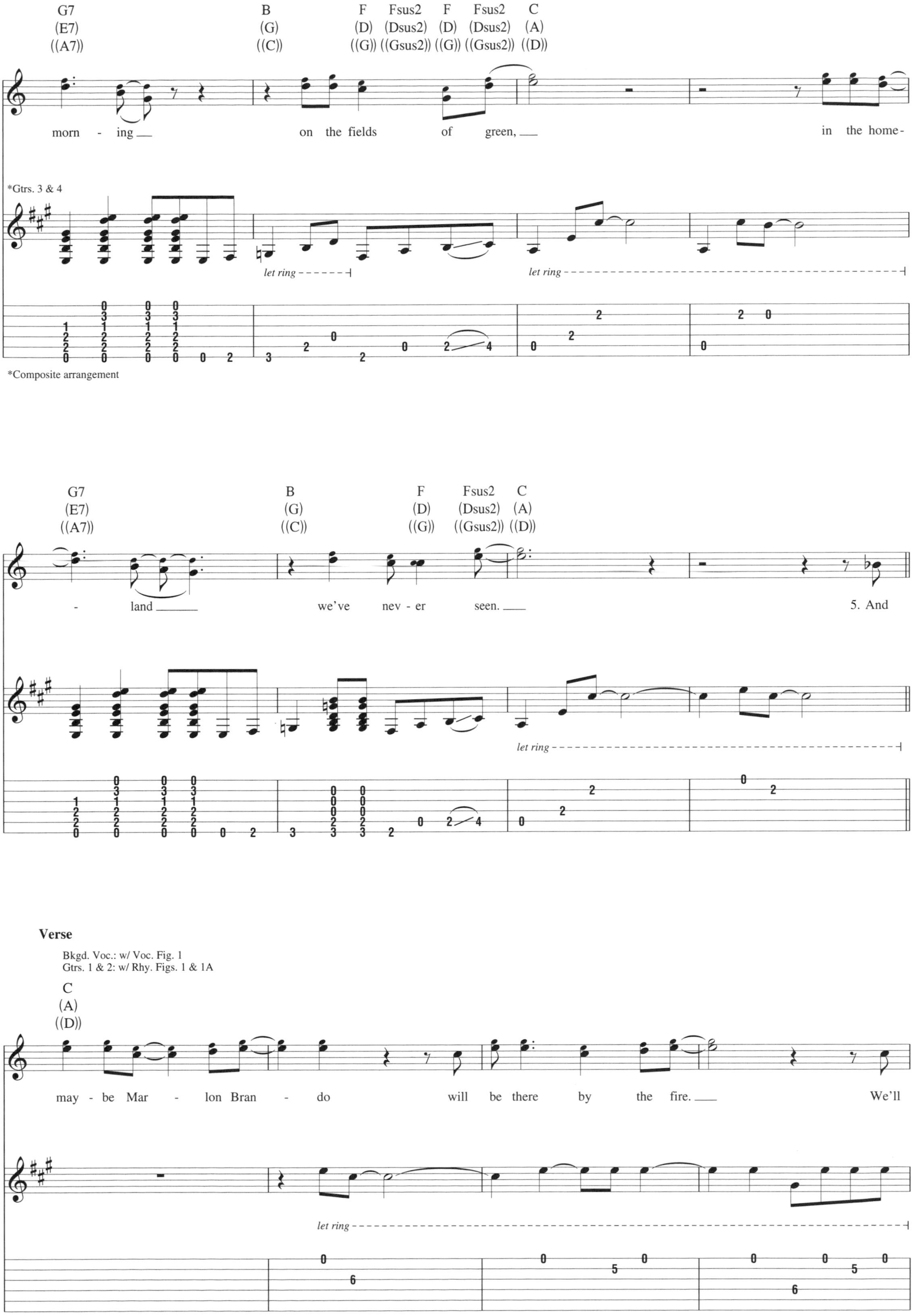
G7 (E7) ((A7))
B (G) ((C))
F (D) ((G))
Fsus2 (Dsus2) ((Gsus2))
F (D) ((G))
Fsus2 (Dsus2) ((Gsus2))
C (A) ((D))
morn - ing on the fields of green, in the home-
*Gtrs. 3 & 4
let ring
let ring
*Composite arrangement
G7 (E7) ((A7))
B (G) ((C))
F (D) ((G))
Fsus2 (Dsus2) ((Gsus2))
C (A) ((D))
- land we've nev - er seen. 5. And
let ring
Verse
Bkgd. Voc.: w/ Voc. Fig. 1
Gtrs. 1 & 2: w/ Rhy. Figs. 1 & 1A
C (A) ((D))
may - be Mar - lon Bran - do will be there by the fire. We'll
let ring

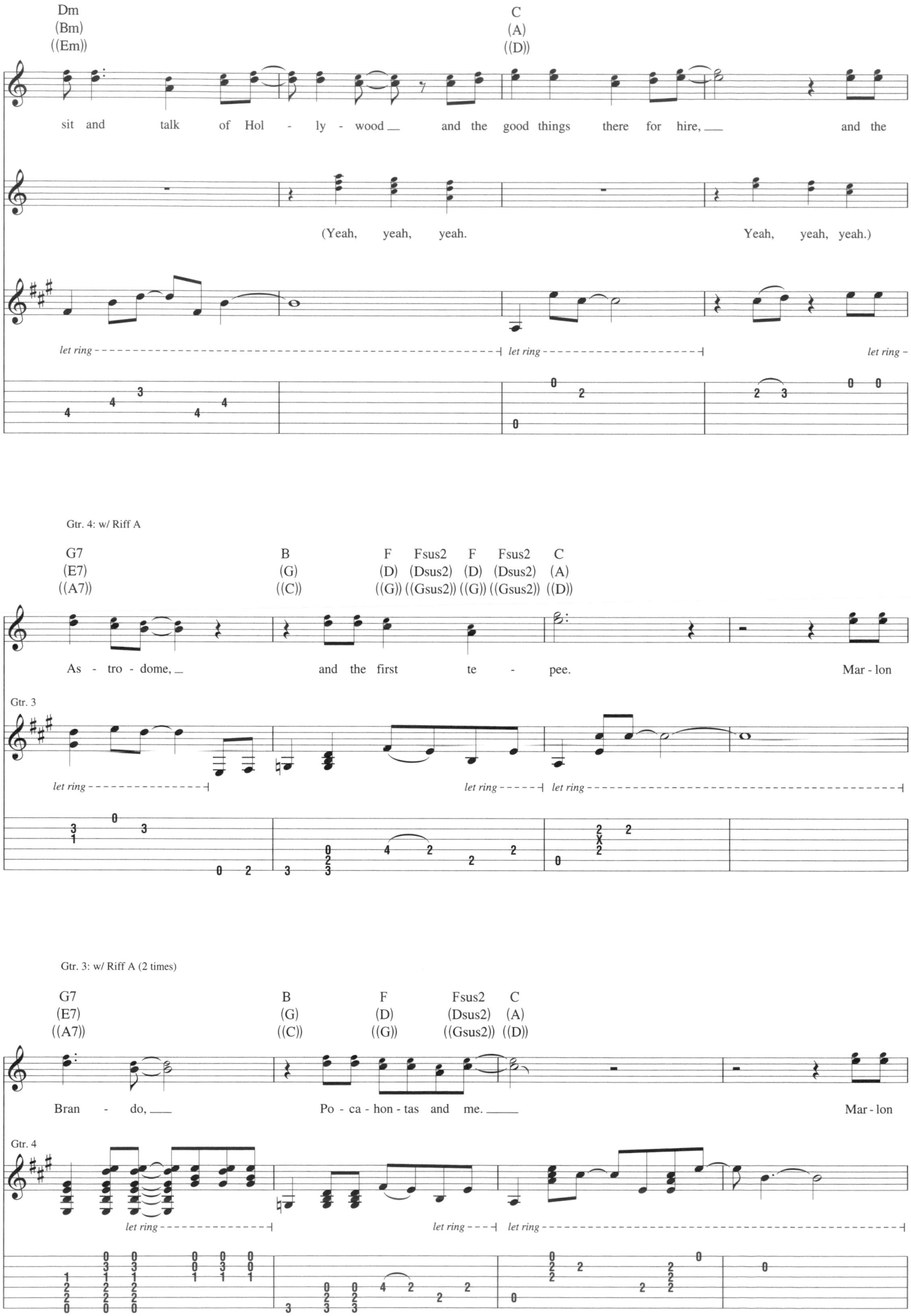
Dm (Bm) ((Em))
C (A) ((D))
sit and talk of Hol - ly - wood __ and the good things there for hire, __ and the
(Yeah, yeah, yeah. Yeah, yeah, yeah.)
let ring
Gtr. 4: w/ Riff A
G7 (E7) ((A7))
B (G) ((C))
F (D) ((G)) Fsus2 (Dsus2) ((Gsus2)) F (D) ((G)) Fsus2 (Dsus2) ((Gsus2)) C (A) ((D))
As - tro - dome, __ and the first te - pee. Mar - lon
Gtr. 3
let ring
Gtr. 3: w/ Riff A (2 times)
G7 (E7) ((A7))
B (G) ((C))
F (D) ((G)) Fsus2 (Dsus2) ((Gsus2)) C (A) ((D))
Bran - do, __ Po - ca - hon - tas and me. __ Mar - lon
Gtr. 4
let ring

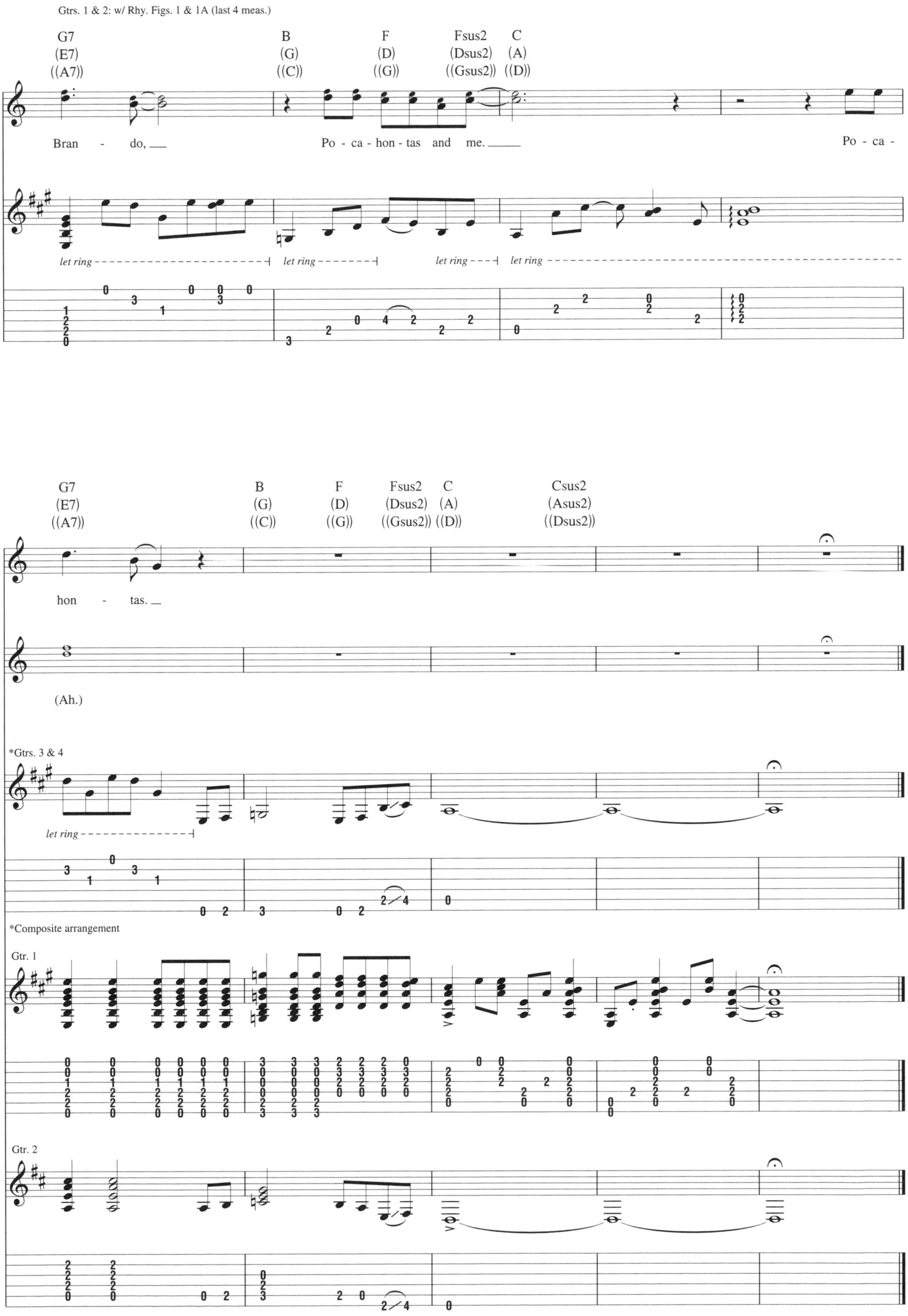
Gtrs. 1 & 2: w/ Rhy. Figs. 1 & 1A (last 4 meas.)
G7 (E7) ((A7))
B (G) ((C))
F (D) ((G))
Fsus2 (Dsus2) ((Gsus2))
C (A) ((D))
Bran - do,
Po - ca - hon - tas and me.
Po - ca -
let ring
hon - tas.
(Ah.)
Csus2 (Asus2) ((Dsus2))
*Gtrs. 3 & 4
*Composite arrangement
Gtr. 1
Gtr. 2

SAIL AWAY

Words and Music by Neil Young

I could live inside a tepee
I could die in Penthouse thirty-five
You could lose me on the freeway
But I would still make it back alive

As long as we can sail away
As long as we can sail away
There'll be wind in the canyon
Moon on the rise
As long as we can sail away

See the losers in the best bars
Meet the winners in the dives
Where the people are the real stars
All the rest of their lives

As long as we can sail away
As long as we can sail away
There'll be wind in the canyon
Moon on the rise
As long as we can sail away.

There's a road stretched out between us
Like a ribbon on the high plain
Down from Phoenix through Salinas
'Round the bend and back again

As long as we can sail away
As long as we can sail away
There'll be wind in the canyon
Moon on the rise
As long as we can sail away
As long as we can sail away
As long as we can sail away
As long as we can sail away

Sail Away

Words and Music by Neil Young

Intro

Moderately slow ♩ = 72

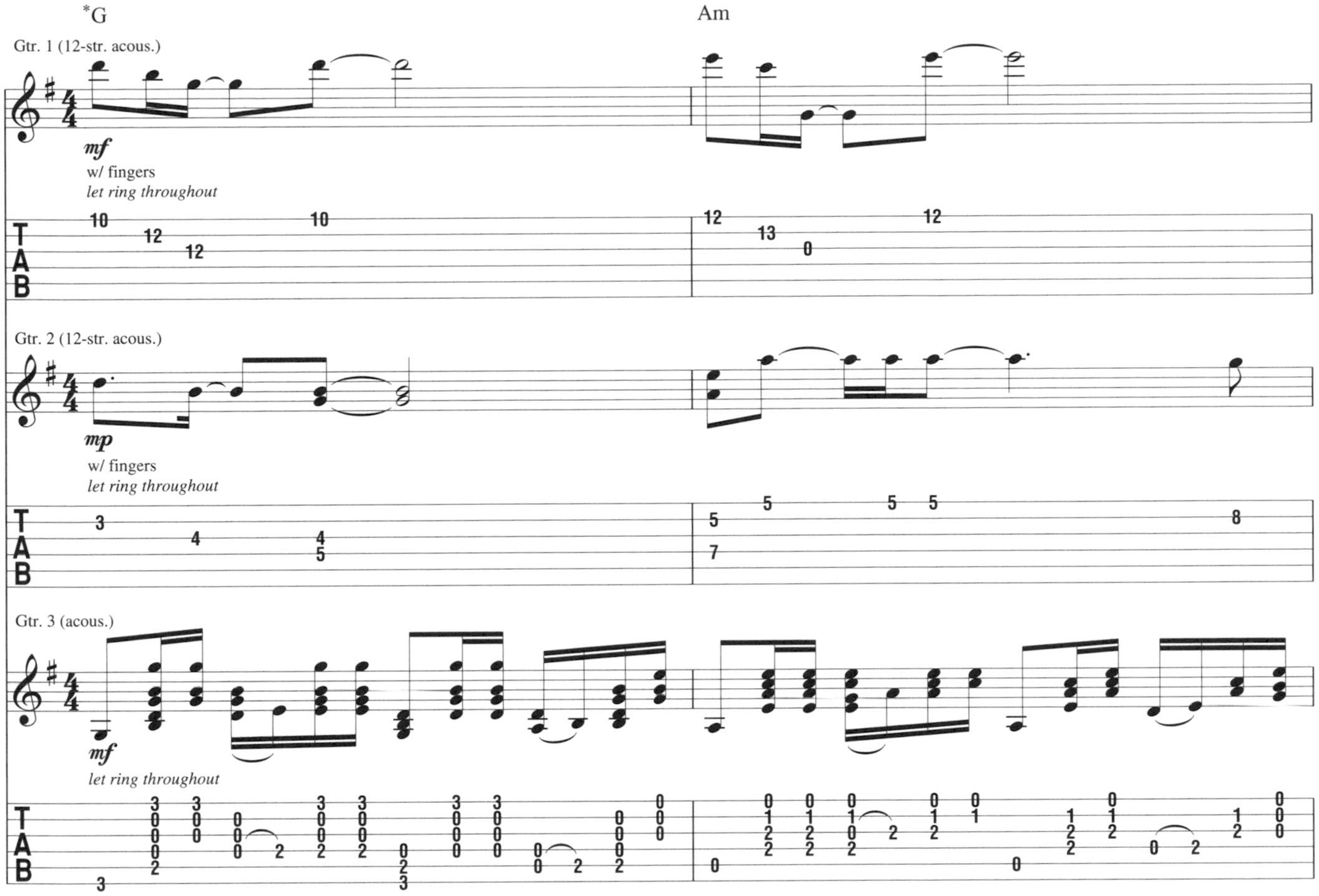

*Chord sumbols reflect basic harmony.

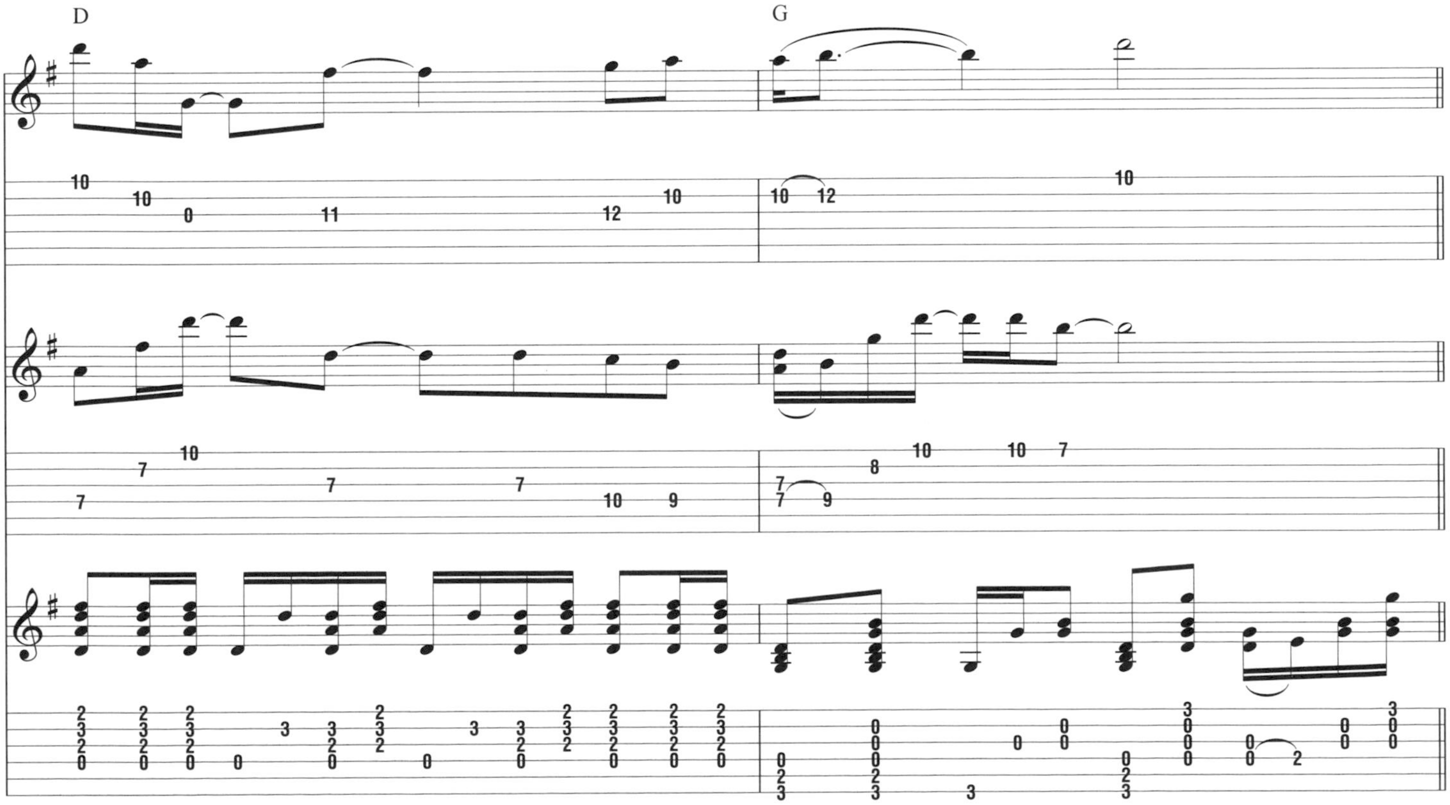

Verse

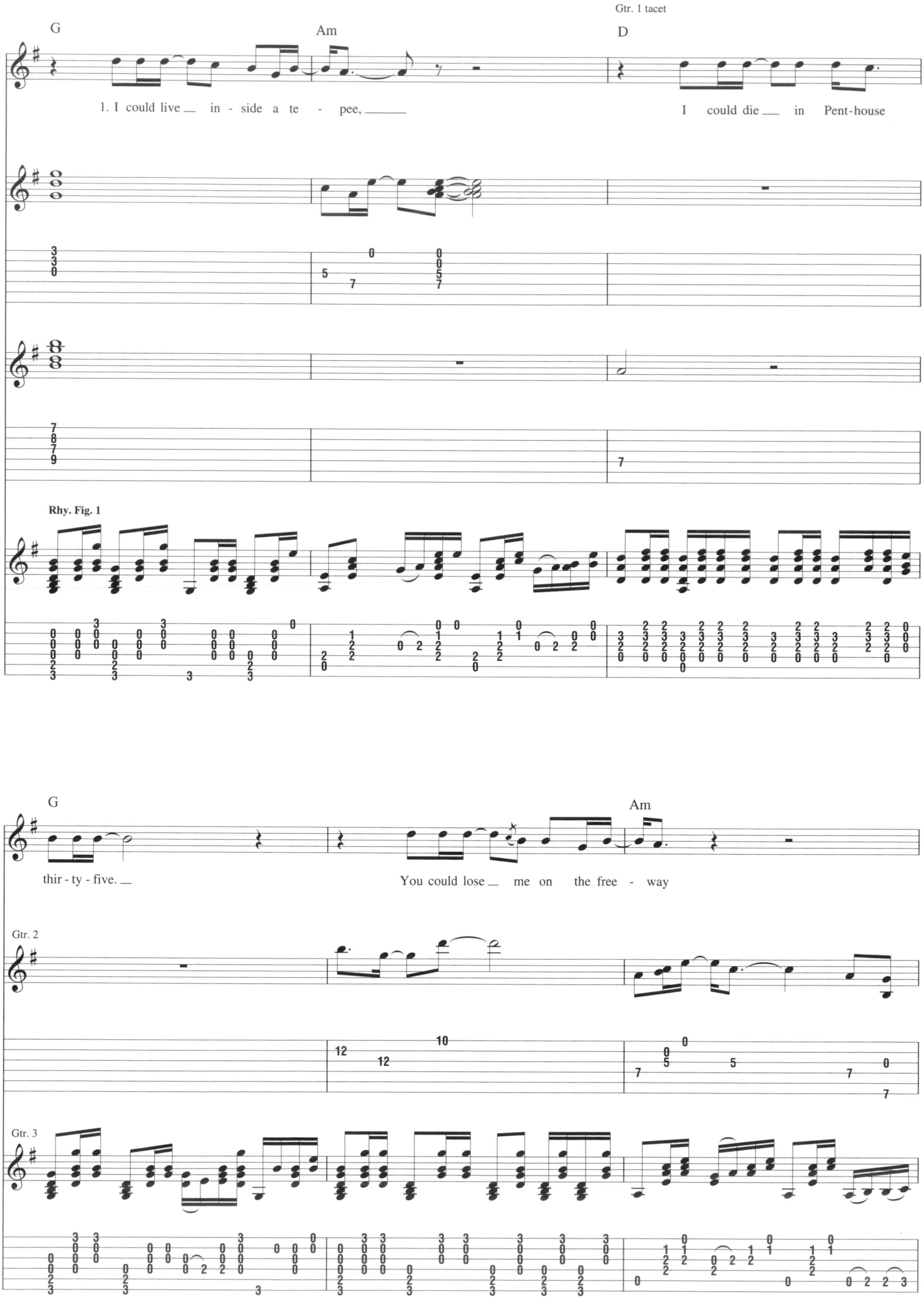
Gtr. 1 tacet
G
Am
D
1. I could live in - side a te - pee,
I could die in Pent-house
Rhy. Fig. 1
G
Am
thir - ty - five.
You could lose me on the free - way
Gtr. 2
Gtr. 3

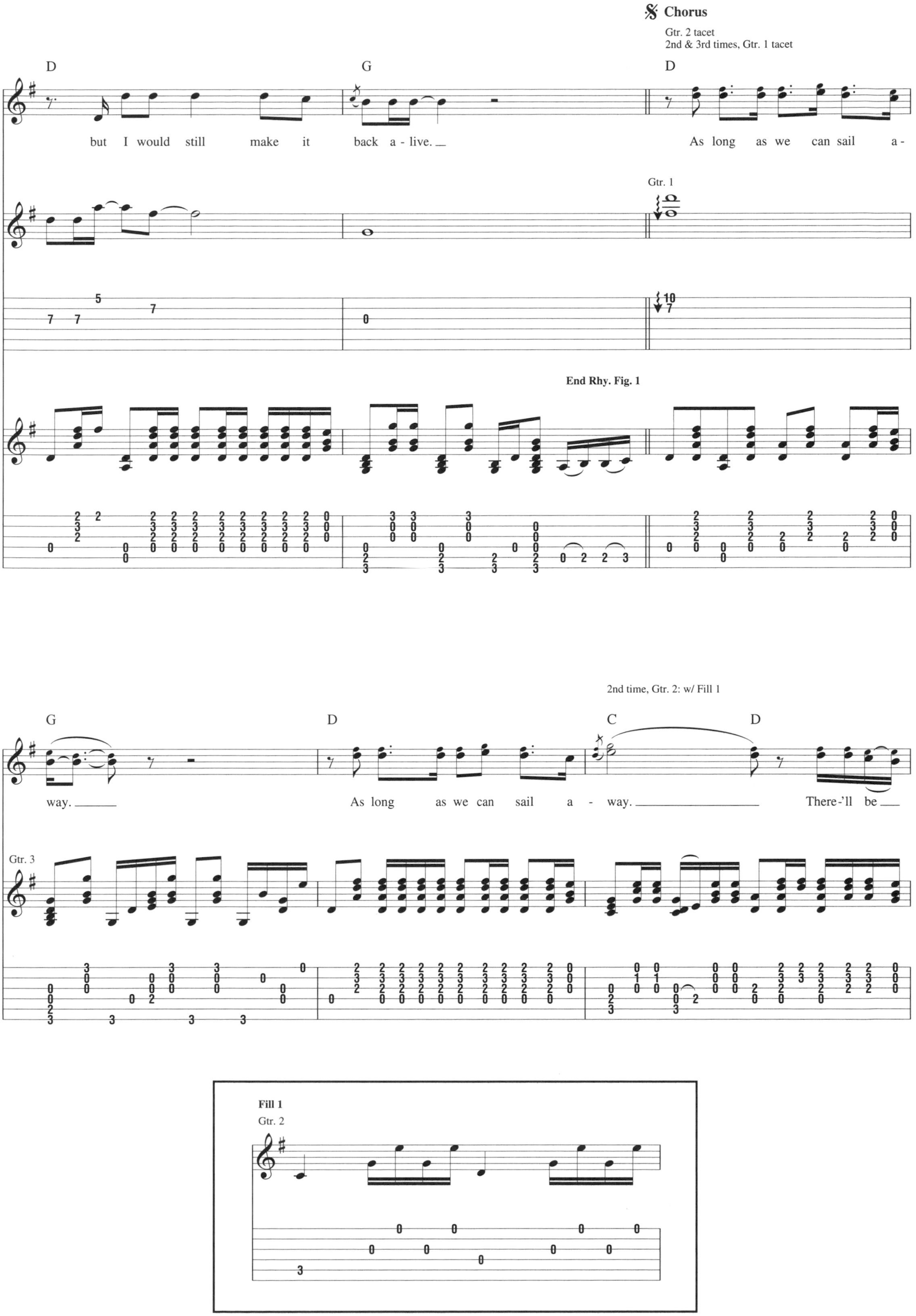
Chorus
Gtr. 2 tacet
2nd & 3rd times, Gtr. 1 tacet
D
G
D
but I would still make it back a - live.
As long as we can sail a -
Gtr. 1
End Rhy. Fig. 1
2nd time, Gtr. 2: w/ Fill 1
G
D
C
D
way.
As long as we can sail a - way.
There-'ll be
Gtr. 3
Fill 1
Gtr. 2

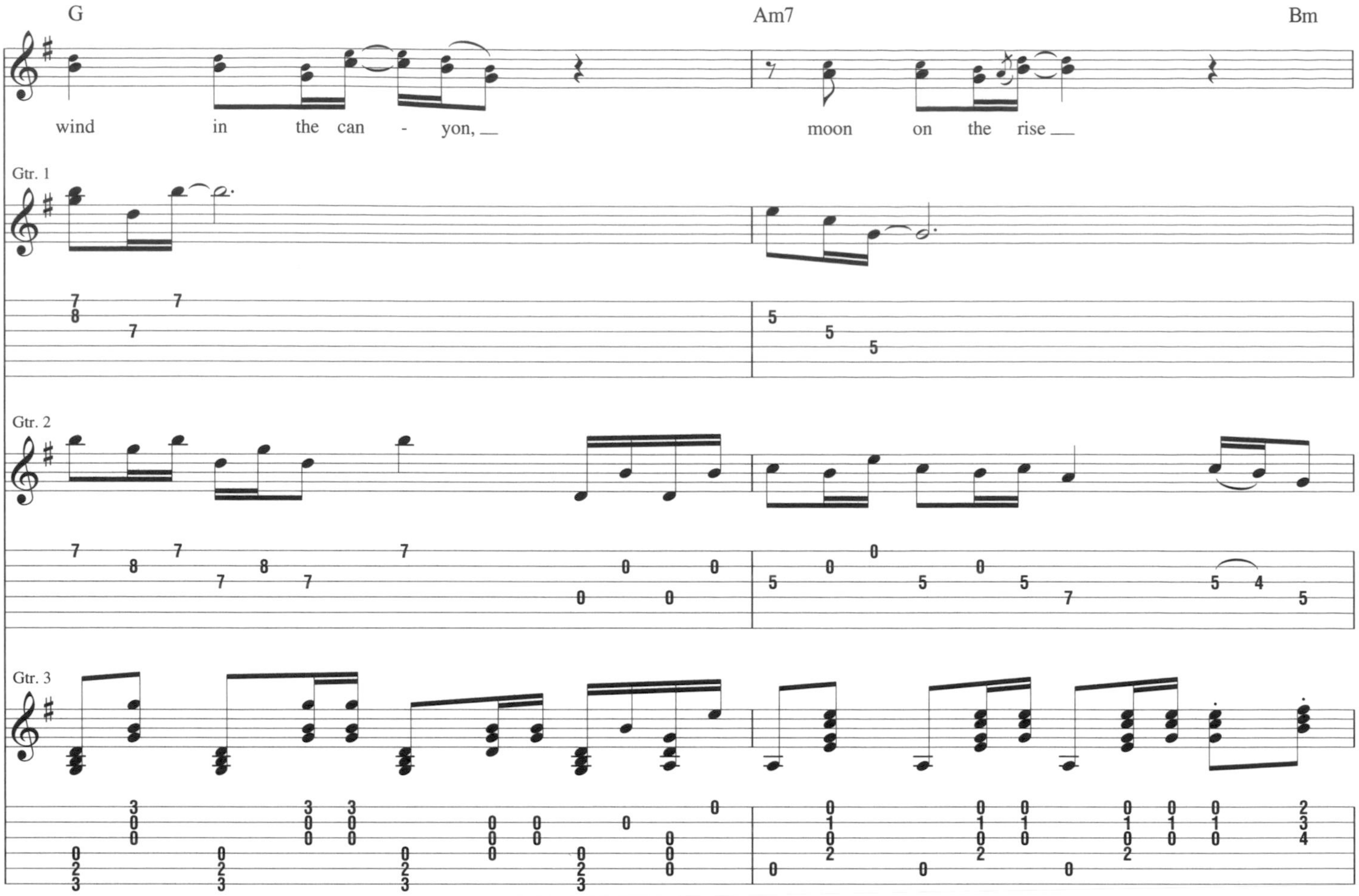
G
Am7
Bm
wind in the can - yon,
moon on the rise
Gtr. 1
Gtr. 2
Gtr. 3

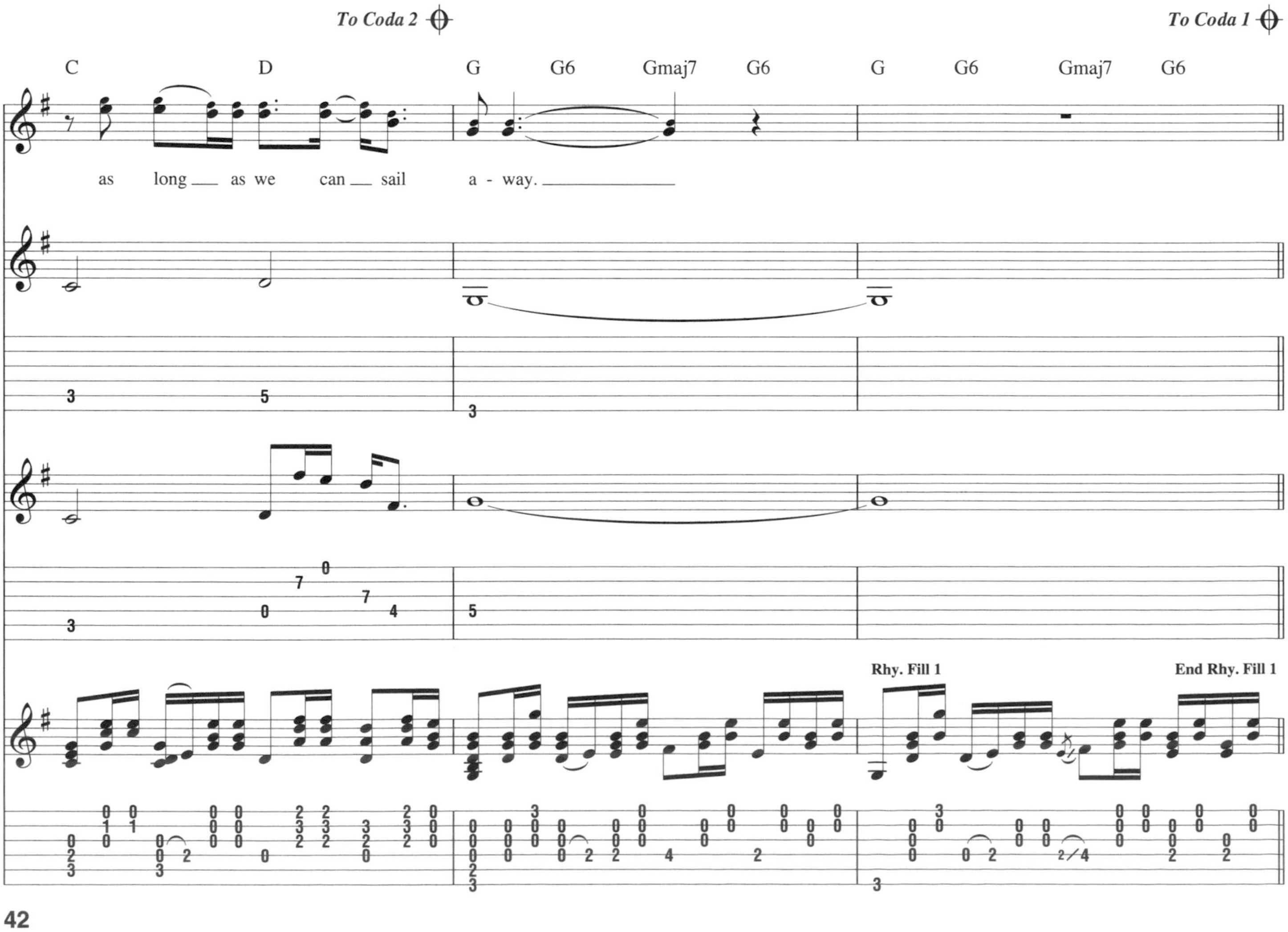
To Coda 2
To Coda 1
C
D
G
G6
Gmaj7
G6
G
G6
Gmaj7
G6
as long as we can sail a - way.
Rhy. Fill 1
End Rhy. Fill 1

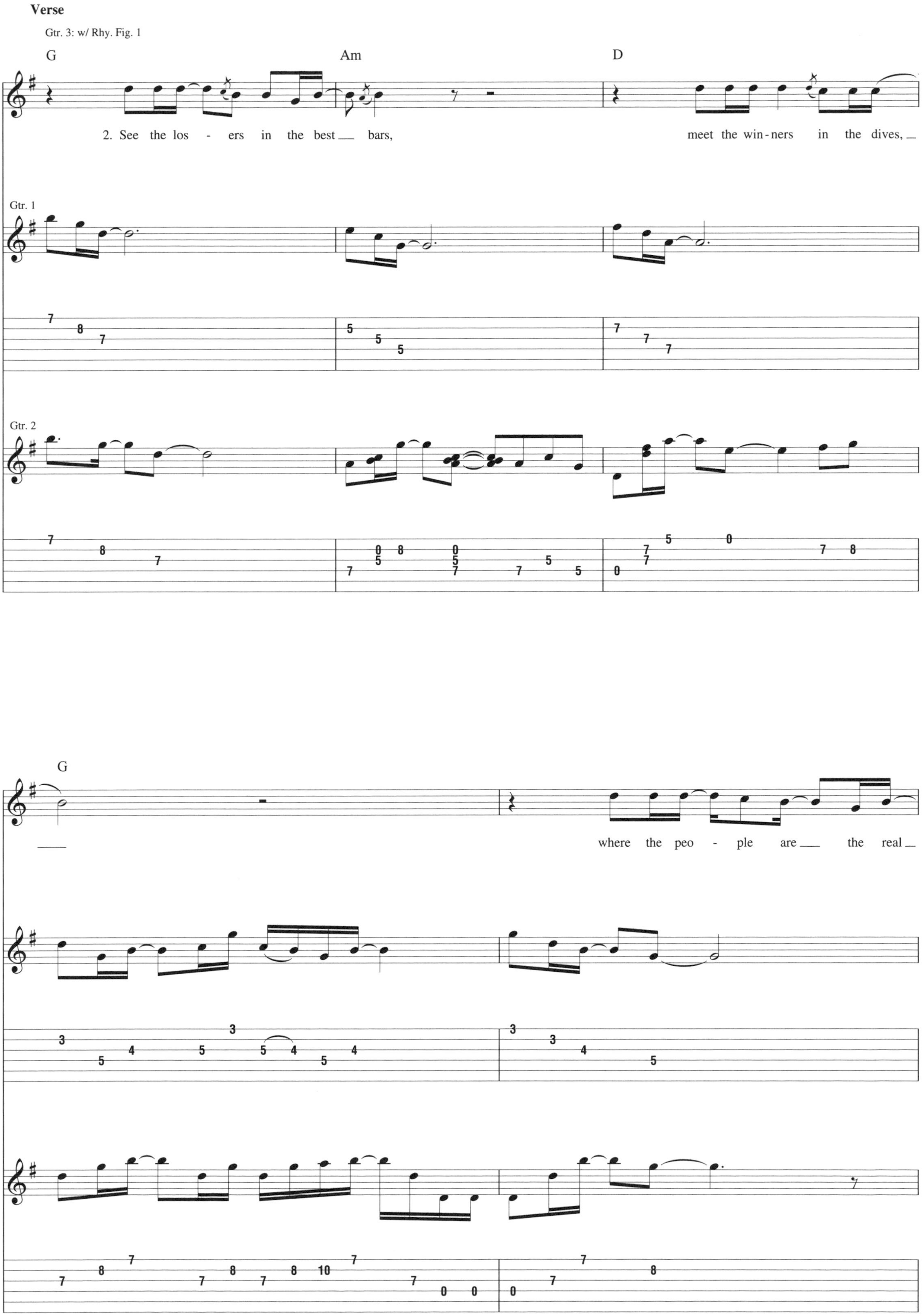
Verse
Gtr. 3: w/ Rhy. Fig. 1
G
Am
D
2. See the los - ers in the best bars,
meet the win-ners in the dives,
Gtr. 1
Gtr. 2
G
where the peo - ple are the real

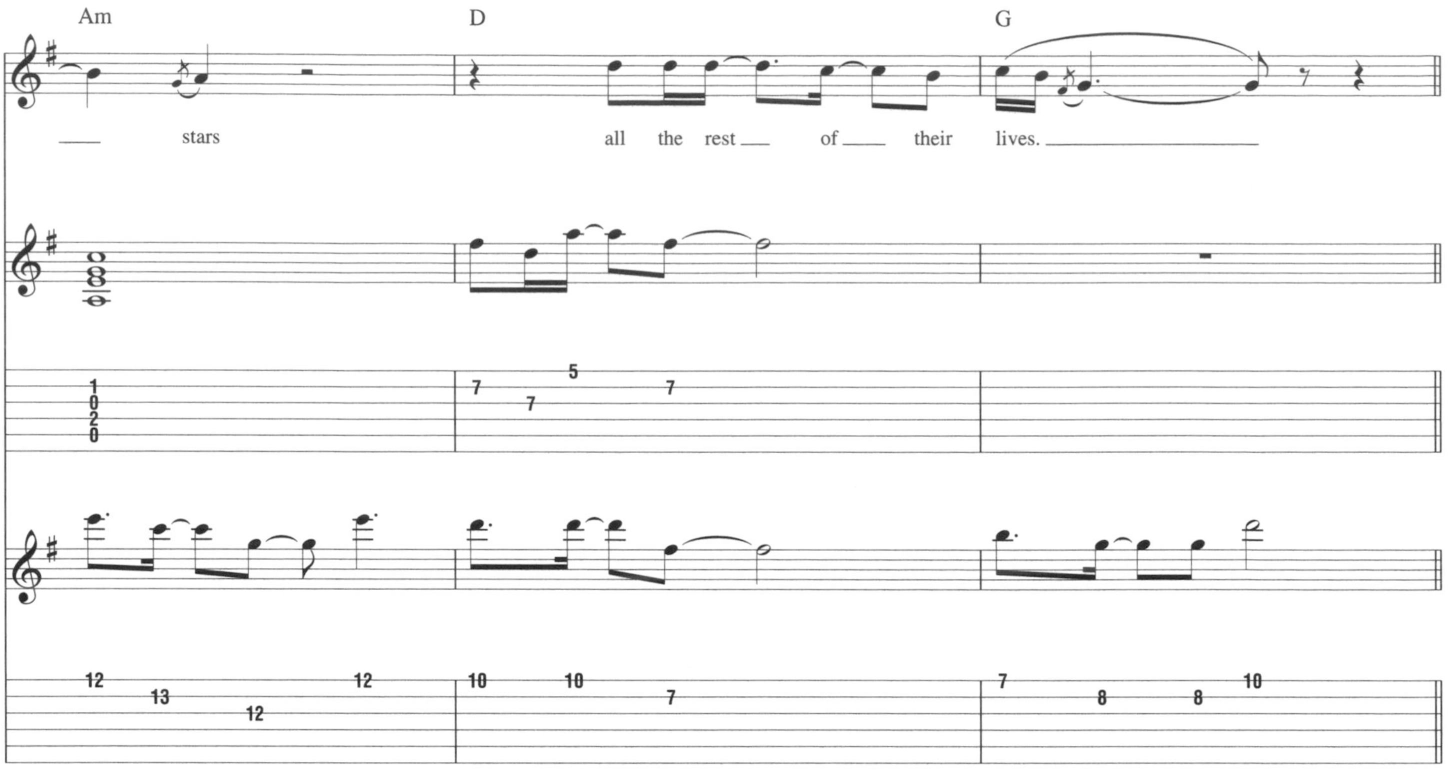

Coda 1

Harmonica Solo

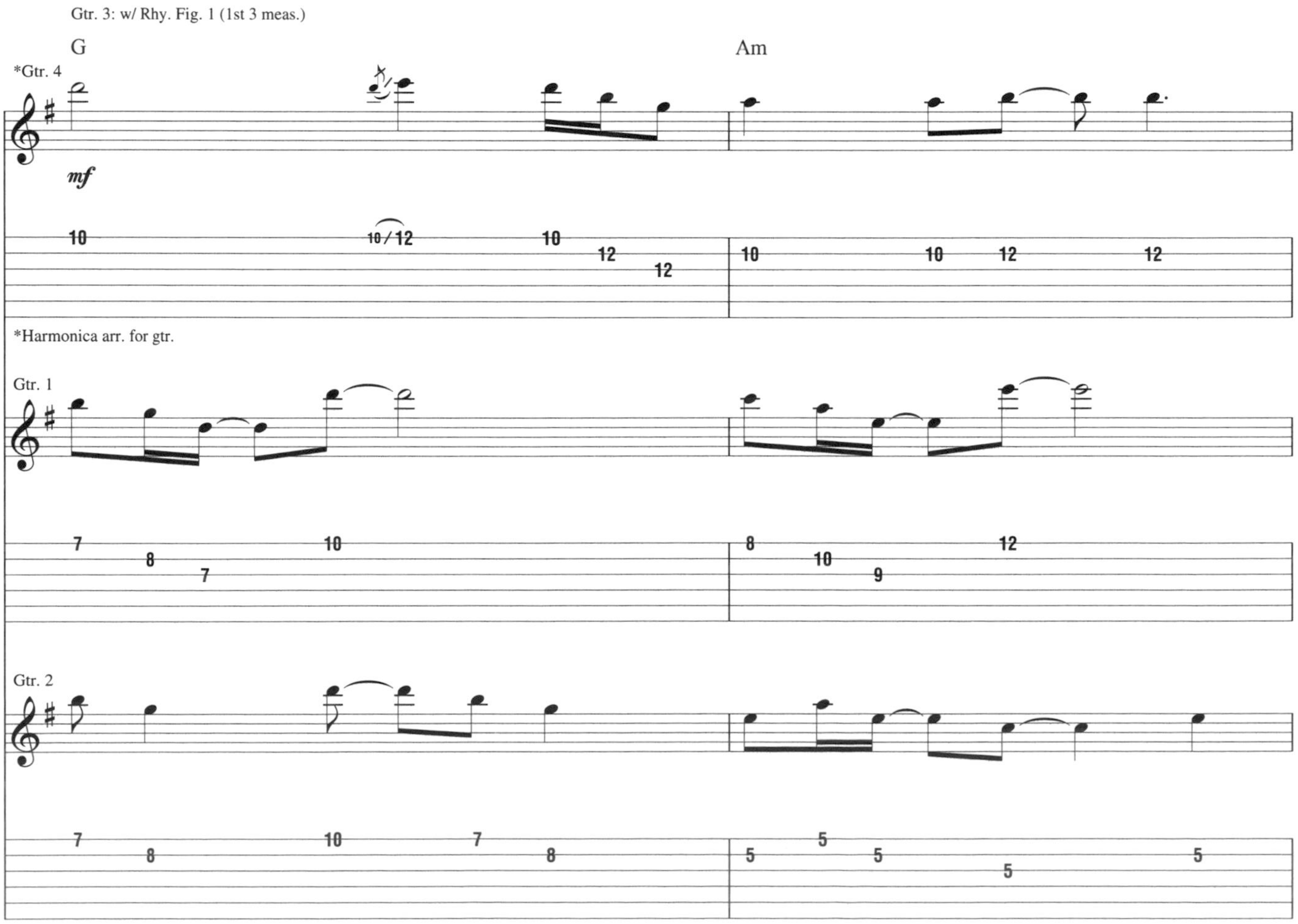

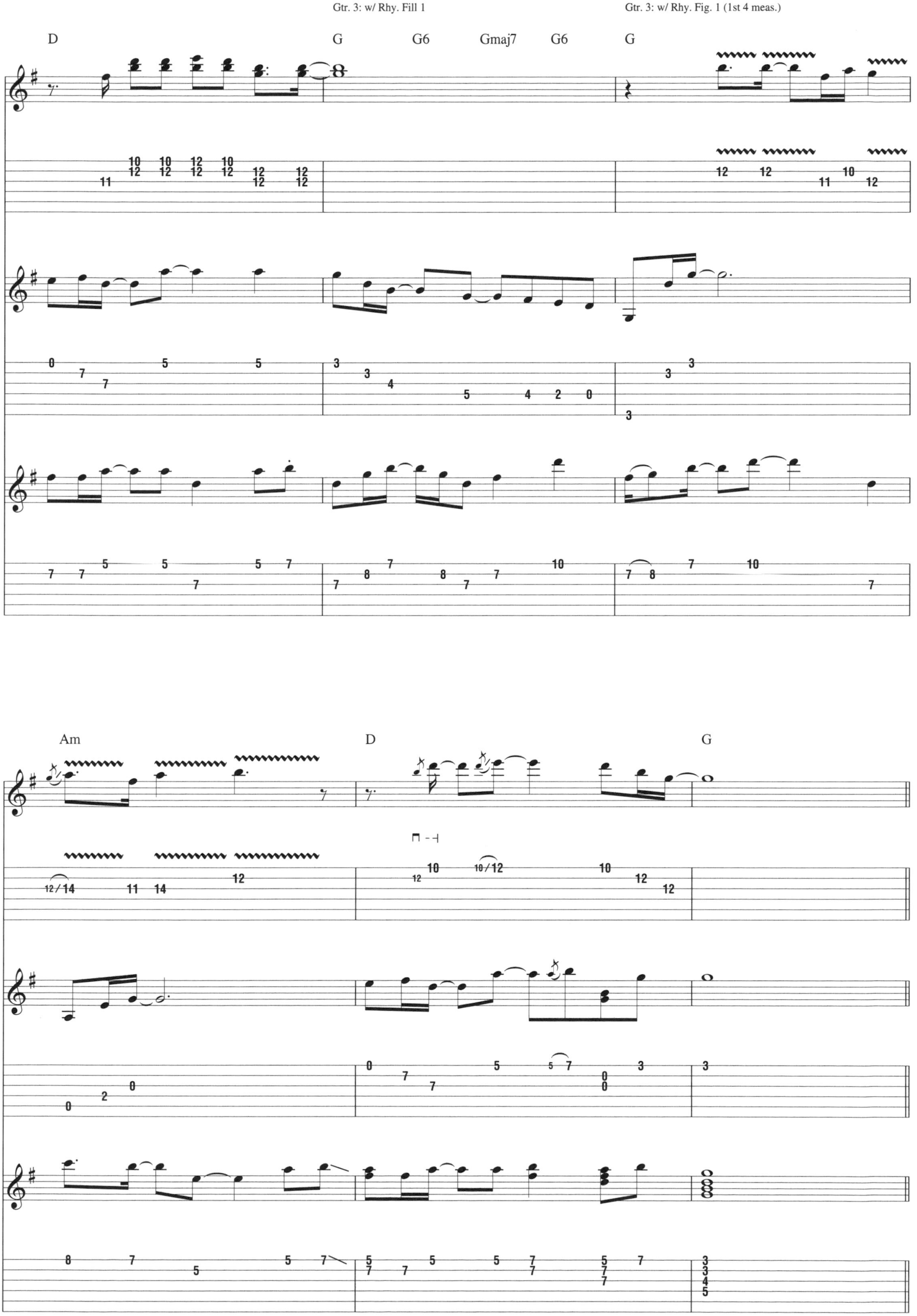
Gtr. 3: w/ Rhy. Fill 1
Gtr. 3: w/ Rhy. Fig. 1 (1st 4 meas.)
D
G
G6
Gmaj7
G6
G
Am
D
G

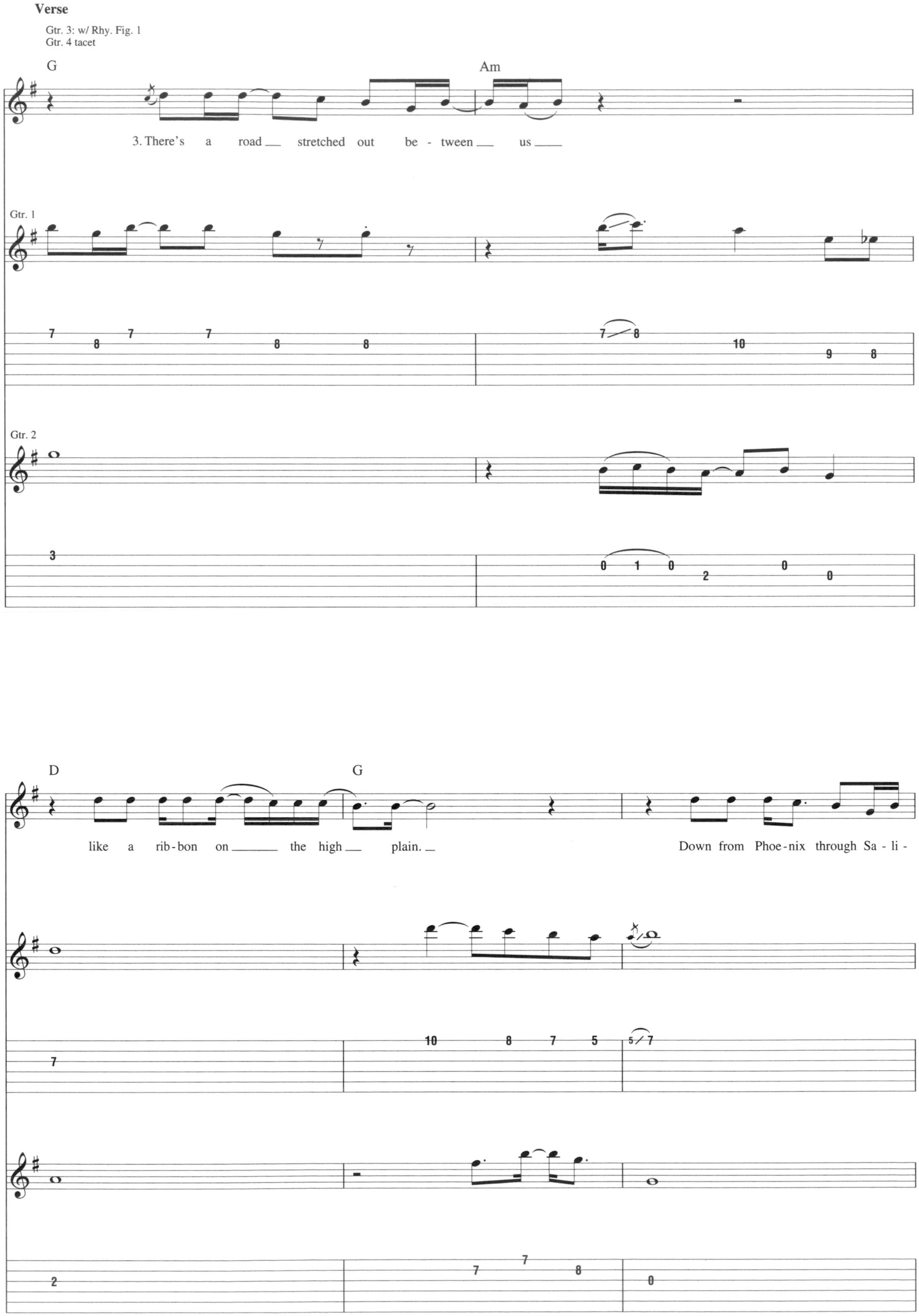
Verse
Gtr. 3: w/ Rhy. Fig. 1
Gtr. 4 tacet
G
Am
3. There's a road stretched out be - tween us
Gtr. 1
Gtr. 2
D
G
like a rib-bon on the high plain.
Down from Phoe-nix through Sa - li -

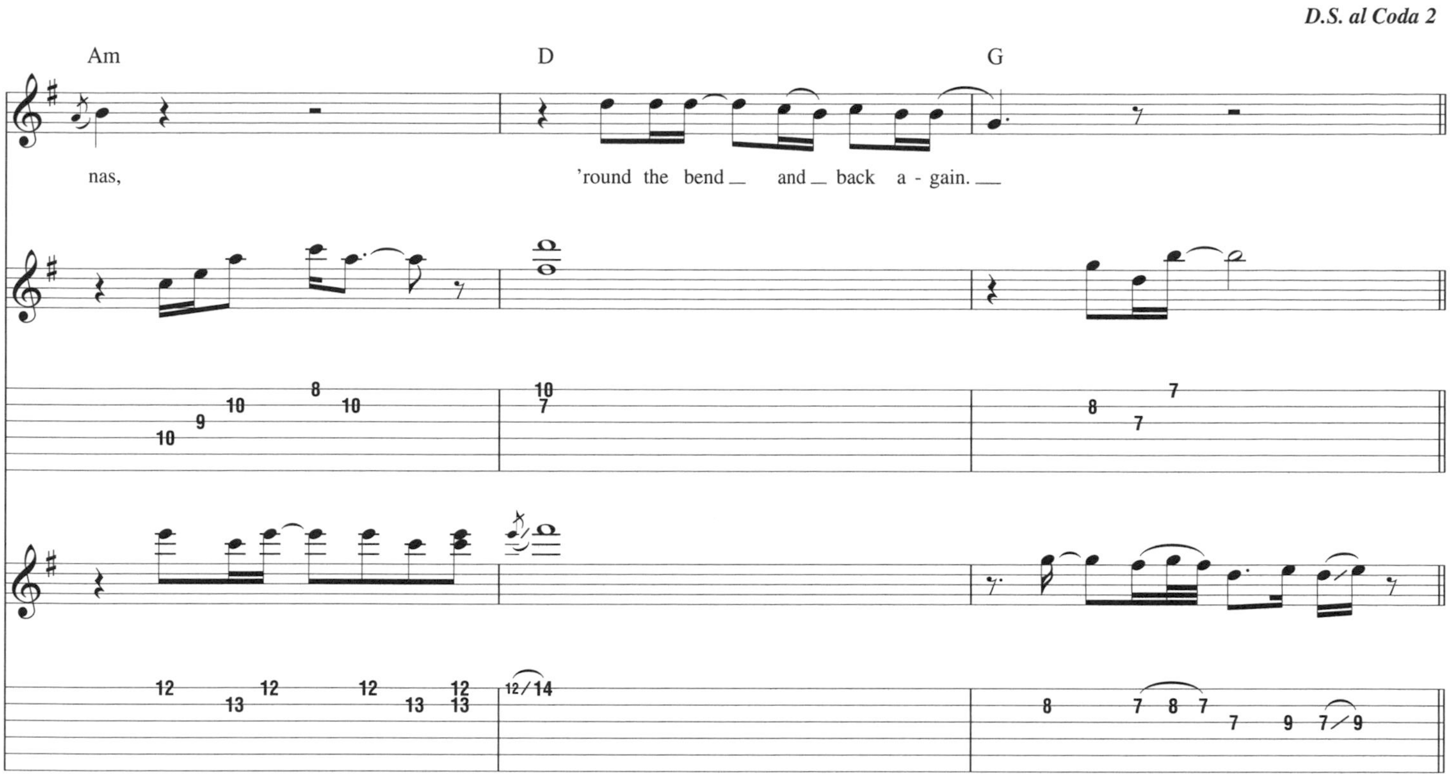
D.S. al Coda 2
Am
D
G
nas,
'round the bend and back a - gain.

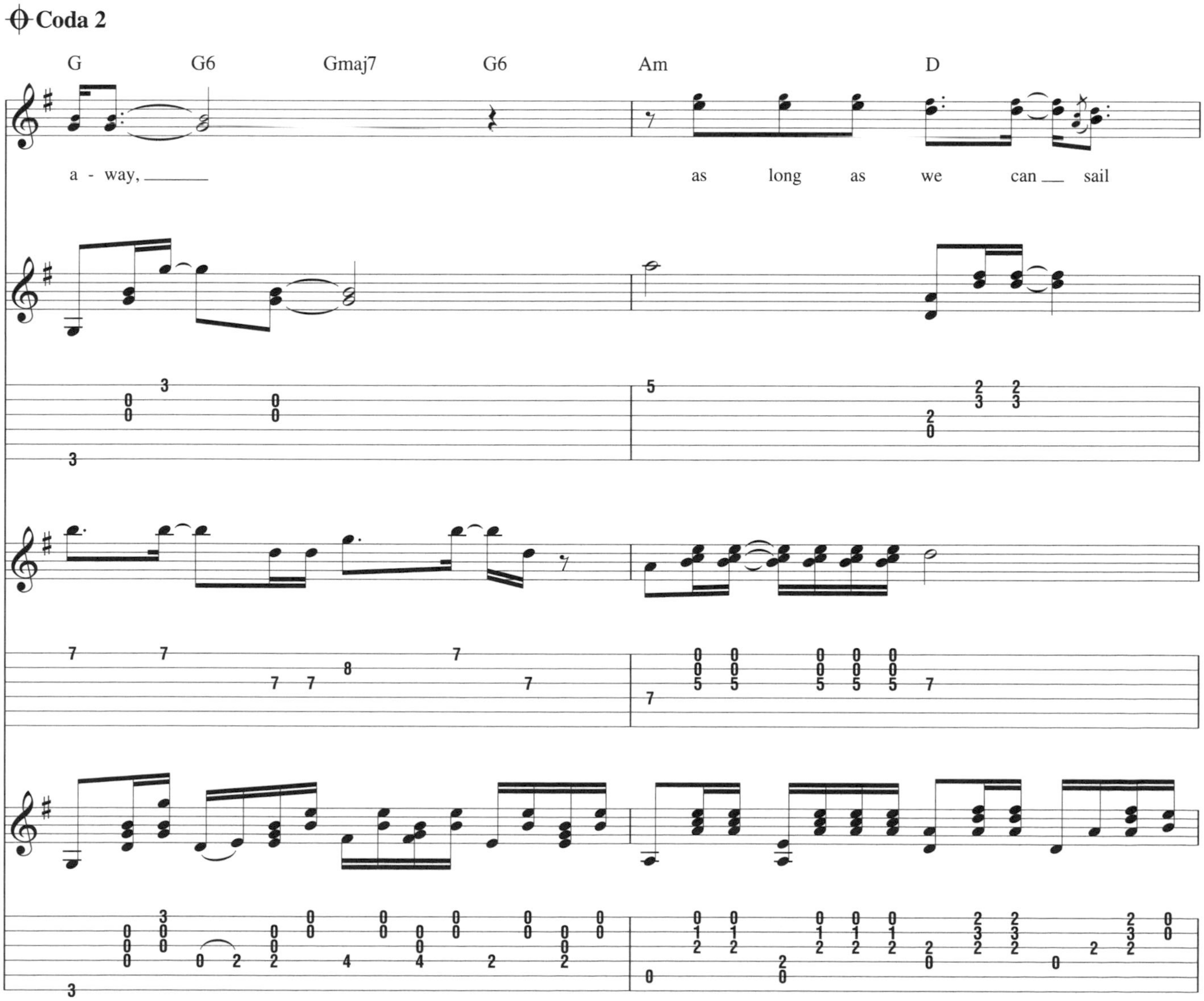
Coda 2
G
G6
Gmaj7
G6
Am
D
a - way,
as long as we can sail

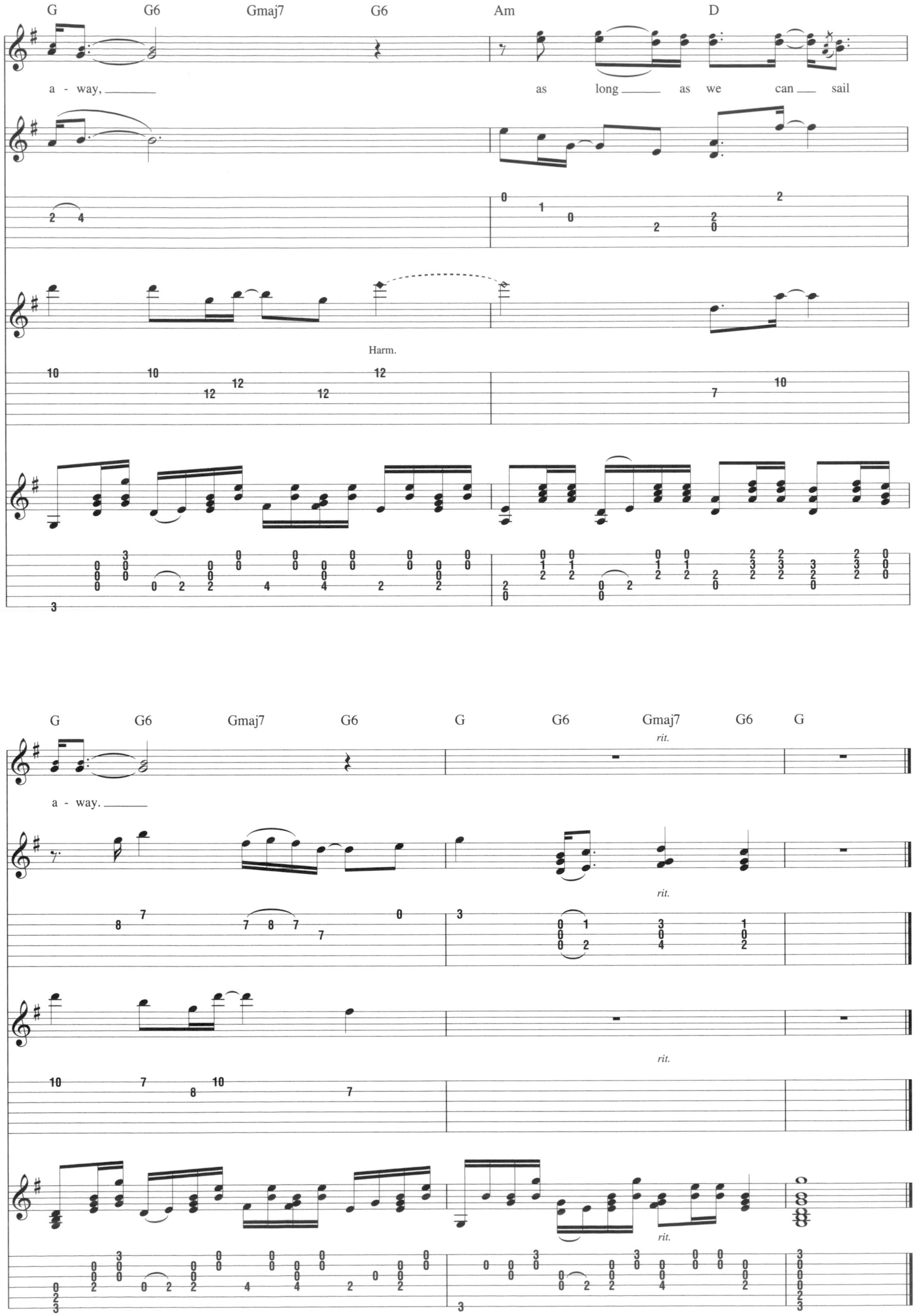
G G6 Gmaj7 G6 Am D
a - way, as long as we can sail
Harm.
G G6 Gmaj7 G6 G G6 Gmaj7 G6 G
rit.
a - way.

POWDERFINGER

Words and Music by Neil Young

Look out, Mama, there's a white boat comin' up the river
With a big red beacon, and a flag, and a man on the rail
I think you'd better call John 'cause it don't
  look like they're here to deliver the mail
And it's less than a mile away
I hope they didn't come to stay
It's got numbers on the side and a gun
  and it's makin' big waves

Daddy's gone, my brother's out
  hunting in the mountains
Big John's been drinking since the river took Emmy Lou
So the Powers That Be left me here to do the thinkin'
And I just turned twenty-two
I was wonderin' what to do
And the closer they got,
The more those feelings grew.

Daddy's rifle in my hand felt reassurin'
He told me, "Red means run, son,
  and numbers add up to nothin'"
When the first shot hit the dock I saw it comin'
Raised my rifle to my eye
Never stopped to wonder why
Then I saw black and my face splashed in the sky

Shelter me from the powder and the finger
Cover me with the thought that pulled the trigger
Think of me as one you never figured
Would fade away so young
With so much left undone
Remember me to my love, I know I'll miss her

Powderfinger

Words and Music by Neil Young

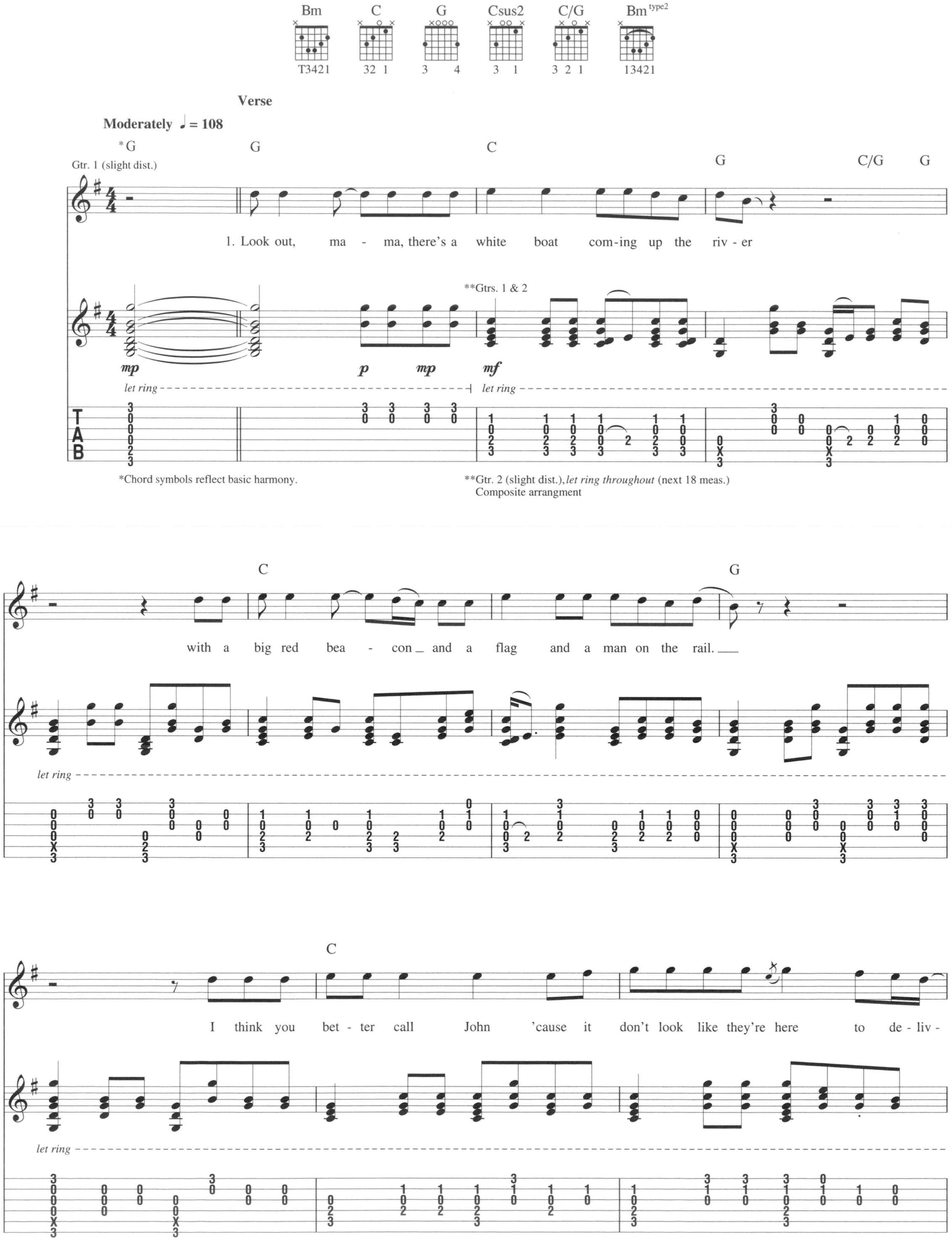

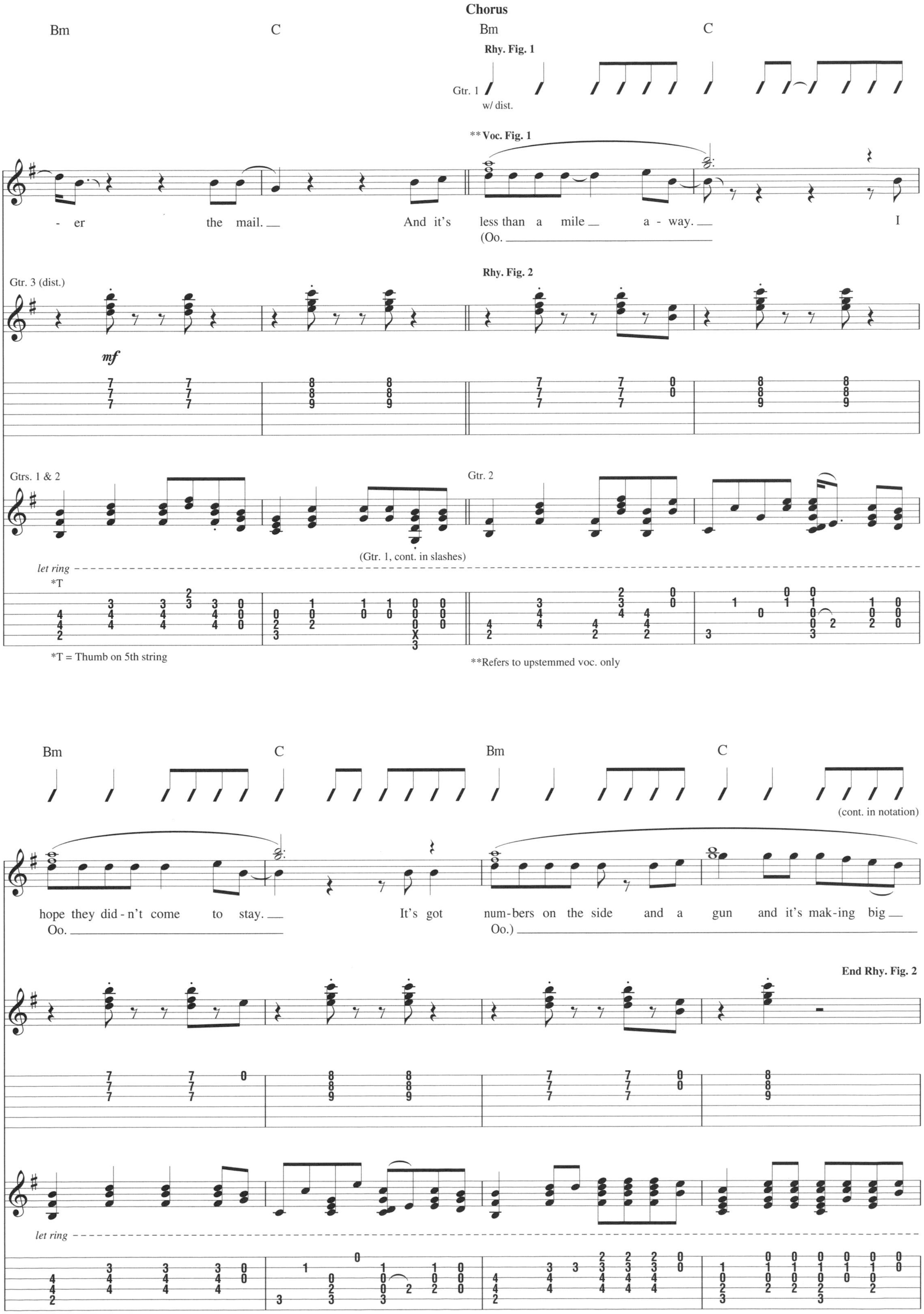
Chorus
Bm
C
Bm
C
Rhy. Fig. 1
Gtr. 1
w/ dist.
** Voc. Fig. 1
- er the mail. And it's less than a mile a - way. I
(Oo.
Gtr. 3 (dist.)
Rhy. Fig. 2
mf
Gtrs. 1 & 2
Gtr. 2
(Gtr. 1, cont. in slashes)
let ring
*T
*T = Thumb on 5th string
**Refers to upstemmed voc. only
Bm
C
Bm
C
(cont. in notation)
hope they did - n't come to stay. It's got num - bers on the side and a gun and it's mak - ing big
Oo.
Oo.)
End Rhy. Fig. 2
let ring

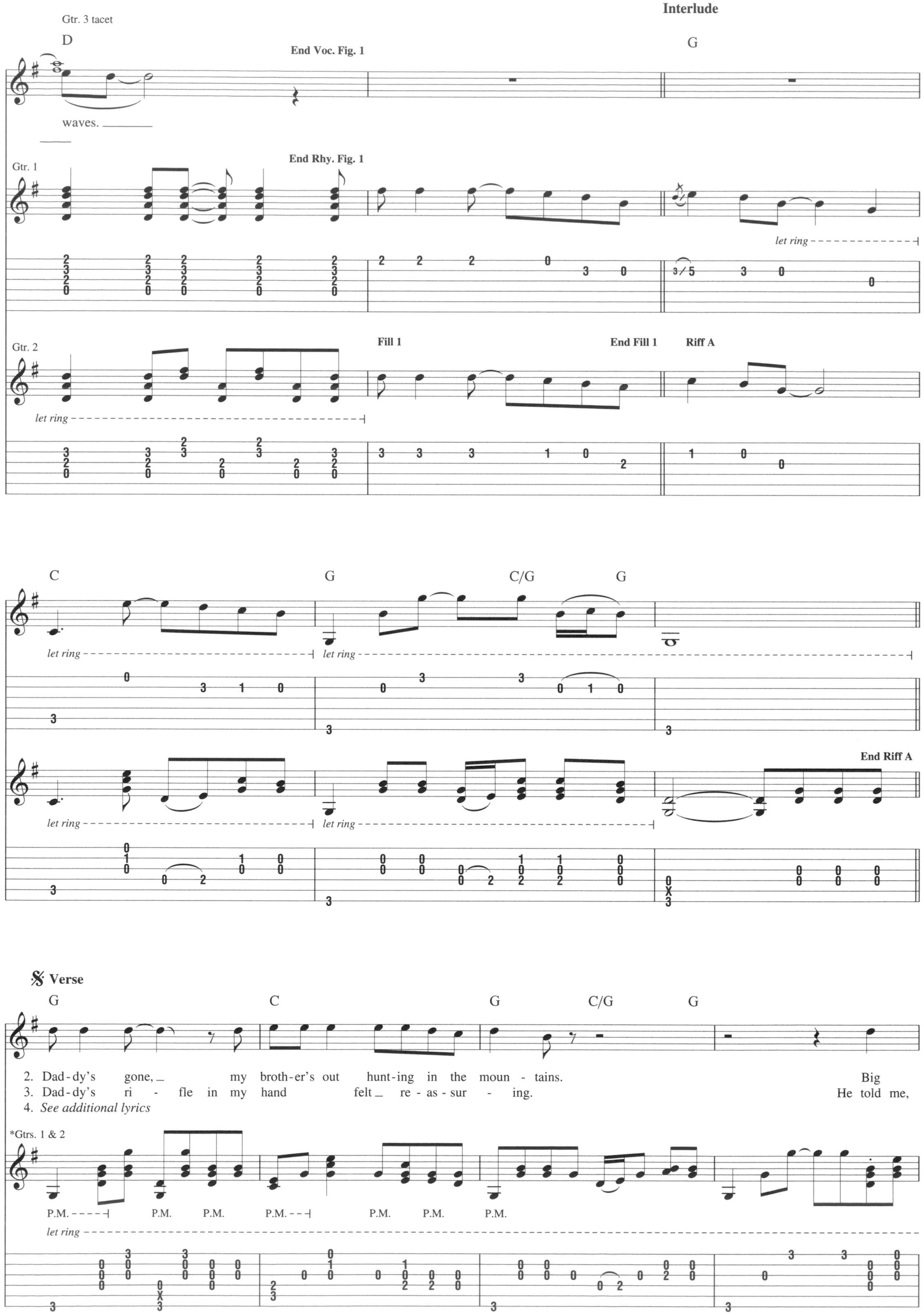
Gtr. 3 tacet
Interlude
D
End Voc. Fig. 1
G
waves.
Gtr. 1
End Rhy. Fig. 1
let ring
Gtr. 2
Fill 1
End Fill 1
Riff A
let ring
C
G
C/G
G
let ring
End Riff A
Verse
G
C
G
C/G
G
2. Dad-dy's gone, my broth-er's out hunt-ing in the moun - tains. Big
3. Dad-dy's ri - fle in my hand felt re - as - sur - ing. He told me,
4. See additional lyrics
*Gtrs. 1 & 2
P.M.
let ring

*Composite arrangement

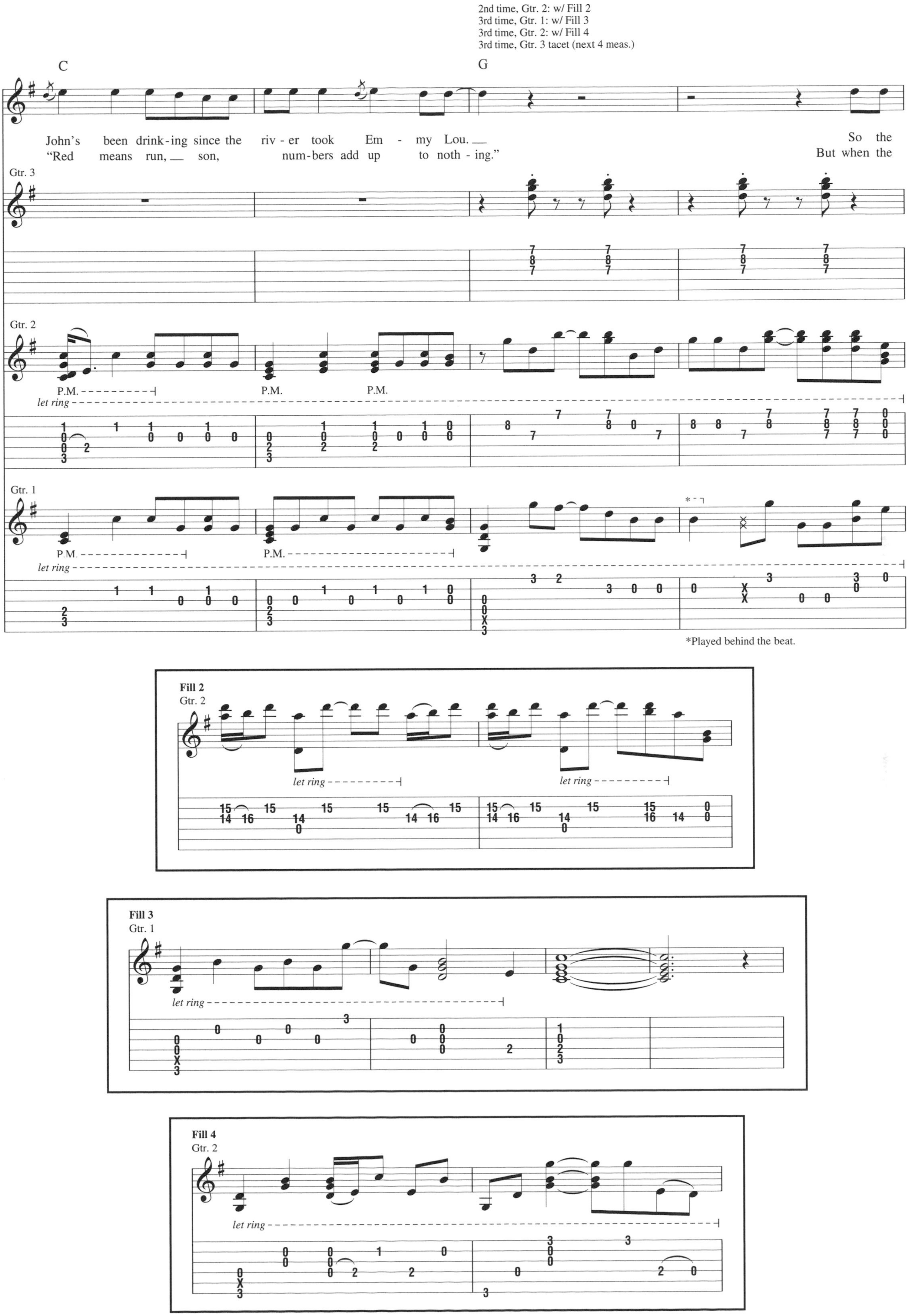
2nd time, Gtr. 2: w/ Fill 2
3rd time, Gtr. 1: w/ Fill 3
3rd time, Gtr. 2: w/ Fill 4
3rd time, Gtr. 3 tacet (next 4 meas.)
C
G
John's been drink-ing since the riv - er took Em - my Lou. So the
"Red means run, son, num-bers add up to noth - ing." But when the
Gtr. 3
Gtr. 2
P.M.
let ring
Gtr. 1
*Played behind the beat.
Fill 2
Gtr. 2
let ring
Fill 3
Gtr. 1
let ring
Fill 4
Gtr. 2
let ring

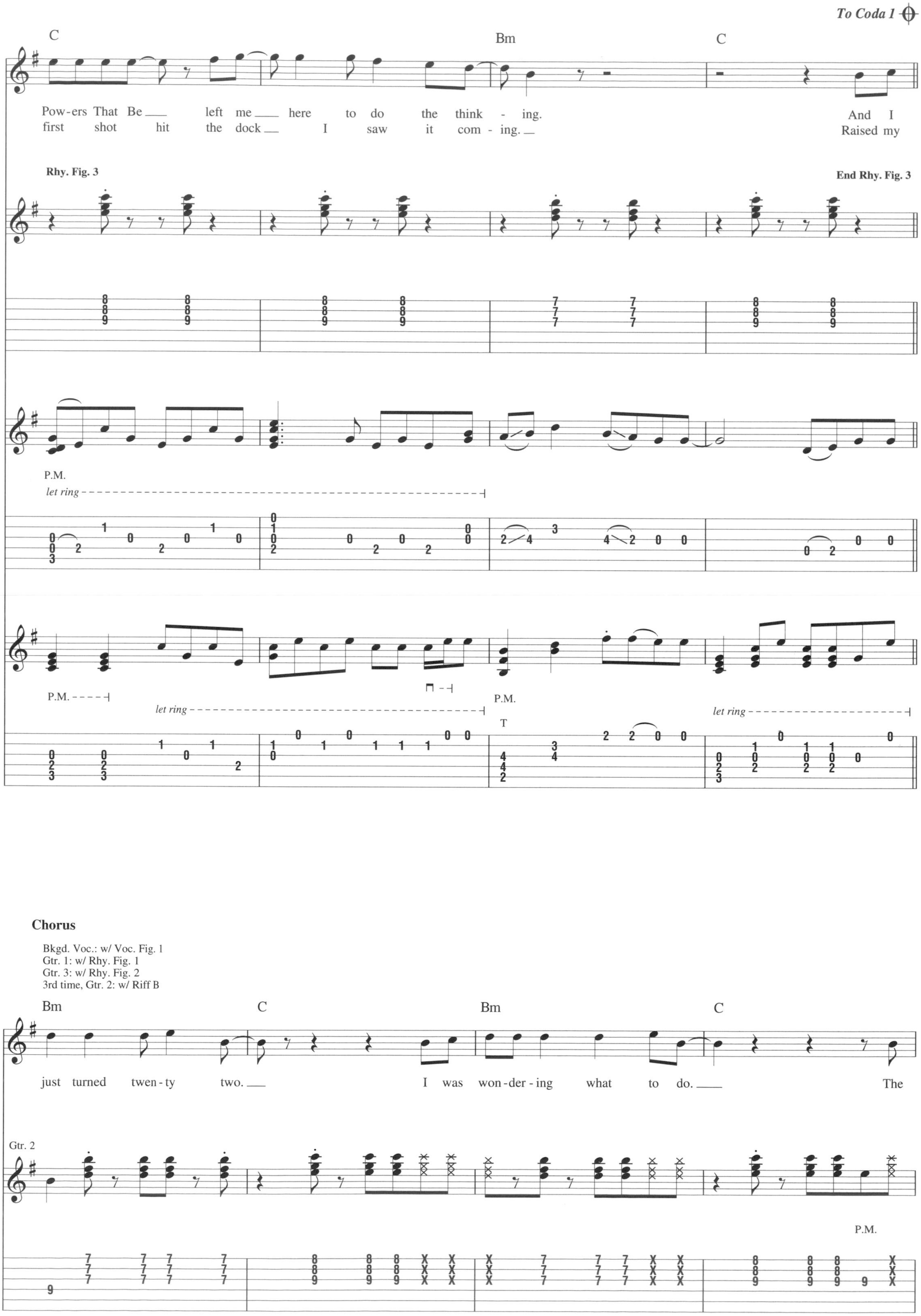
To Coda 1
C
Bm
C
Pow-ers That Be ___ left me ___ here to do the think - ing. And I
first shot hit the dock ___ I saw it com - ing. ___ Raised my
Rhy. Fig. 3
End Rhy. Fig. 3
P.M.
let ring
P.M.
let ring
P.M.
T
let ring
Chorus
Bkgd. Voc.: w/ Voc. Fig. 1
Gtr. 1: w/ Rhy. Fig. 1
Gtr. 3: w/ Rhy. Fig. 2
3rd time, Gtr. 2: w/ Riff B
Bm
C
Bm
C
just turned twen-ty two. ___ I was won-der-ing what to do. ___ The
Gtr. 2
P.M.

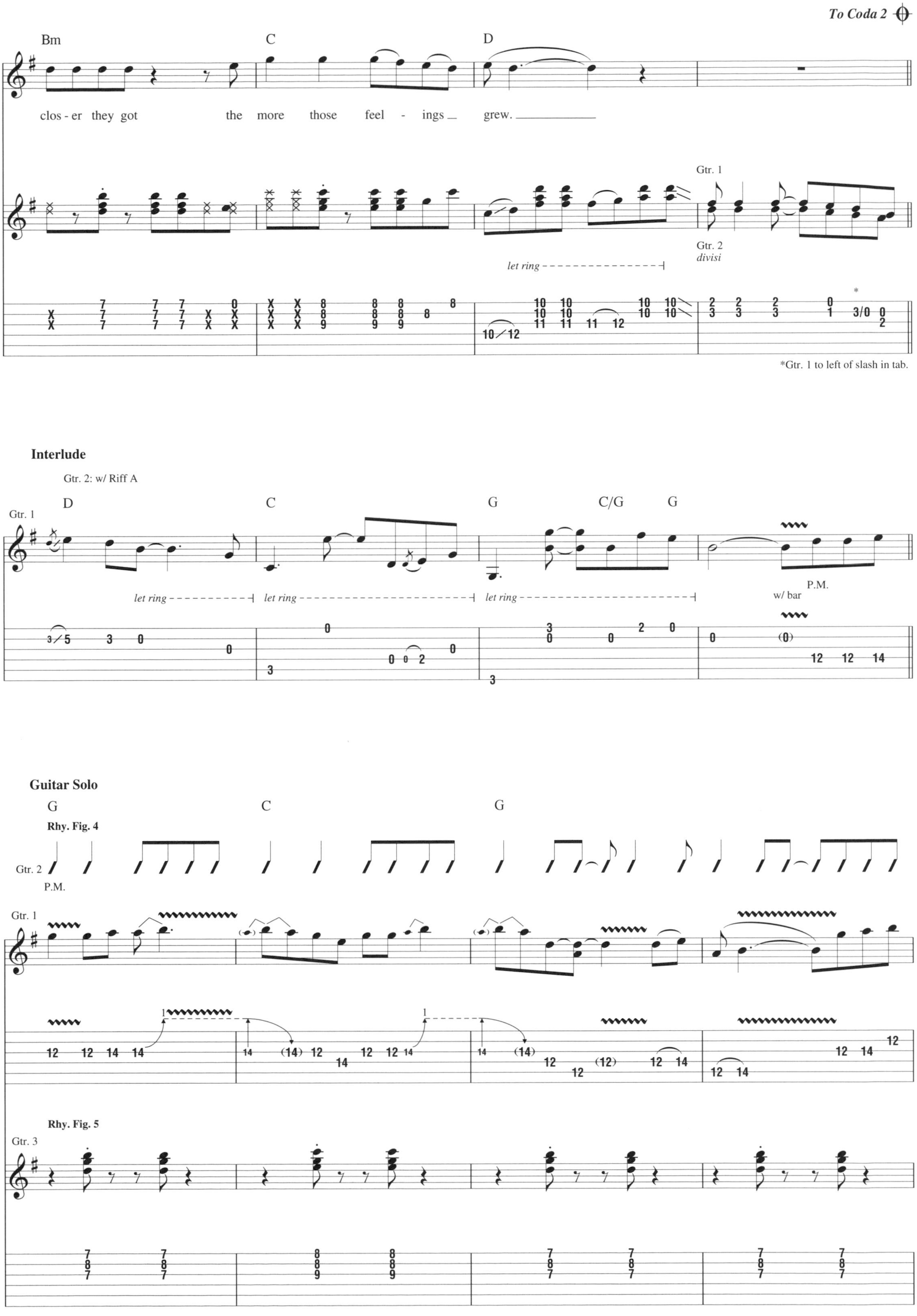
To Coda 2
Bm
C
D
clos - er they got the more those feel - ings grew.
Gtr. 1
Gtr. 2
divisi
let ring
*Gtr. 1 to left of slash in tab.
Interlude
Gtr. 2: w/ Riff A
Gtr. 1
D
C
G
C/G
G
let ring
w/ bar
P.M.
Guitar Solo
Rhy. Fig. 4
Gtr. 2
P.M.
Gtr. 1
Rhy. Fig. 5
Gtr. 3

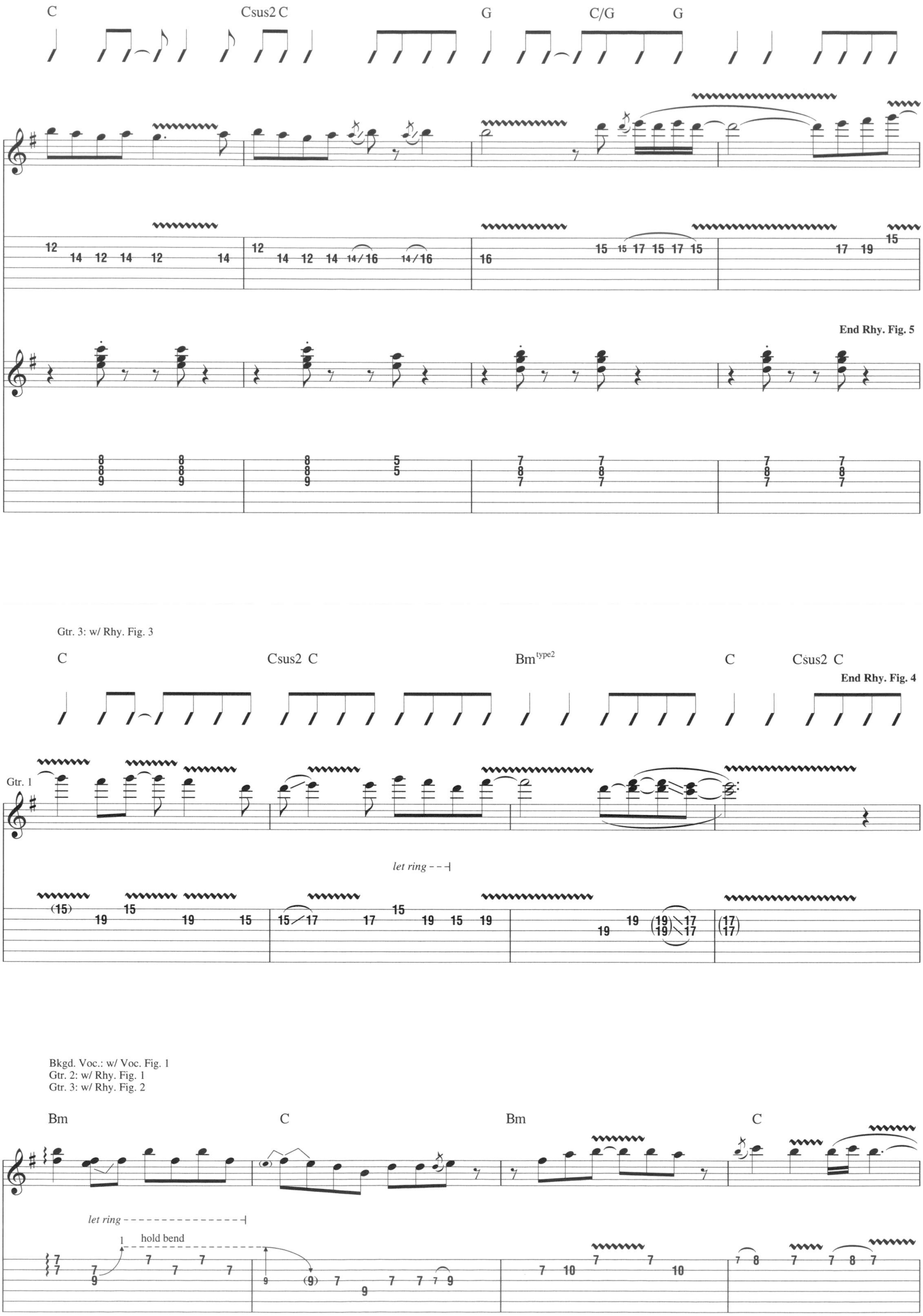
C
Csus2 C
G
C/G
G
End Rhy. Fig. 5
Gtr. 3: w/ Rhy. Fig. 3
C
Csus2 C
Bm type2
C
Csus2 C
End Rhy. Fig. 4
Gtr. 1
let ring
Bkgd. Voc.: w/ Voc. Fig. 1
Gtr. 2: w/ Rhy. Fig. 1
Gtr. 3: w/ Rhy. Fig. 2
Bm
C
Bm
C
let ring
hold bend

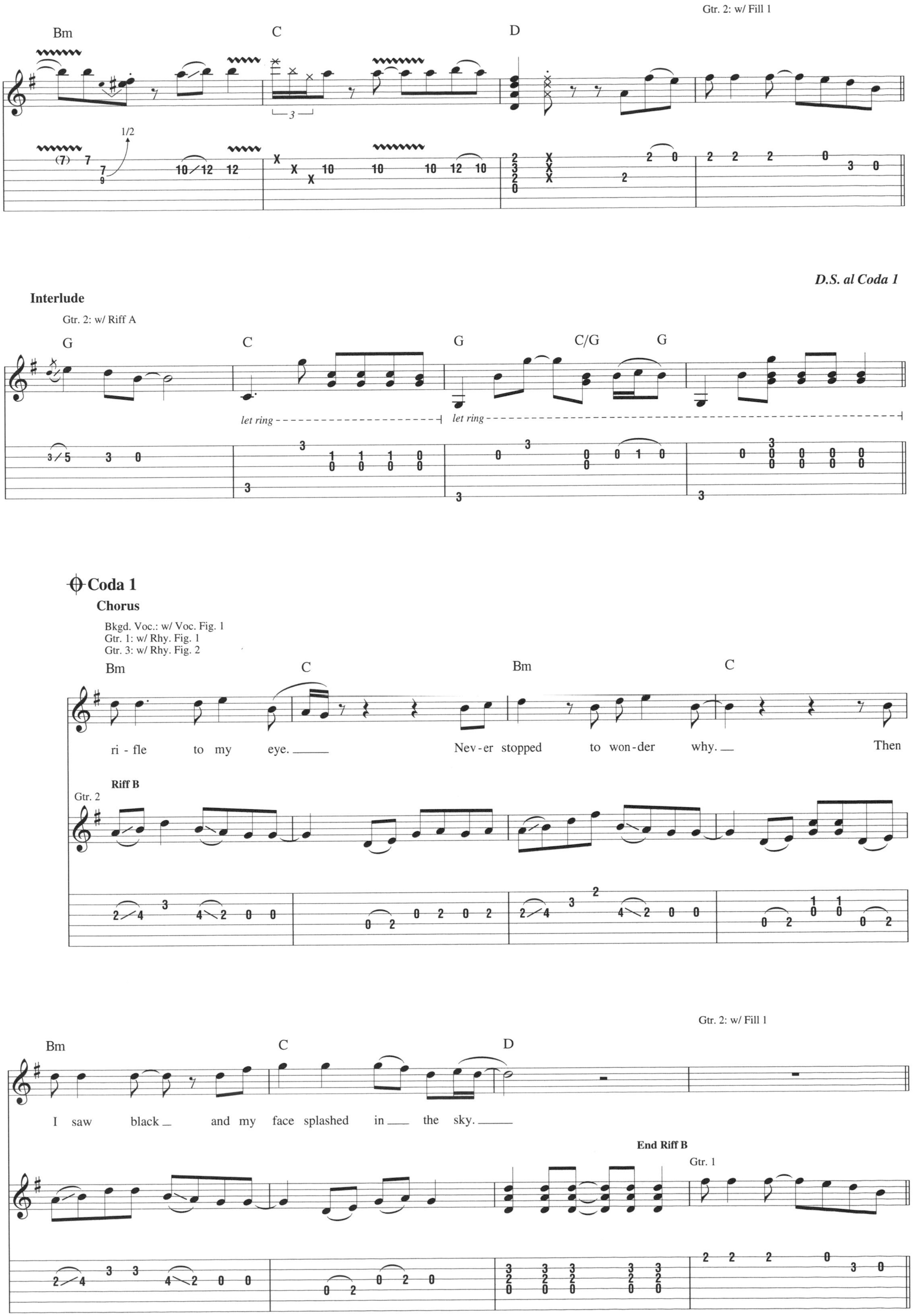
Gtr. 2: w/ Fill 1
Bm
C
D
1/2
D.S. al Coda 1
Interlude
Gtr. 2: w/ Riff A
G
C
G
C/G
G
let ring
let ring
Coda 1
Chorus
Bkgd. Voc.: w/ Voc. Fig. 1
Gtr. 1: w/ Rhy. Fig. 1
Gtr. 3: w/ Rhy. Fig. 2
Bm
C
Bm
C
ri - fle to my eye. Nev-er stopped to won-der why. Then
Riff B
Gtr. 2
Gtr. 2: w/ Fill 1
Bm
C
D
I saw black and my face splashed in the sky.
End Riff B
Gtr. 1

Interlude

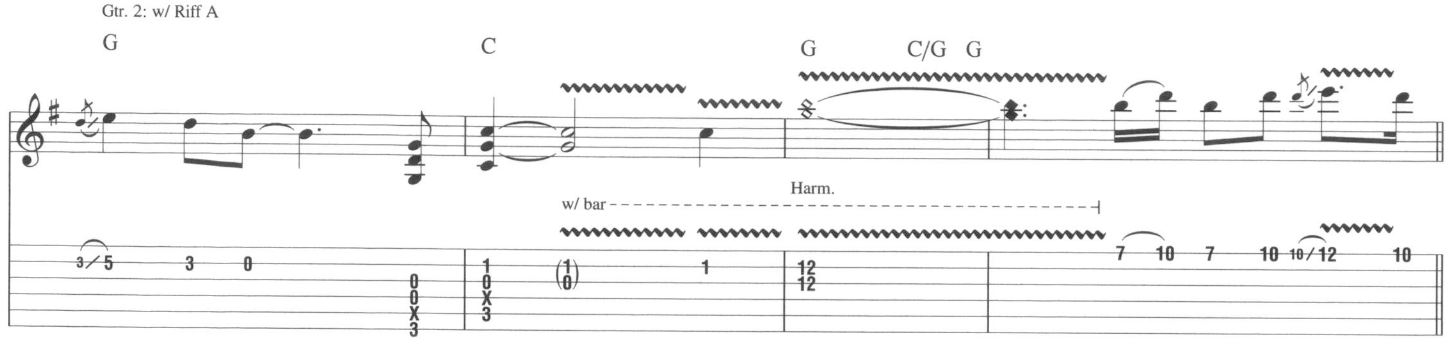

Guitar Solo

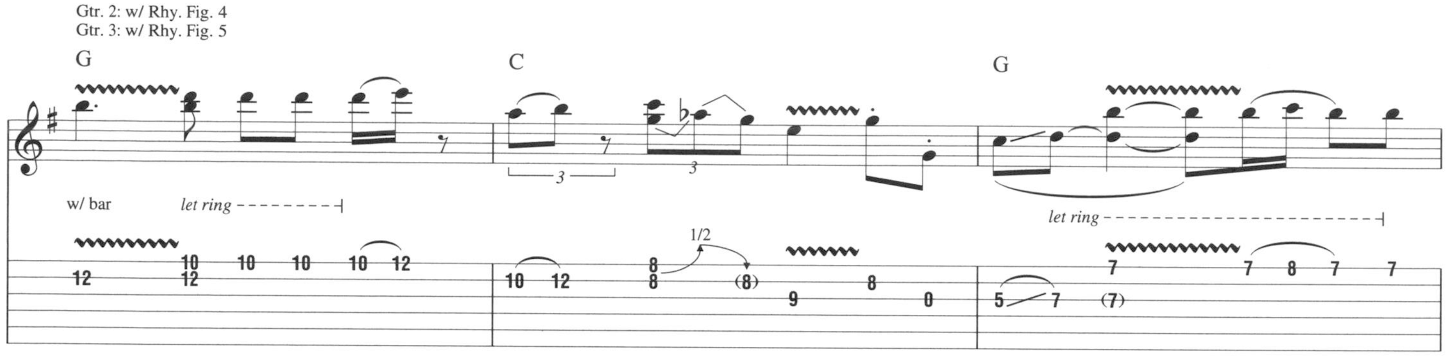

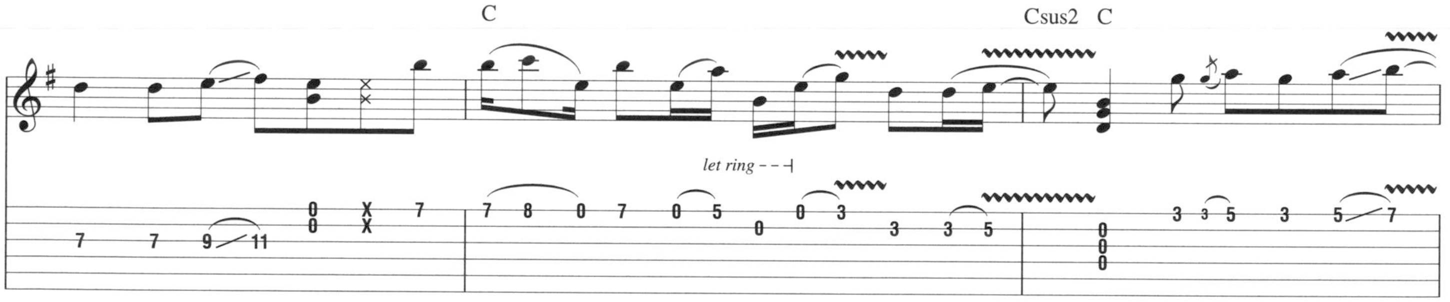

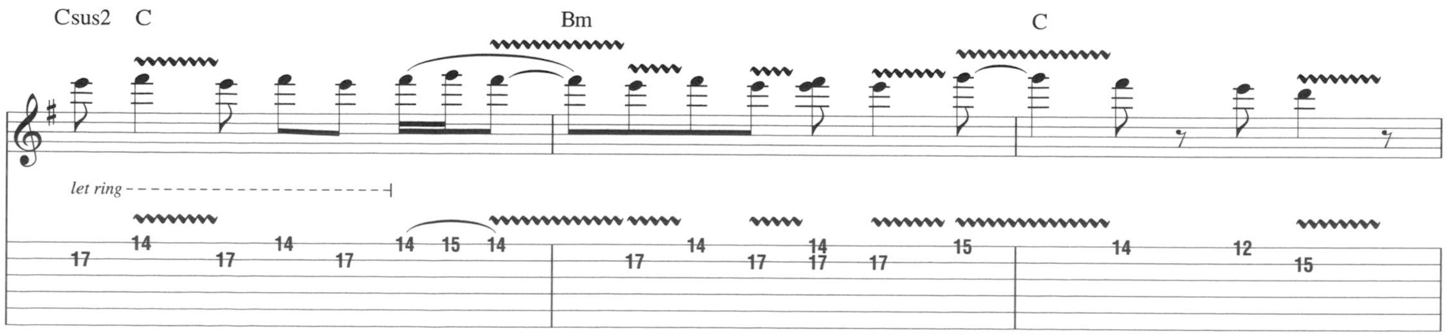

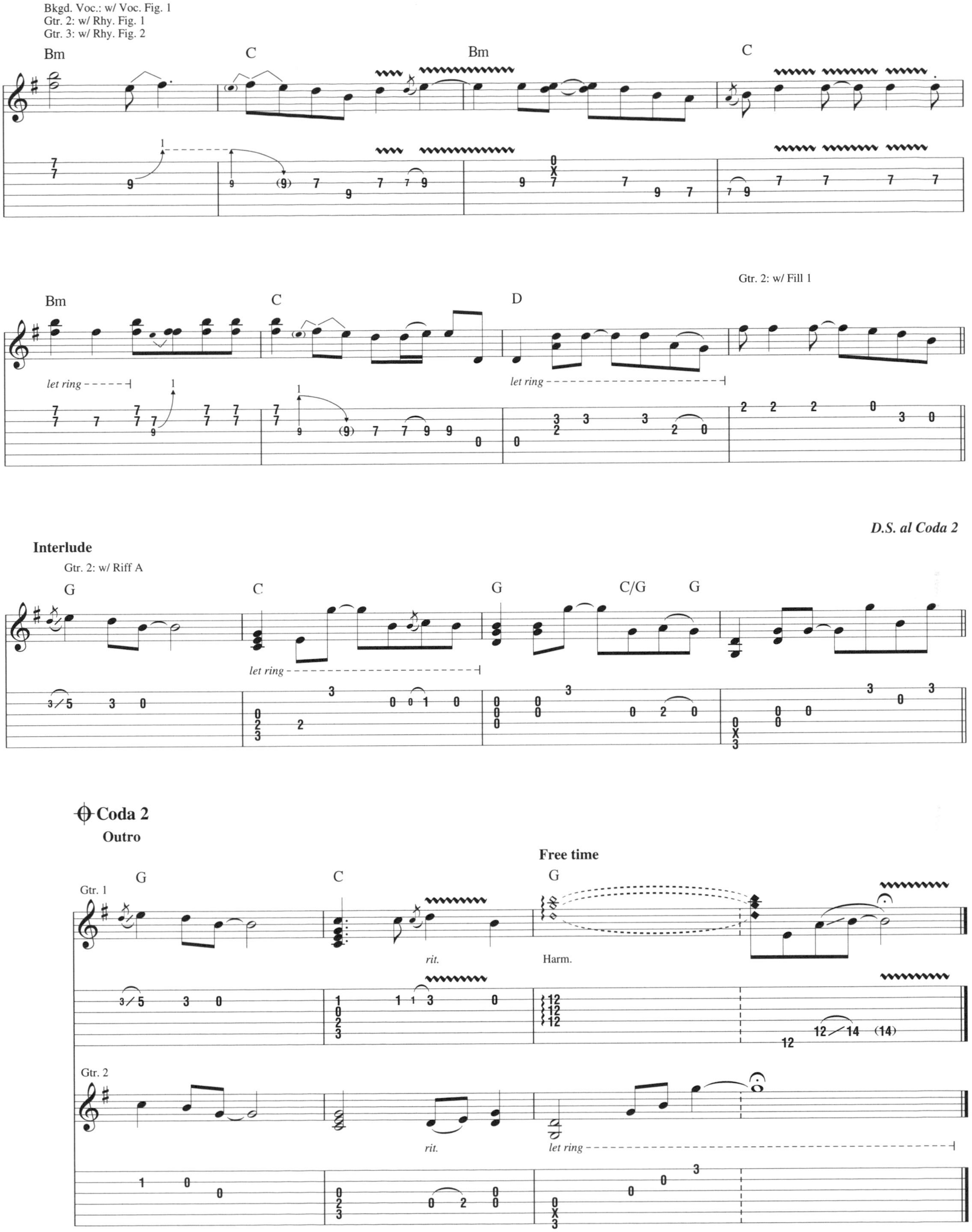

Additional Lyrics

4. Shelter me from the powder and the finger.
   Cover me with the thought that pulled the trigger.
   Just think of me as one you never figured
   Would fade away so young,
   With so much left undone.
   Remember me to my love, I know I'll miss her.

WELFARE MOTHERS

Words and Music by Neil Young

People, pick up on what I'm puttin' down now
Welfare mothers make better lovers
Down at every laundromat in town now
Welfare mothers make better lovers
While they're washin' you can hear this sound now
Welfare mothers make better lovers
DEE VORR CEE!

Hard to believe that love is free now
Welfare mothers make better lovers
Out on the street with the whole family now
Welfare mothers make better lovers
Hard to believe that love is free now
Welfare mothers make better lovers
DEE VORR CEEE!

People, pick up on what I'm puttin' down now
Welfare mothers make better lovers
Down in every laundromat in town now
Welfare mothers make better lovers
While they're washin' you can hear this sound now
Welfare mothers make better lovers
DEE VORR CEEE!

Welfare Mothers

Words and Music by Neil Young

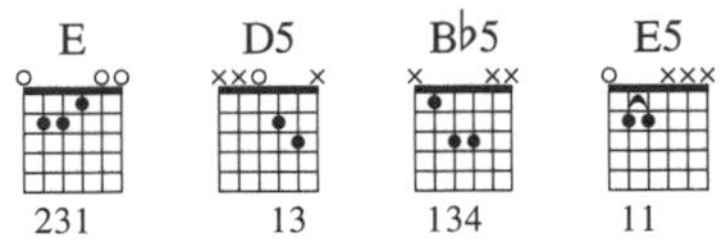

Intro

Moderate Rock ♩ = 127 (♫ = ♩♪ triplet)

*Chord symbols reflect implied harmony.

**Set for one octave below.

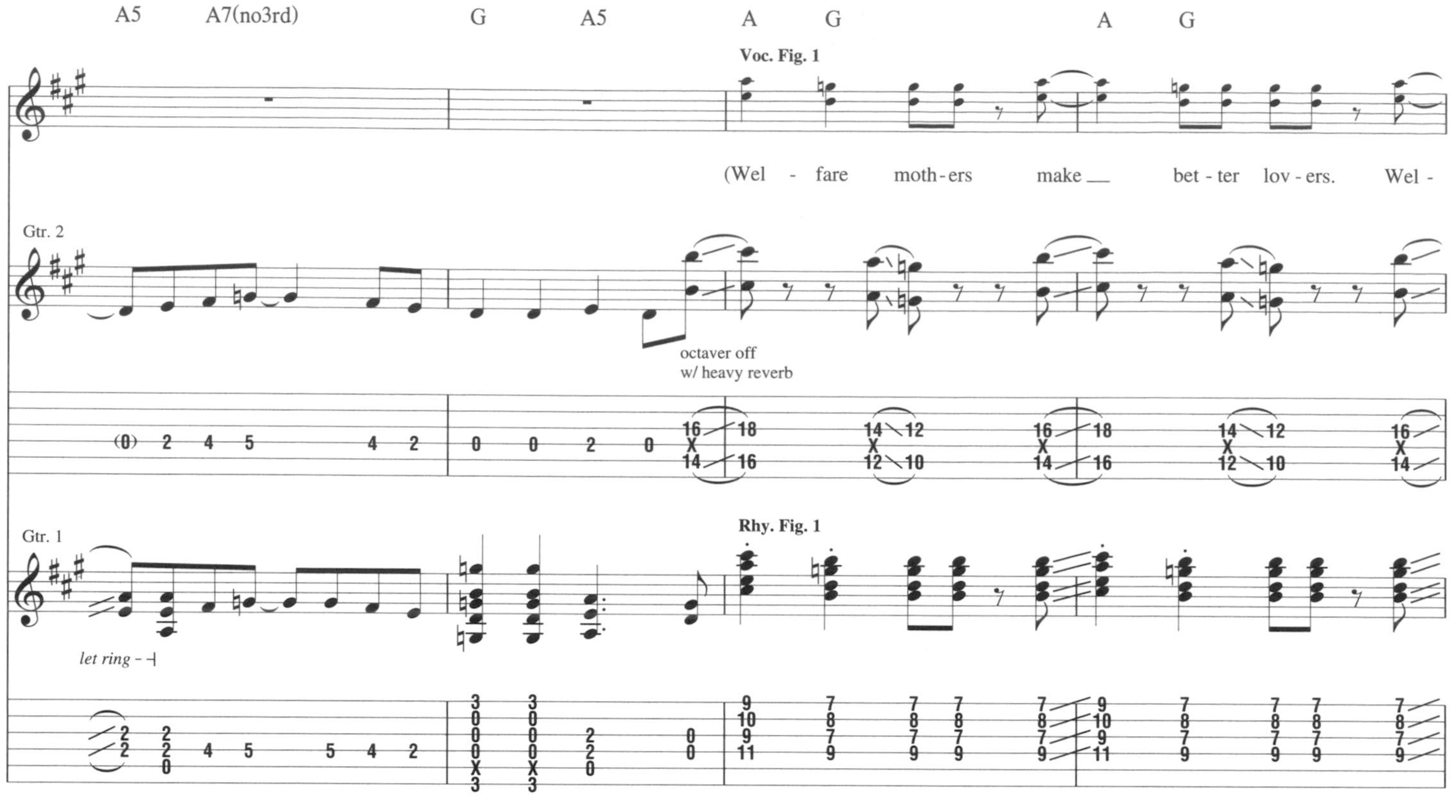
A5 A7(no3rd) G A5 A G A G
Voc. Fig. 1
(Wel - fare moth-ers make __ bet-ter lov-ers. Wel -
Gtr. 2
octaver off
w/ heavy reverb
Gtr. 1
Rhy. Fig. 1
let ring

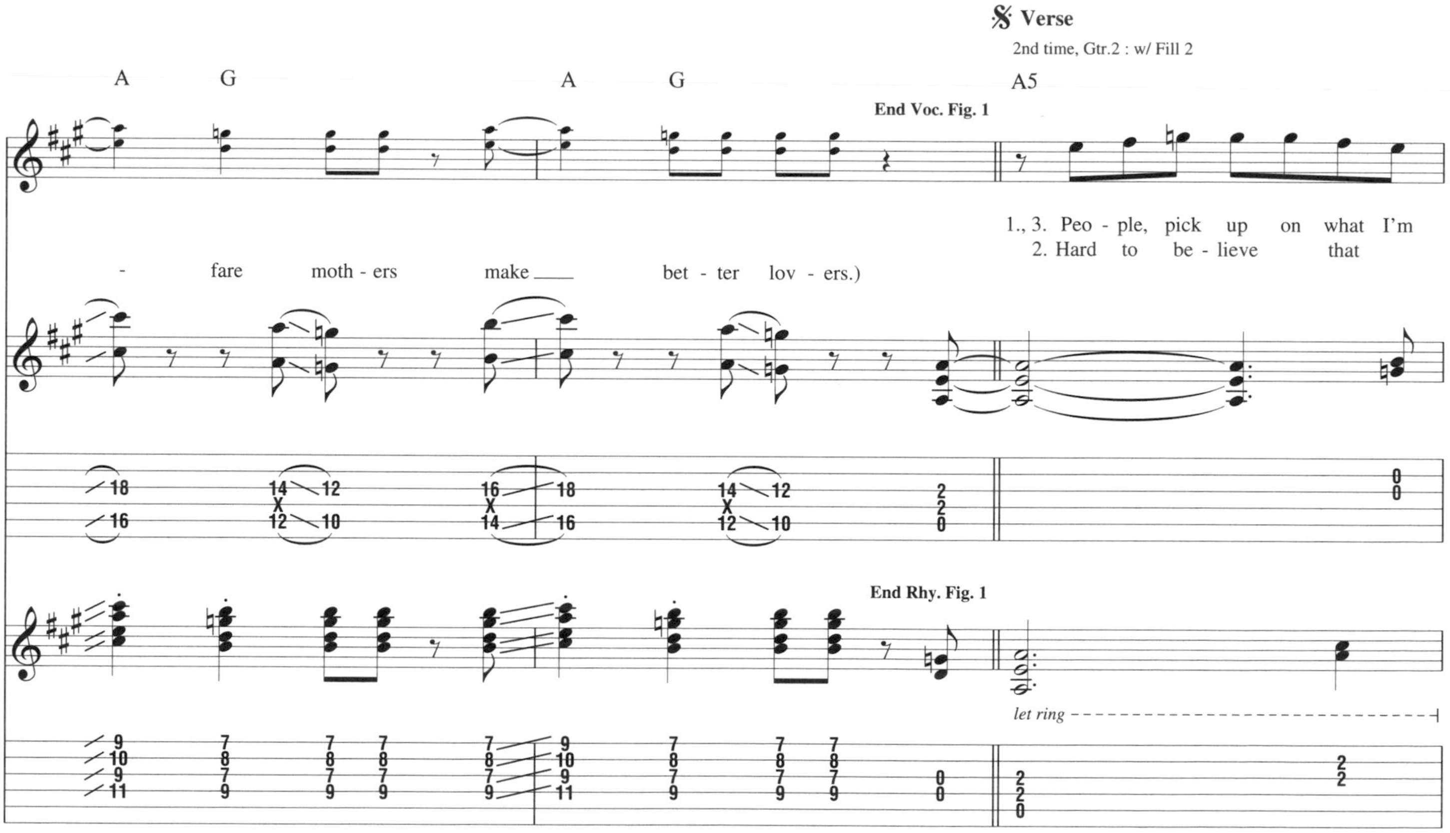
Verse
2nd time, Gtr. 2 : w/ Fill 2
A G A G A5
End Voc. Fig. 1
- fare moth-ers make __ bet-ter lov-ers.)
1., 3. Peo - ple, pick up on what I'm
2. Hard to be - lieve that
End Rhy. Fig. 1
let ring

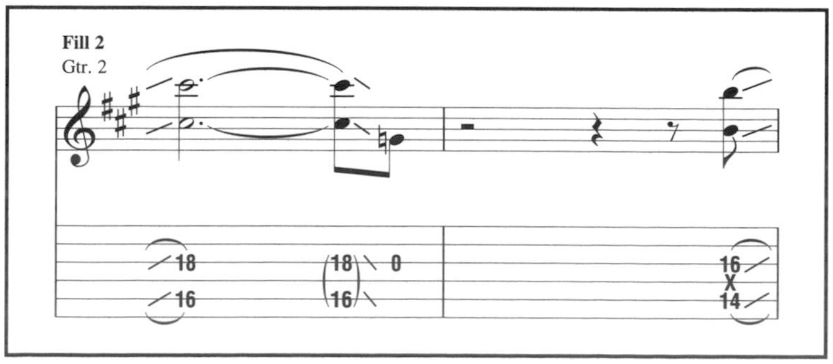
Fill 2
Gtr. 2

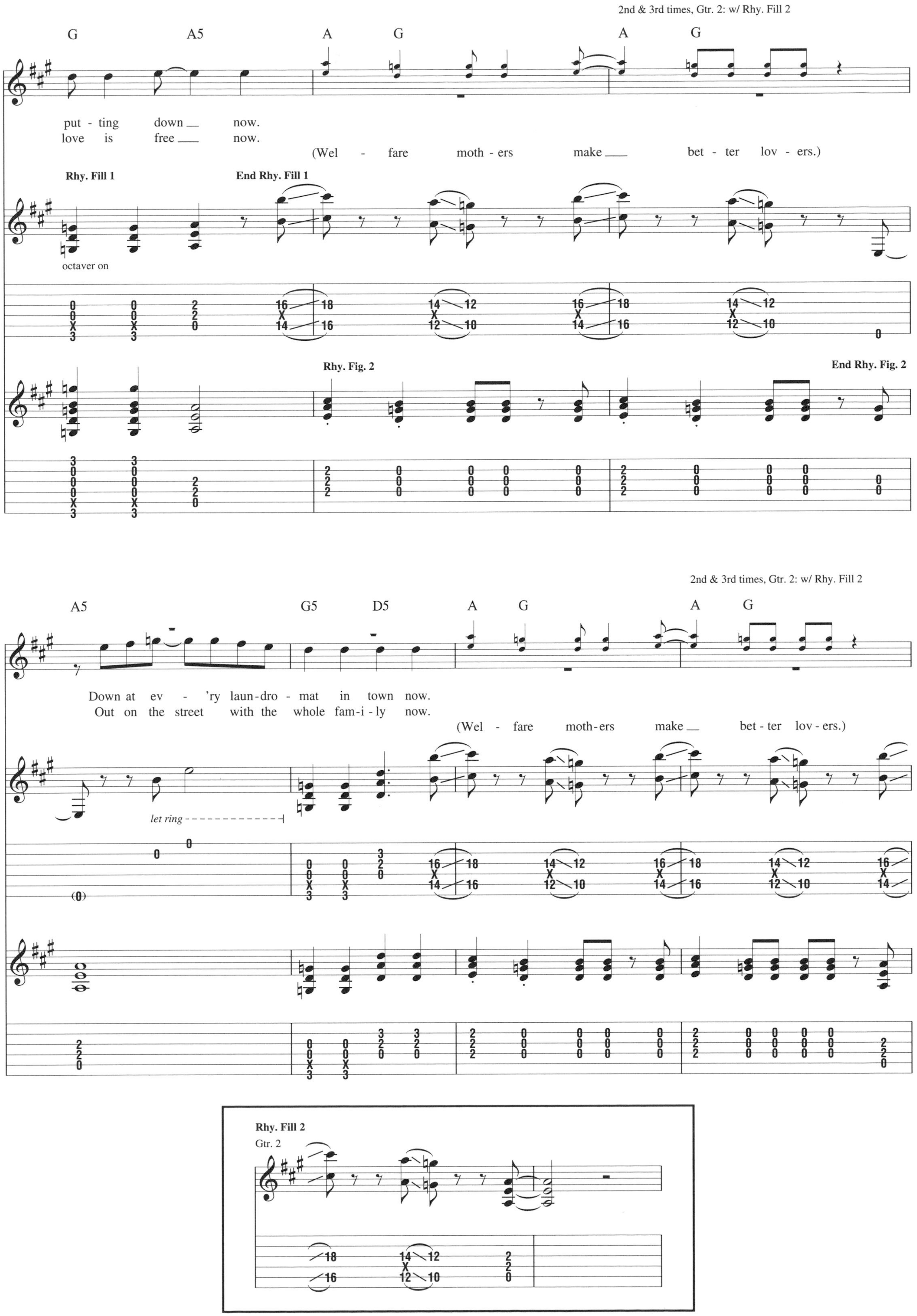
2nd & 3rd times, Gtr. 2: w/ Rhy. Fill 2
G A5 A G A G
put - ting down now.
love is free now.
(Wel - fare moth - ers make bet - ter lov - ers.)
Rhy. Fill 1
End Rhy. Fill 1
octaver on
Rhy. Fig. 2
End Rhy. Fig. 2
2nd & 3rd times, Gtr. 2: w/ Rhy. Fill 2
A5 G5 D5 A G A G
Down at ev - 'ry laun - dro - mat in town now.
Out on the street with the whole fam - i - ly now.
(Wel - fare moth - ers make bet - ter lov - ers.)
let ring
Rhy. Fill 2
Gtr. 2

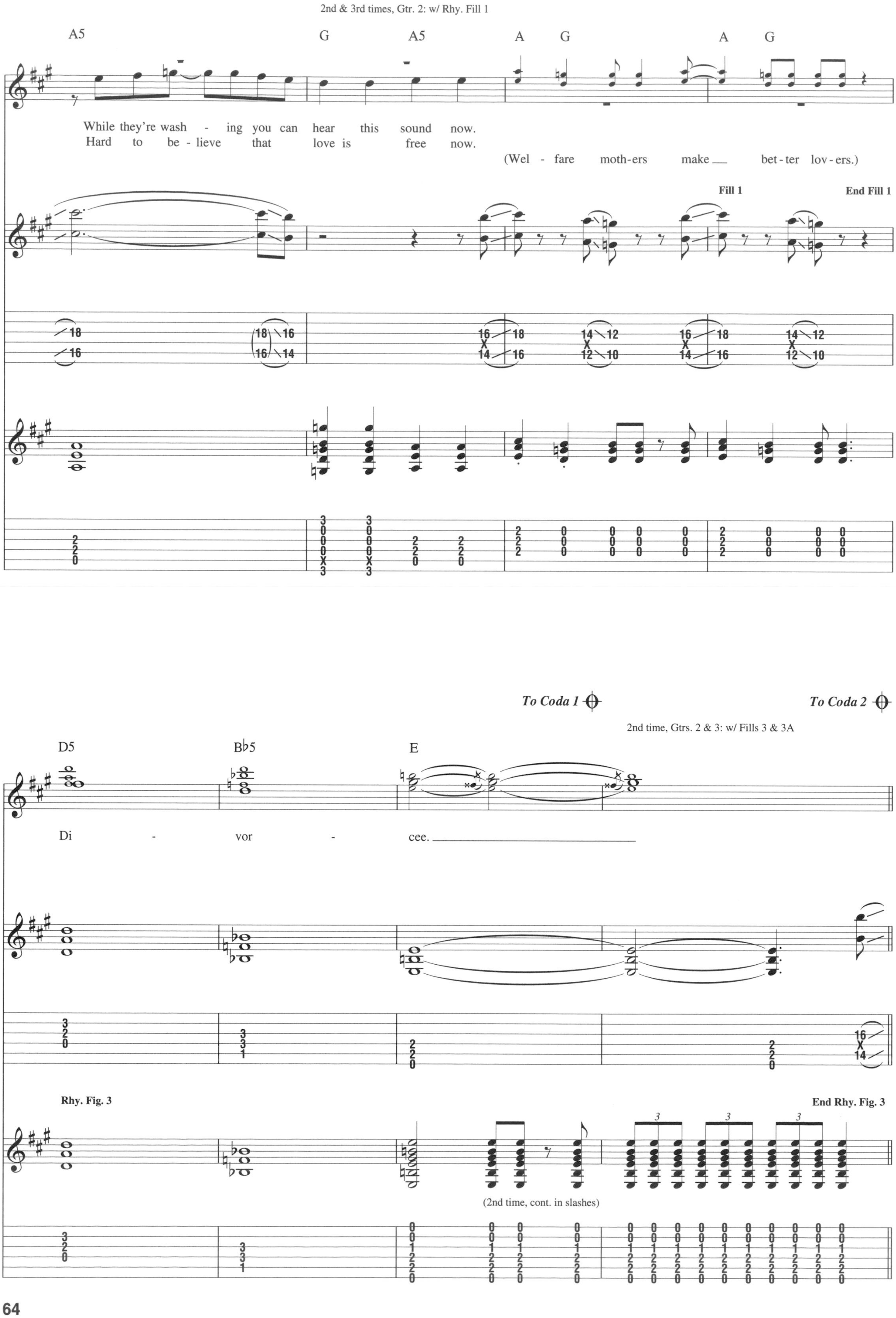
2nd & 3rd times, Gtr. 2: w/ Rhy. Fill 1
A5
G
A5
A
G
A
G
While they're wash - ing you can hear this sound now.
Hard to be - lieve that love is free now.
(Wel - fare moth-ers make better lov-ers.)
Fill 1
End Fill 1
To Coda 1
To Coda 2
2nd time, Gtrs. 2 & 3: w/ Fills 3 & 3A
D5
B♭5
E
Di - vor - cee.
Rhy. Fig. 3
End Rhy. Fig. 3
(2nd time, cont. in slashes)

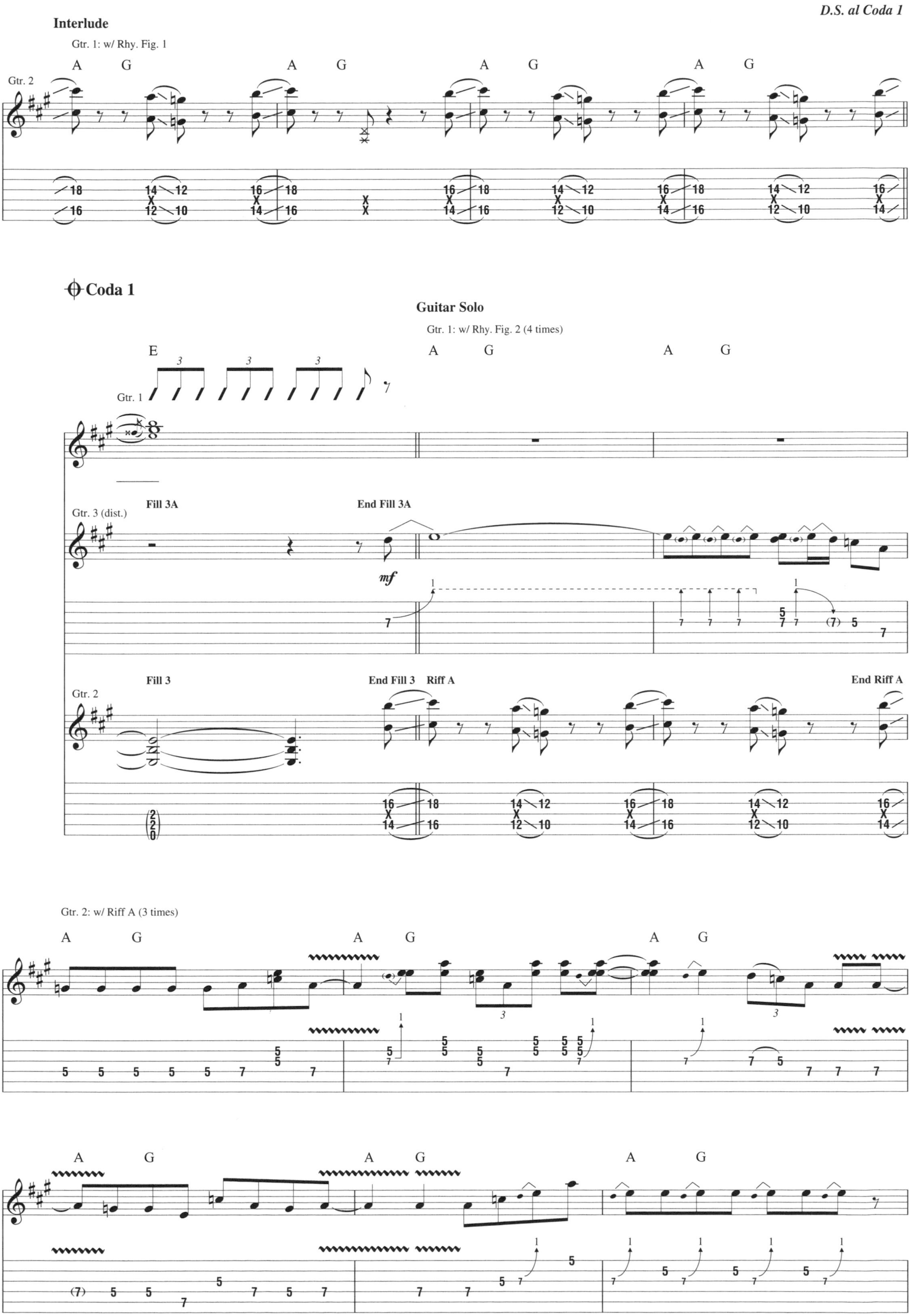
D.S. al Coda 1
Interlude
Gtr. 1: w/ Rhy. Fig. 1
A G A G A G A G
Gtr. 2
Coda 1
Guitar Solo
Gtr. 1: w/ Rhy. Fig. 2 (4 times)
E
A G A G
Gtr. 1
Gtr. 3 (dist.)
Fill 3A
End Fill 3A
mf
Gtr. 2
Fill 3
End Fill 3
Riff A
End Riff A
Gtr. 2: w/ Riff A (3 times)
A G A G A G
A G A G A G

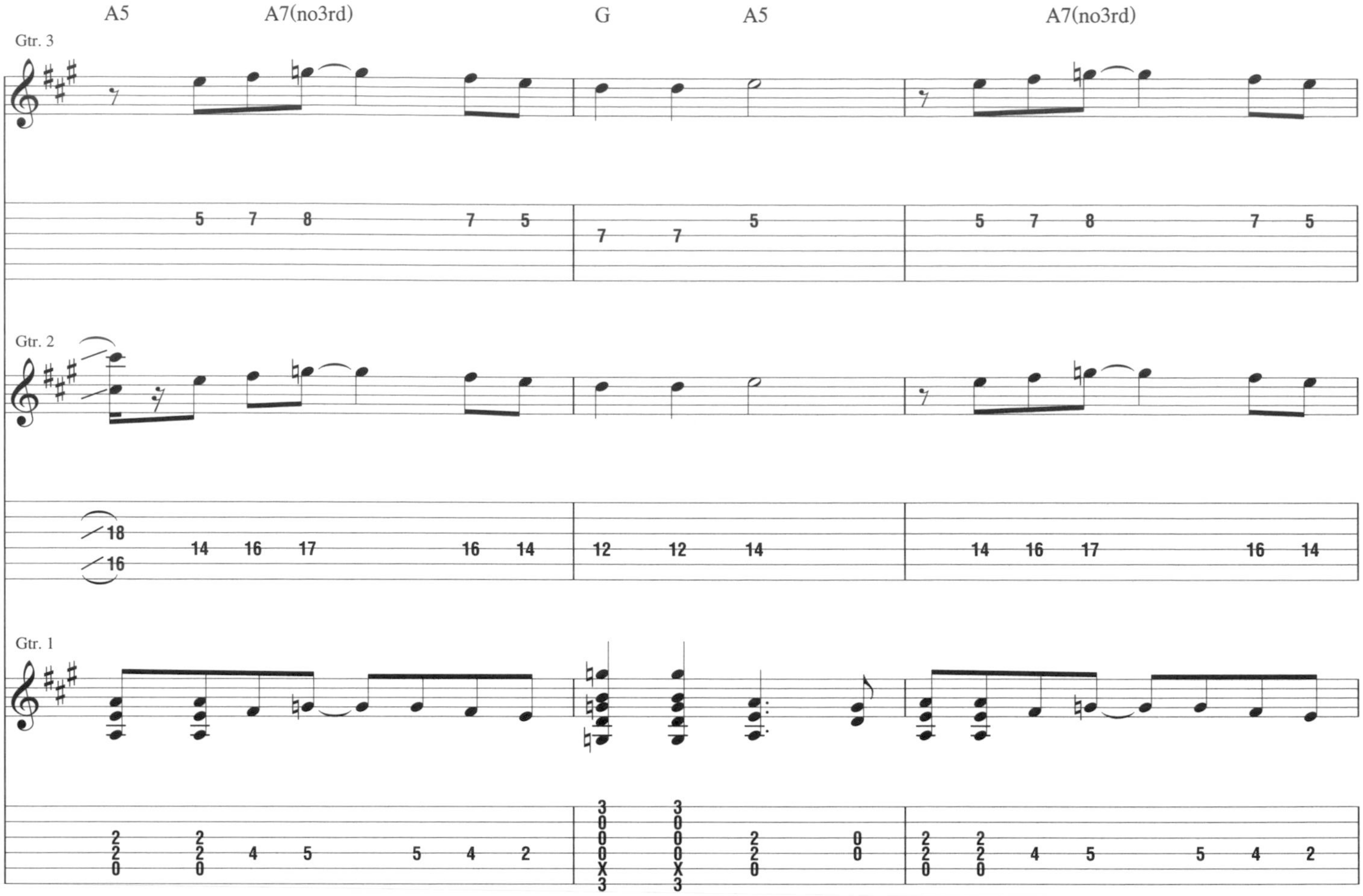
A5
A7(no3rd)
G
A5
A7(no3rd)
Gtr. 3
Gtr. 2
Gtr. 1

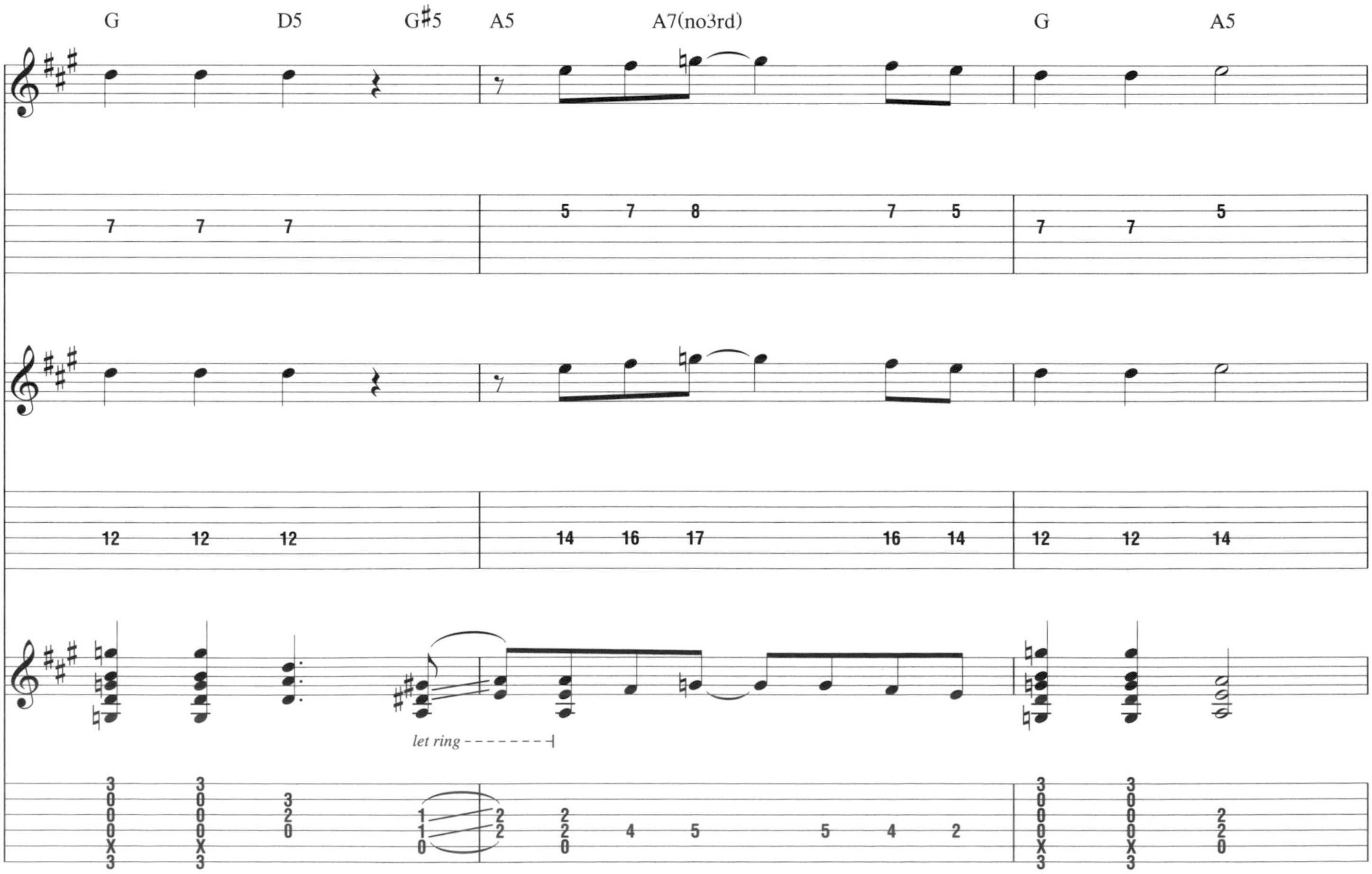
G
D5
G♯5
A5
A7(no3rd)
G
A5
let ring

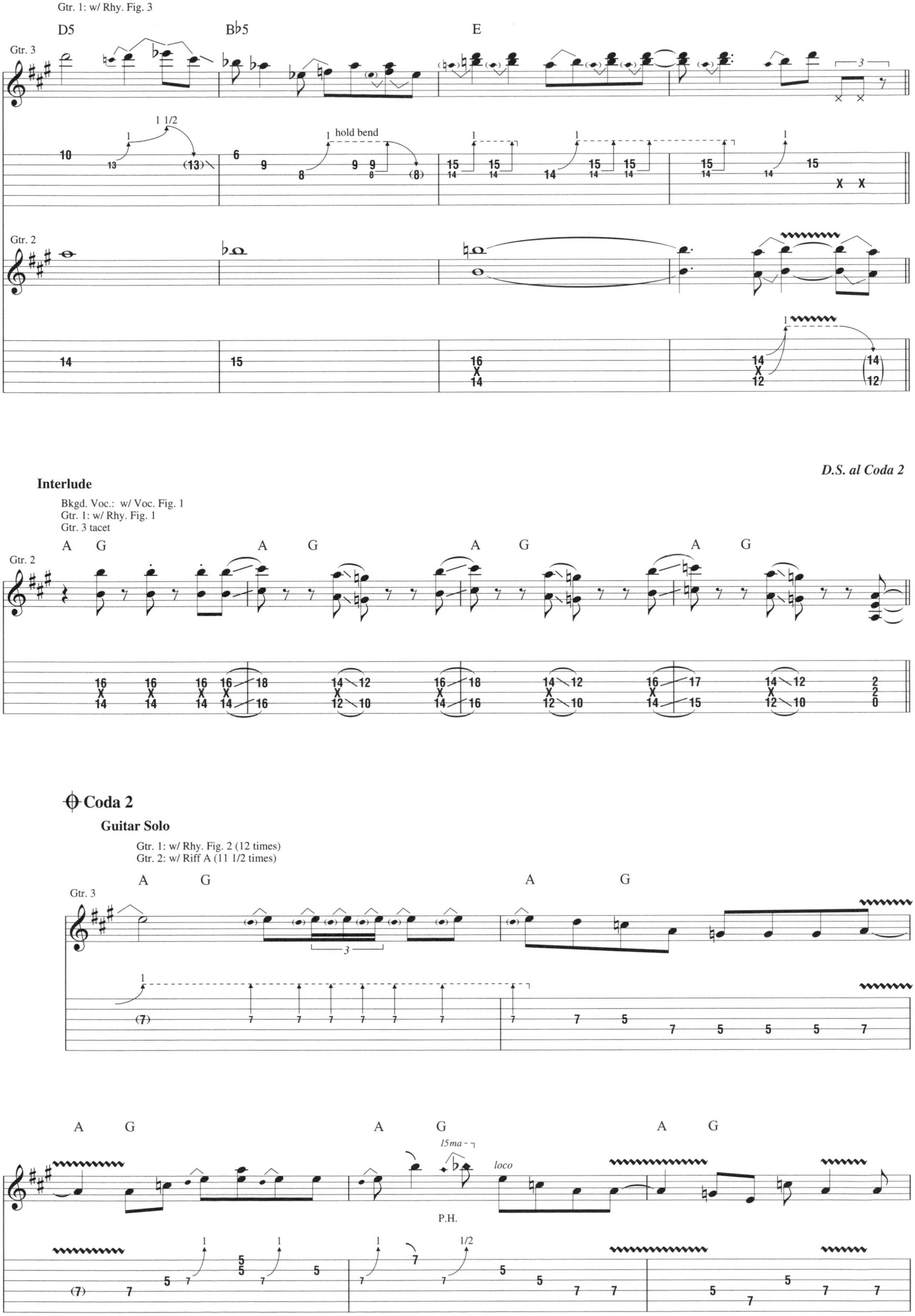
Gtr. 1: w/ Rhy. Fig. 3
D5
B♭5
E
Gtr. 3
1 1/2
hold bend
Gtr. 2
D.S. al Coda 2
Interlude
Bkgd. Voc.: w/ Voc. Fig. 1
Gtr. 1: w/ Rhy. Fig. 1
Gtr. 3 tacet
A G
Coda 2
Guitar Solo
Gtr. 1: w/ Rhy. Fig. 2 (12 times)
Gtr. 2: w/ Riff A (11 1/2 times)
15ma
loco
P.H.

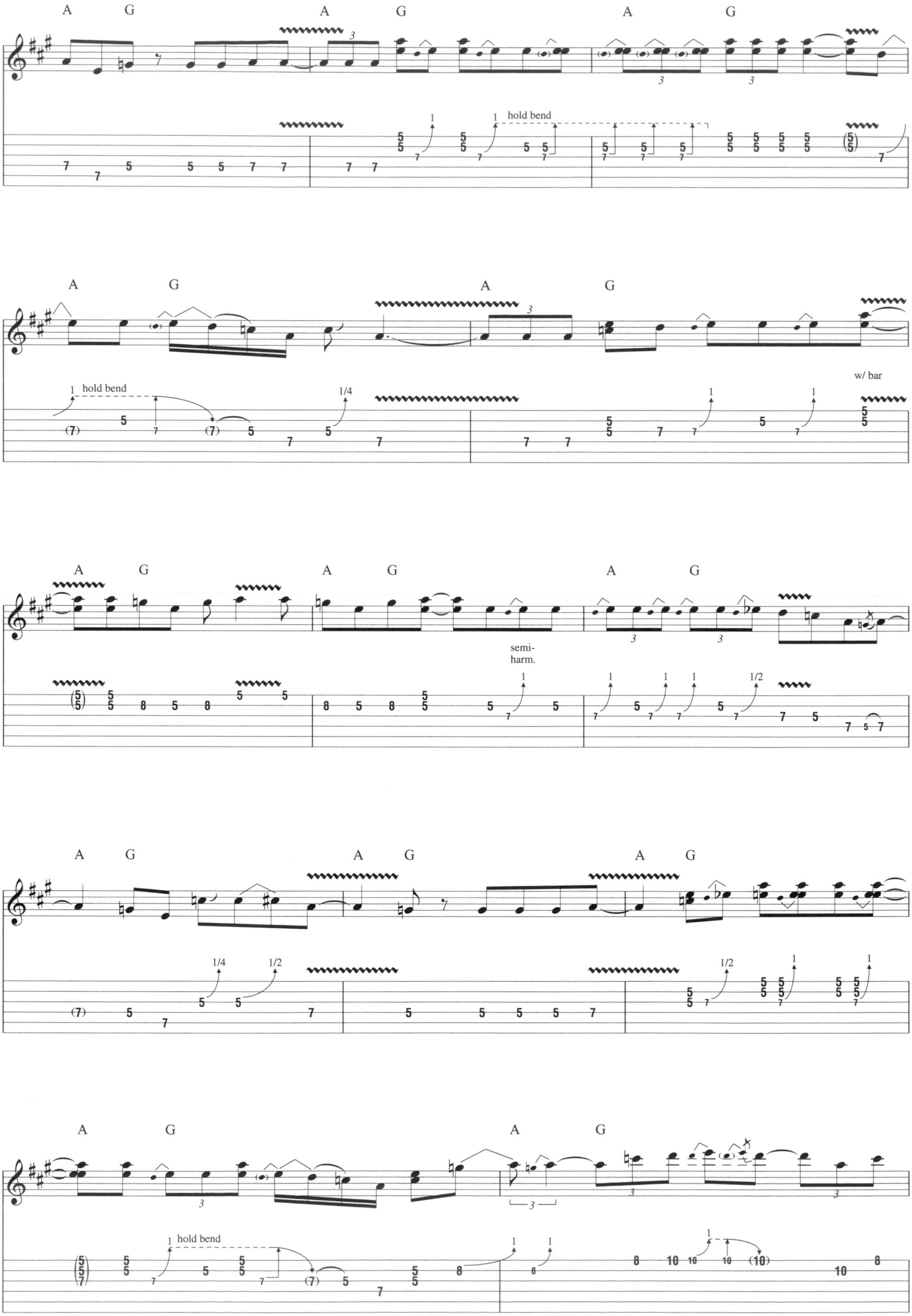
A G A G A G
hold bend
A G A G
hold bend
w/ bar
A G A G A G
semi-
harm.
A G A G A G
A G A G
hold bend

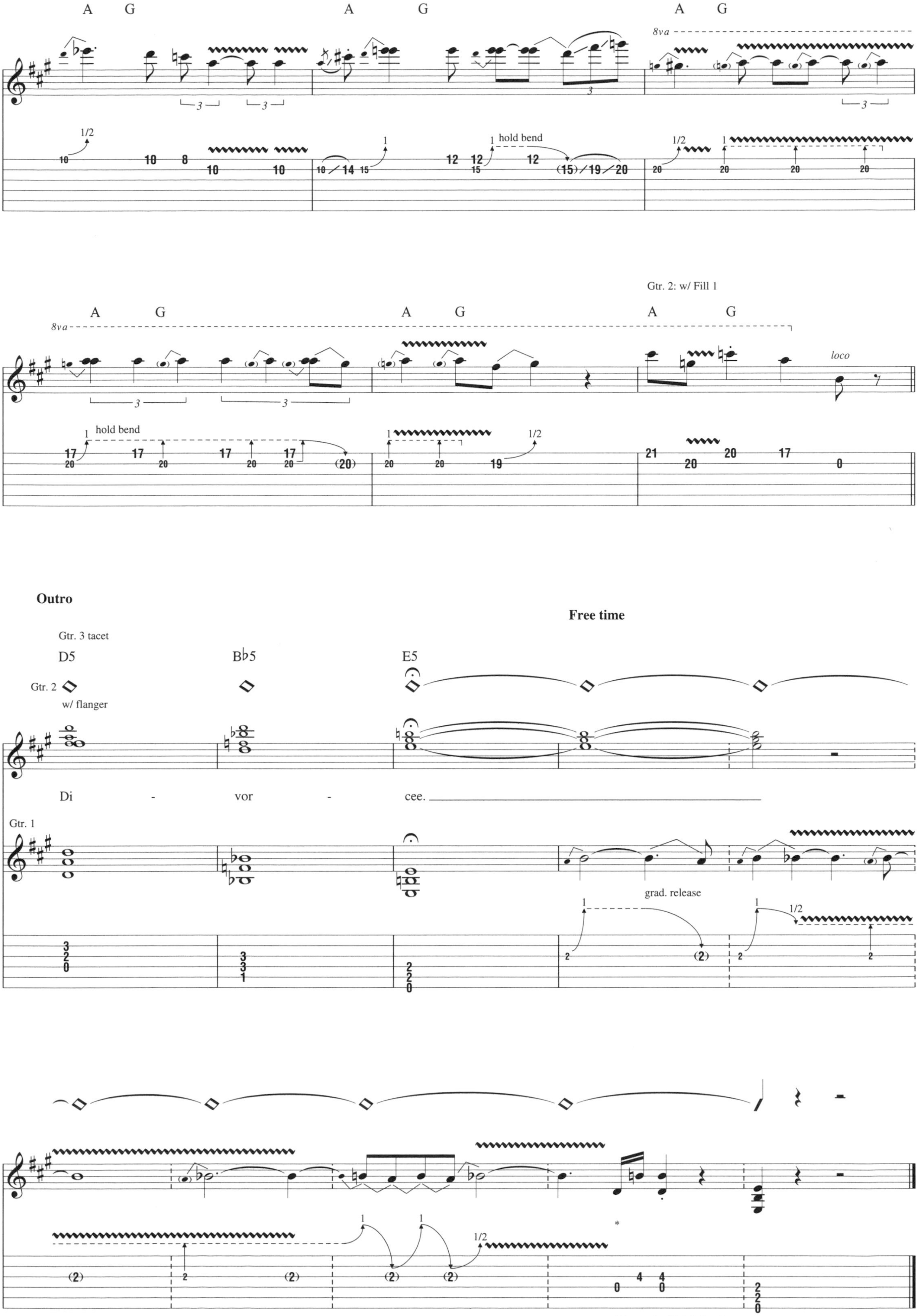

*Bumped with left hand.

SEDAN DELIVERY

Words and Music by Neil Young

Last night I was cool at the pool hall
Held the table for eleven games
Nothing was easier than the first seven
I beat a woman with varicose veins
She stopped to see herself in the mirror
Fix her hair and hide heir veins
And she lost the game.

Next day I went to the dentist
He pulled some teeth and I lost some blood
We'd like to thank you for the cards you sent us
My wives and I were all choked up

I recall how Caesar and Cleo
Made love in the Milky Way
They needed boats and armies to get there
I know there's a better way

I saw the movie and I read the book
But when it happened to me
I sure was glad I had what it took
To get away

Gotta get away
Gotta get away
Gotta get away
Gotta get away

I'm makin' another delivery
Of chemicals and sacred roots
I'll hold what you have to give me
But I'll use what I have to use
The lasers are in the lab
The old man is dressed in white clothes
Everybody says he's mad
No one knows the things that he knows

No one knows
No one knows
No one knows
No one knows

I'm sleepin' in every hallway
I still can't accept the stares
I'm sleepin' with many covers
I'm warm now so I don't care
I'm thinkin' of no one in my mind
Sedan delivery is a job I know I'll keep
It sure was hard to find

Hard to find
Hard to find
Hard to find
Hard to find

Sedan Delivery

Words and Music by Neil Young

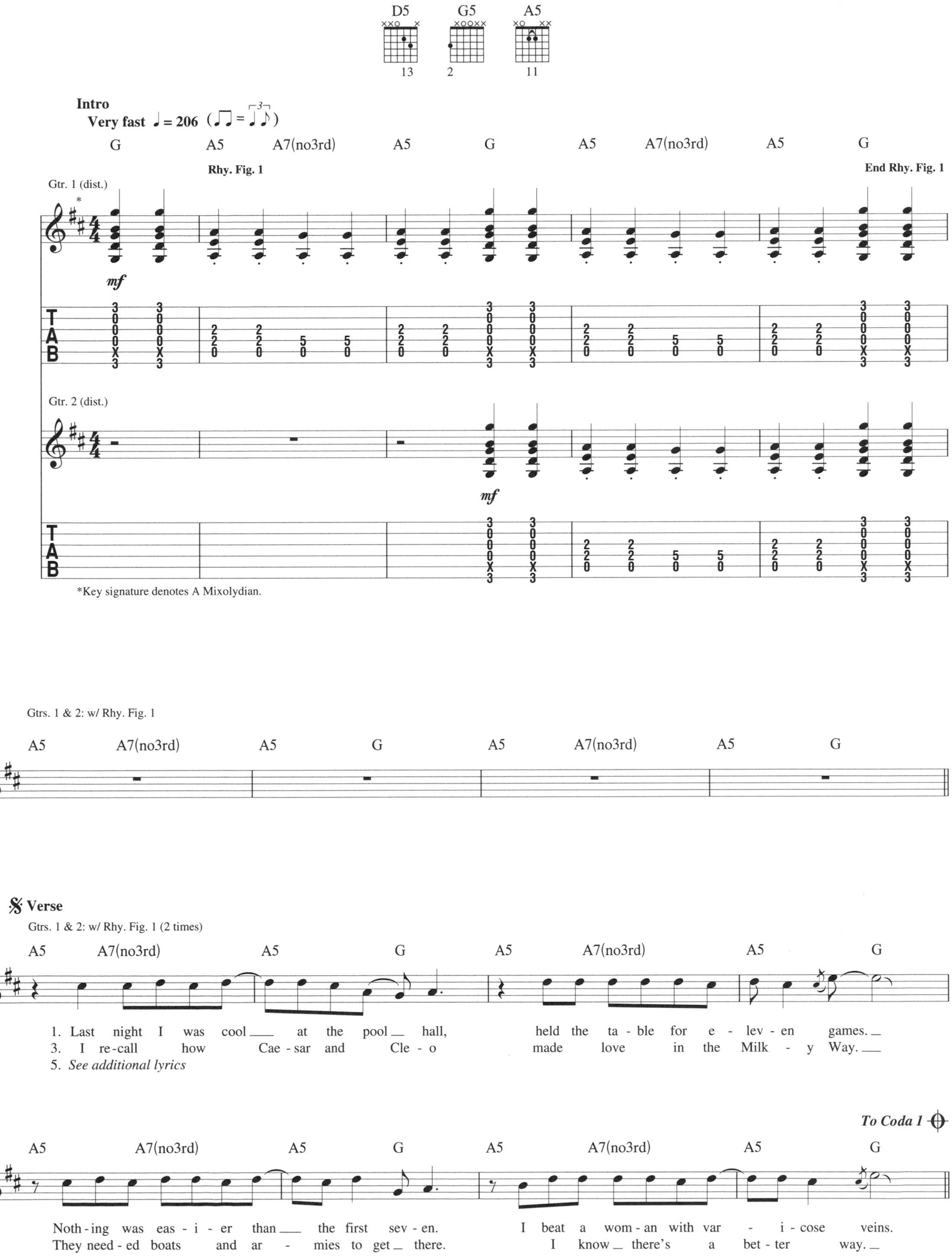

Chorus

Quarter-time feel

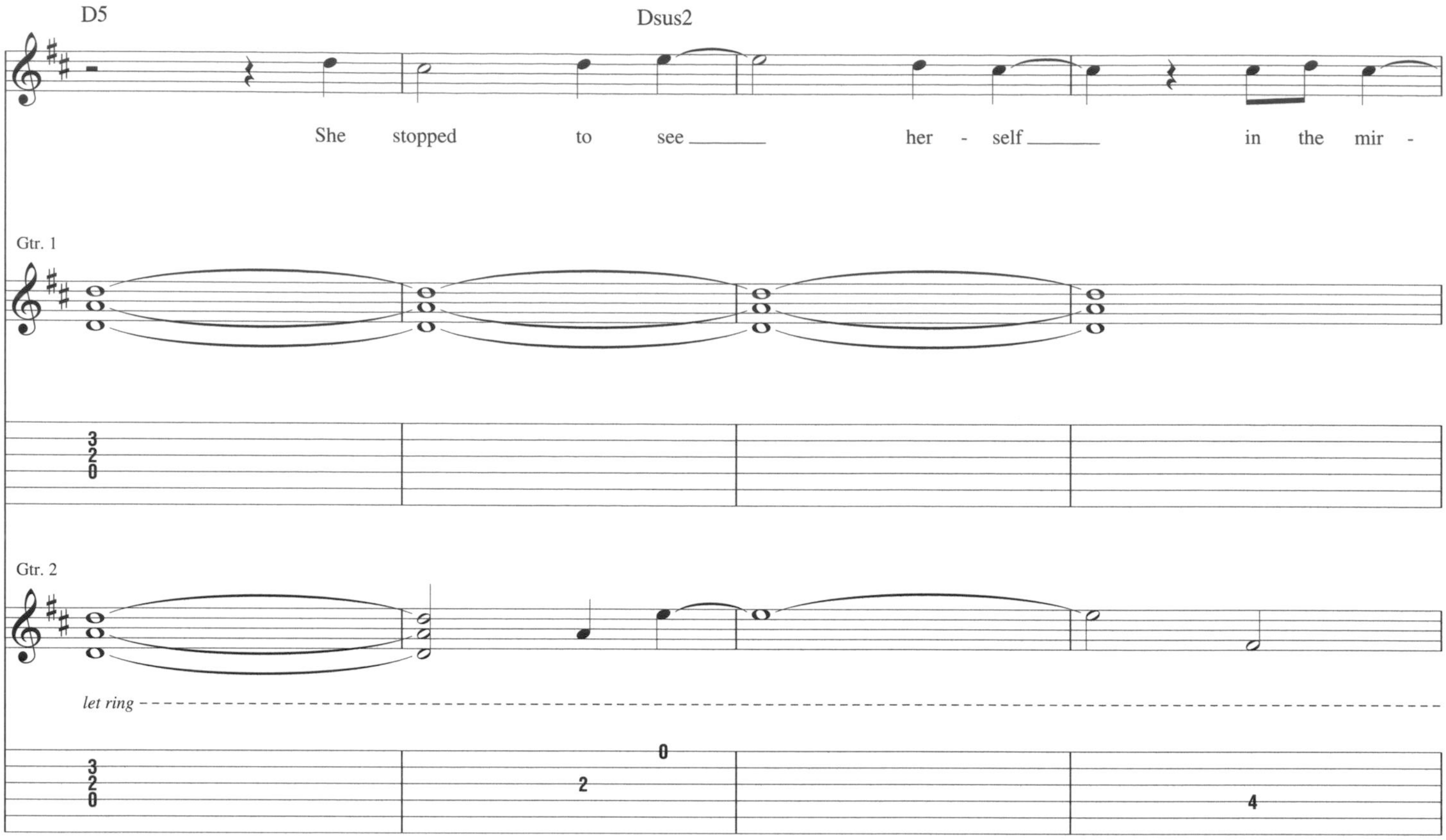
D5
Dsus2
She stopped to see her - self in the mir -
Gtr. 1
Gtr. 2
let ring

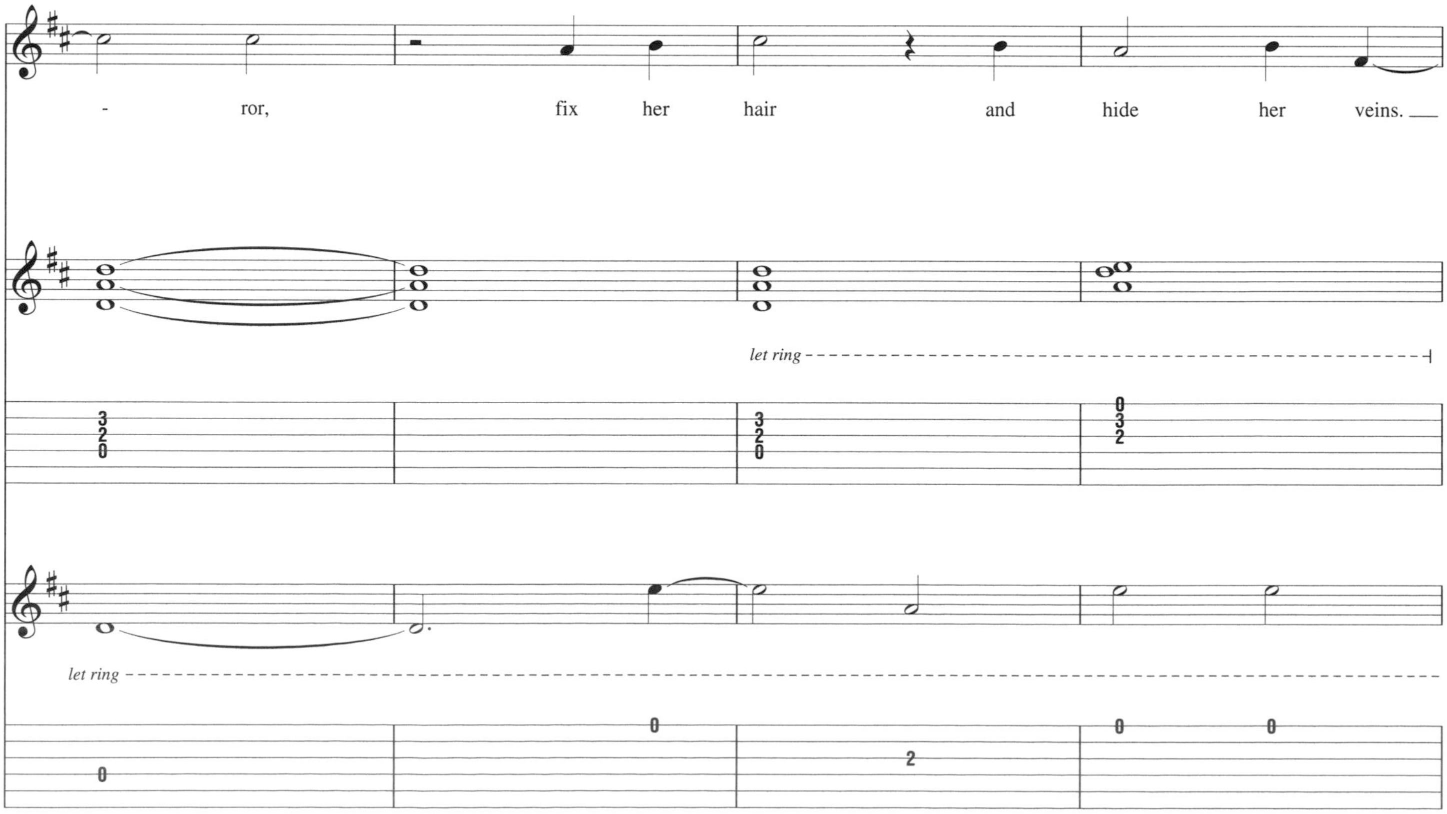
- ror, fix her hair and hide her veins.
let ring
let ring

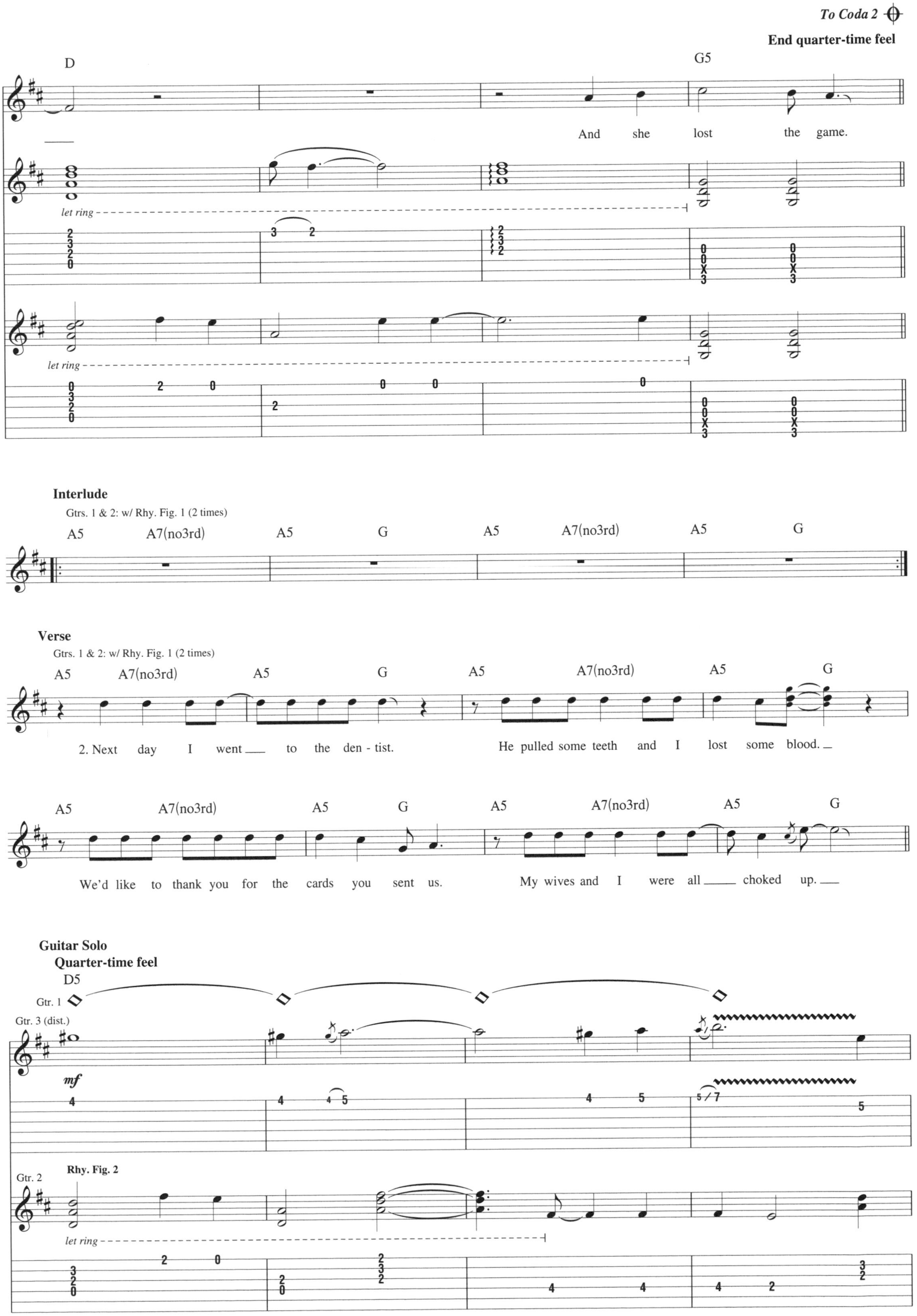
To Coda 2
End quarter-time feel
D
G5
And she lost the game.
let ring
Interlude
Gtrs. 1 & 2: w/ Rhy. Fig. 1 (2 times)
A5 A7(no3rd) A5 G A5 A7(no3rd) A5 G
Verse
Gtrs. 1 & 2: w/ Rhy. Fig. 1 (2 times)
A5 A7(no3rd) A5 G A5 A7(no3rd) A5 G
2. Next day I went to the den - tist. He pulled some teeth and I lost some blood.
A5 A7(no3rd) A5 G A5 A7(no3rd) A5 G
We'd like to thank you for the cards you sent us. My wives and I were all choked up.
Guitar Solo
Quarter-time feel
D5
Gtr. 1
Gtr. 3 (dist.)
mf
Gtr. 2
Rhy. Fig. 2
let ring

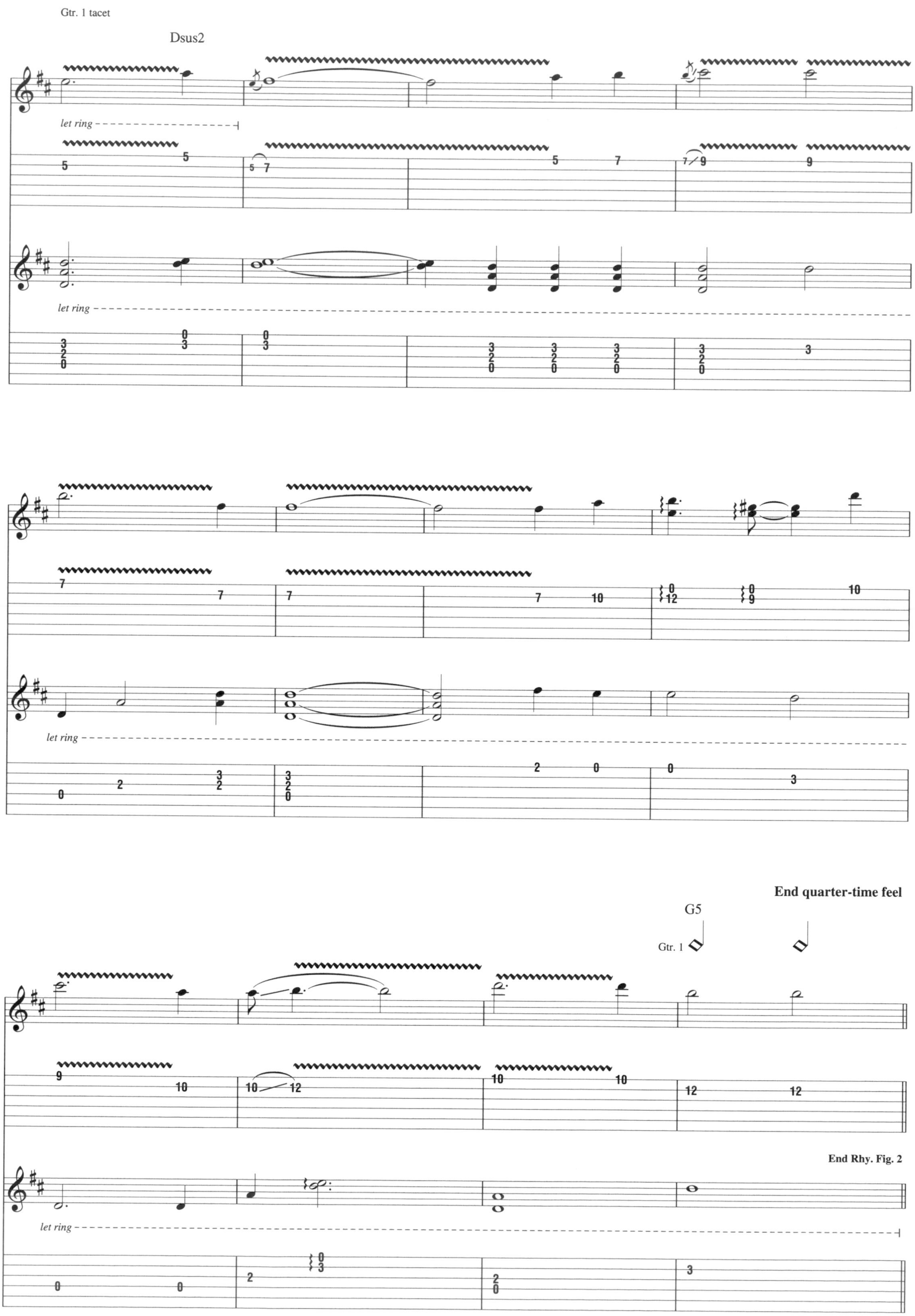
Gtr. 1 tacet
Dsus2
let ring
let ring
let ring
End quarter-time feel
G5
Gtr. 1
End Rhy. Fig. 2
let ring

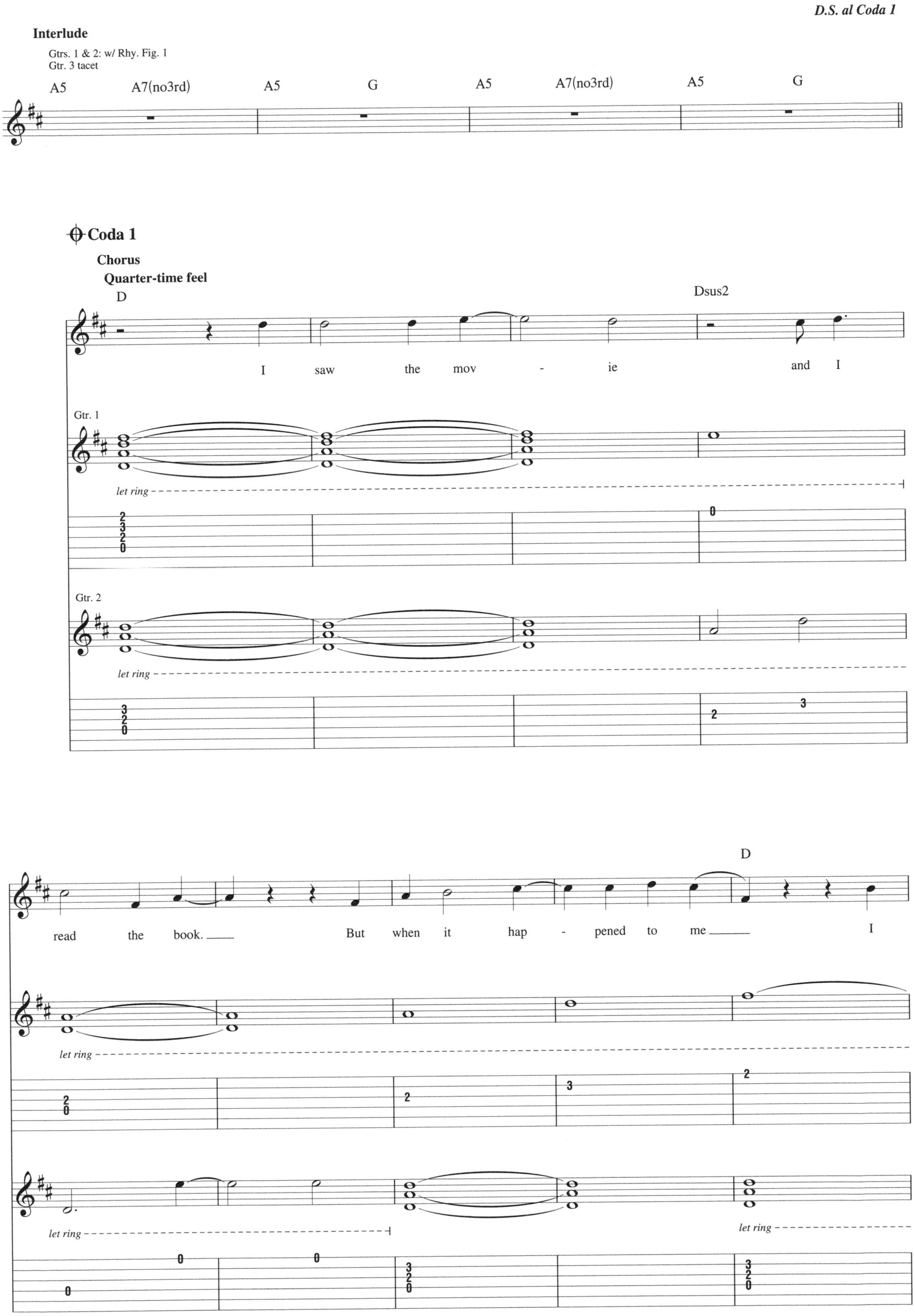
D.S. al Coda 1
Interlude
Gtrs. 1 & 2: w/ Rhy. Fig. 1
Gtr. 3 tacet
A5 A7(no3rd) A5 G A5 A7(no3rd) A5 G
Coda 1
Chorus
Quarter-time feel
D
Dsus2
I saw the mov - ie and I
Gtr. 1
let ring
Gtr. 2
let ring
D
read the book. But when it hap - pened to me I
let ring
let ring
let ring

End quarter-time feel

Interlude

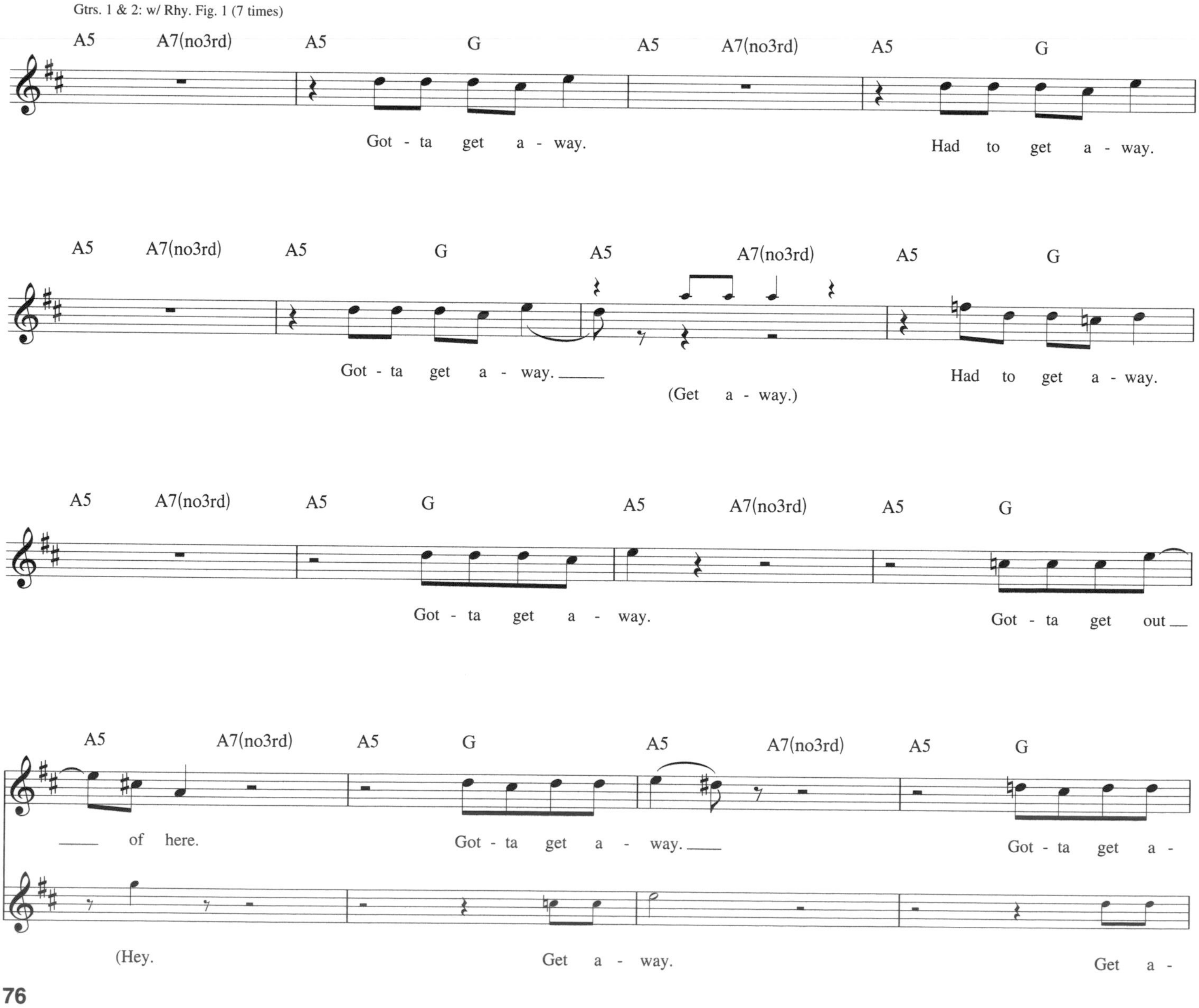

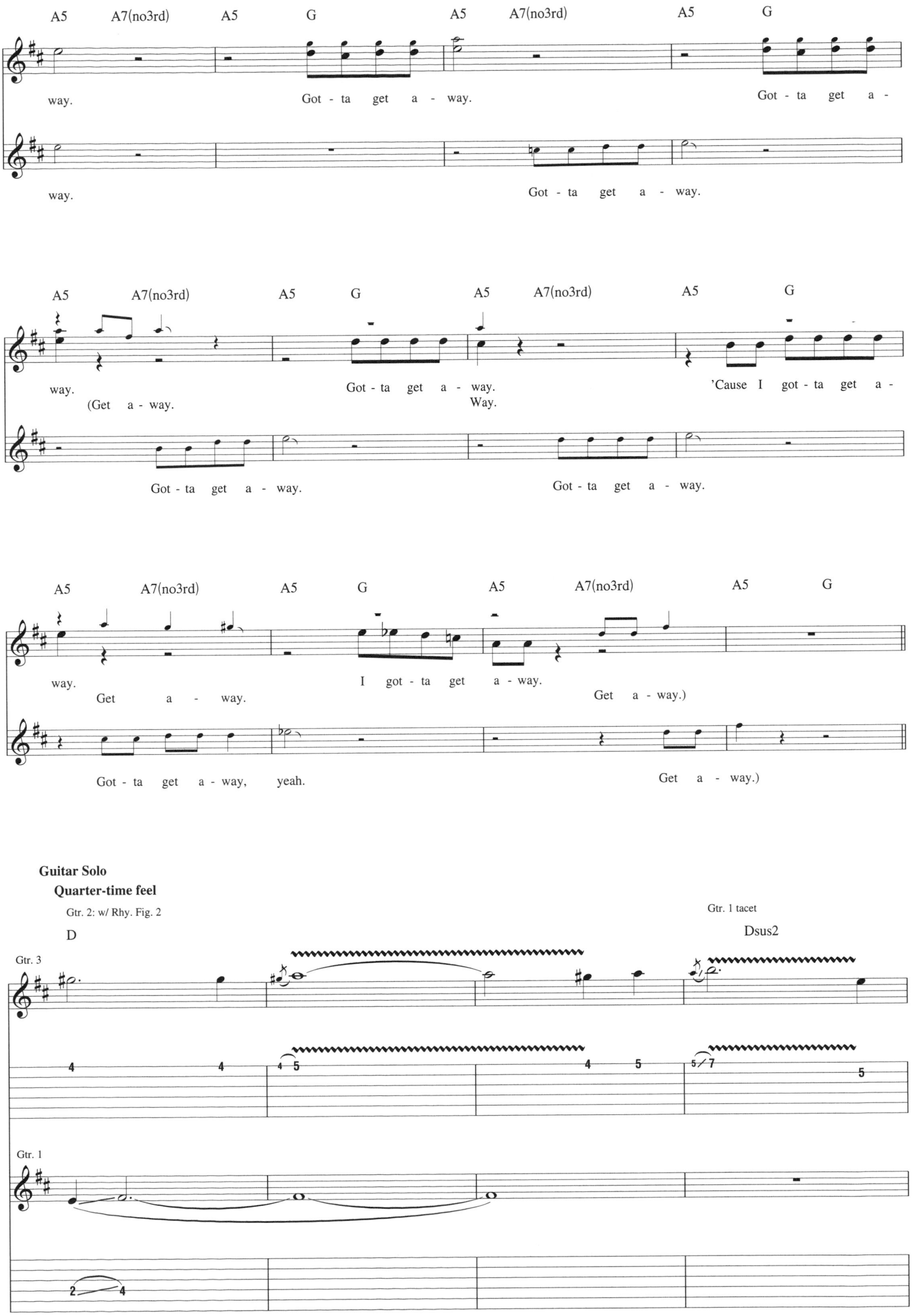
A5 A7(no3rd) A5 G A5 A7(no3rd) A5 G
way. Got - ta get a - way. Got - ta get a -
way. Got - ta get a - way.
A5 A7(no3rd) A5 G A5 A7(no3rd) A5 G
way. Got - ta get a - way. 'Cause I got - ta get a -
(Get a - way. Way.
Got - ta get a - way. Got - ta get a - way.
A5 A7(no3rd) A5 G A5 A7(no3rd) A5 G
way. I got - ta get a - way.
Get a - way. Get a - way.)
Got - ta get a - way, yeah. Get a - way.)
Guitar Solo
Quarter-time feel
Gtr. 2: w/ Rhy. Fig. 2
Gtr. 1 tacet
D
Dsus2
Gtr. 3
Gtr. 1

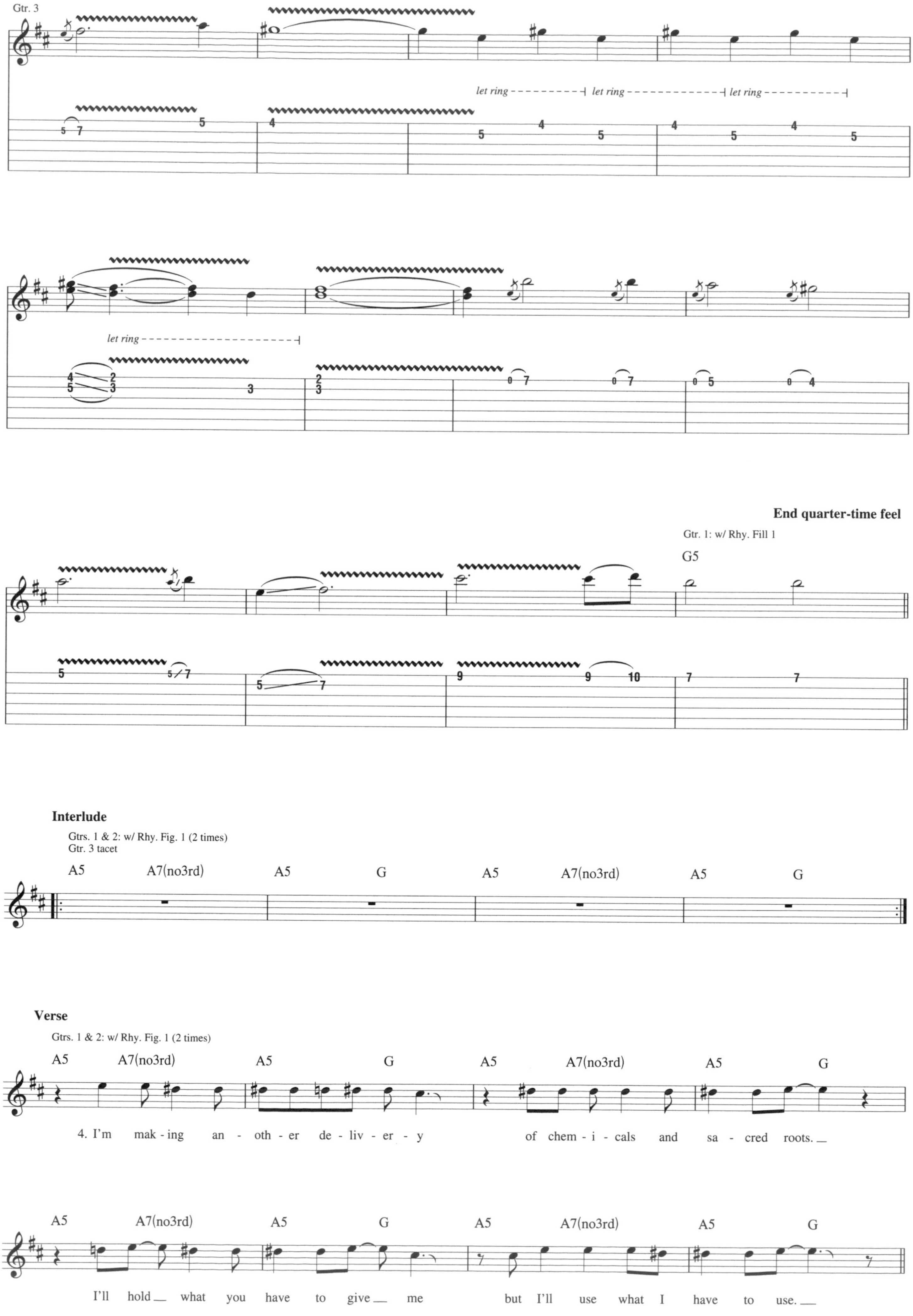
Gtr. 3
let ring
End quarter-time feel
Gtr. 1: w/ Rhy. Fill 1
G5
Interlude
Gtrs. 1 & 2: w/ Rhy. Fig. 1 (2 times)
Gtr. 3 tacet
A5 A7(no3rd) A5 G A5 A7(no3rd) A5 G
Verse
Gtrs. 1 & 2: w/ Rhy. Fig. 1 (2 times)
A5 A7(no3rd) A5 G A5 A7(no3rd) A5 G
4. I'm mak - ing an - oth - er de - liv - er - y of chem - i - cals and sa - cred roots.
A5 A7(no3rd) A5 G A5 A7(no3rd) A5 G
I'll hold what you have to give me but I'll use what I have to use.

Chorus

Quarter-time feel

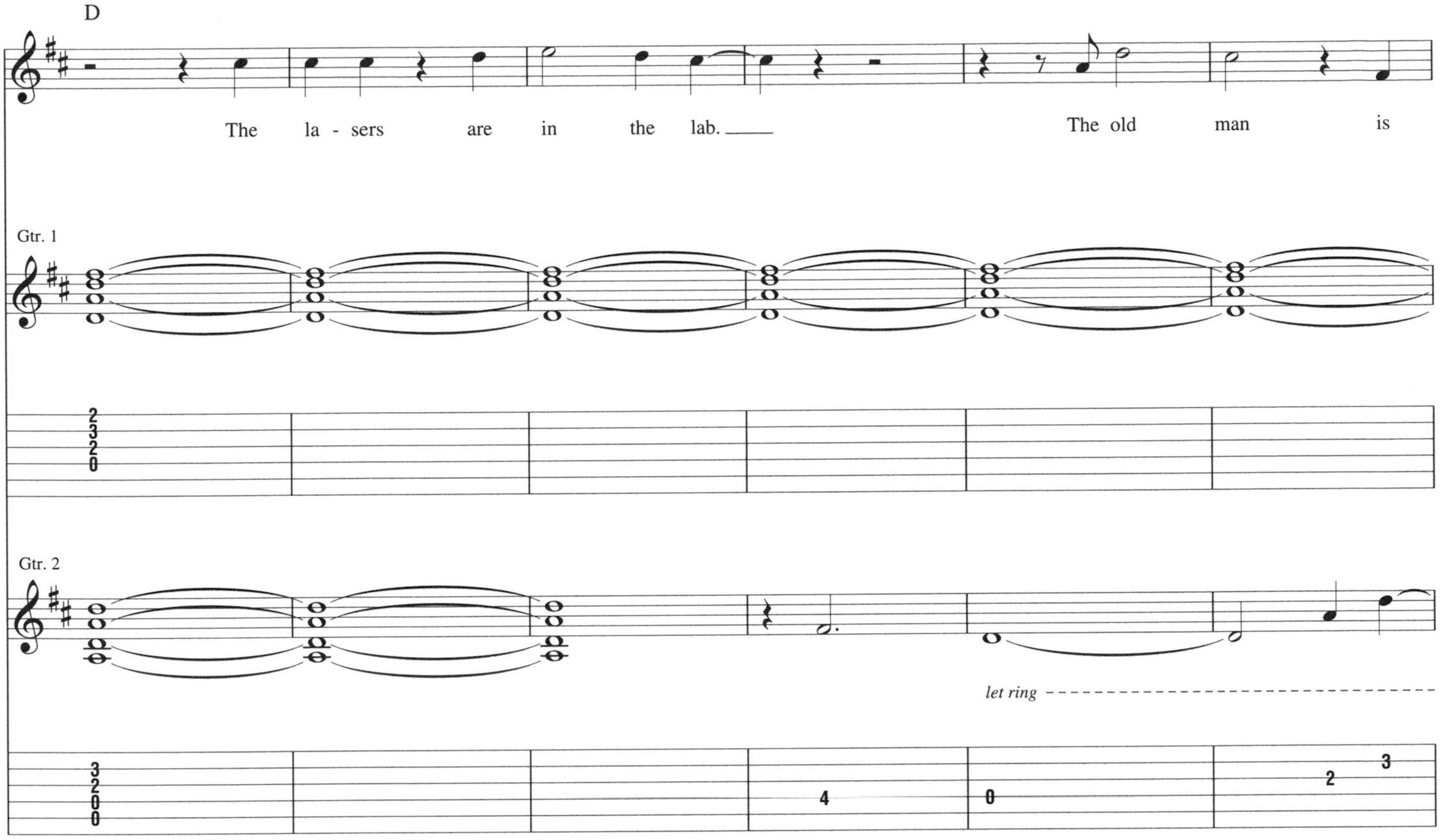

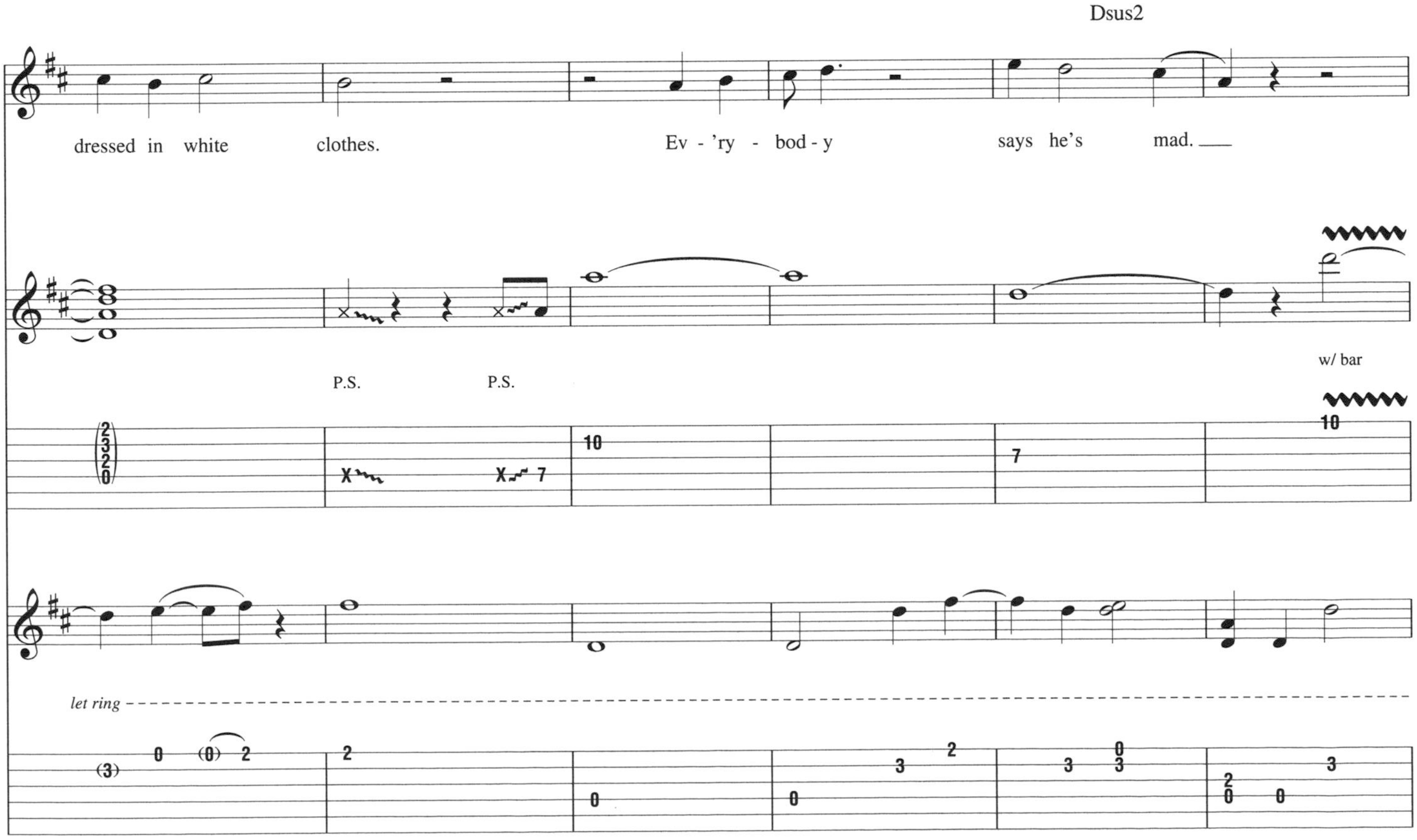

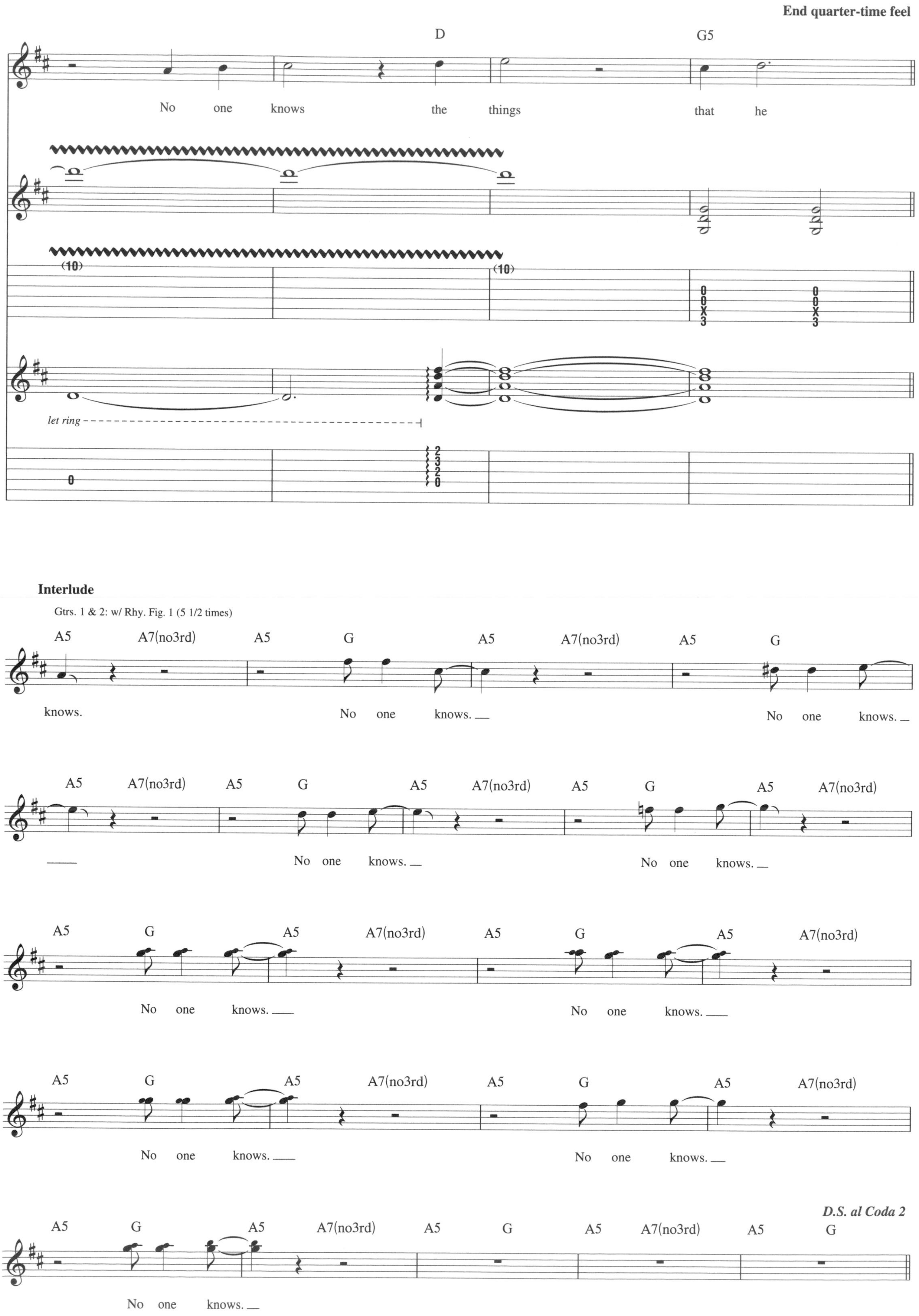
End quarter-time feel
D
G5
No one knows the things that he
let ring
Interlude
Gtrs. 1 & 2: w/ Rhy. Fig. 1 (5 1/2 times)
A5 A7(no3rd) A5 G A5 A7(no3rd) A5 G
knows. No one knows. No one knows.
A5 A7(no3rd) A5 G A5 A7(no3rd) A5 G A5 A7(no3rd)
No one knows. No one knows.
A5 G A5 A7(no3rd) A5 G A5 A7(no3rd)
No one knows. No one knows.
A5 G A5 A7(no3rd) A5 G A5 A7(no3rd)
No one knows. No one knows.
D.S. al Coda 2
A5 G A5 A7(no3rd) A5 G A5 A7(no3rd) A5 G
No one knows.

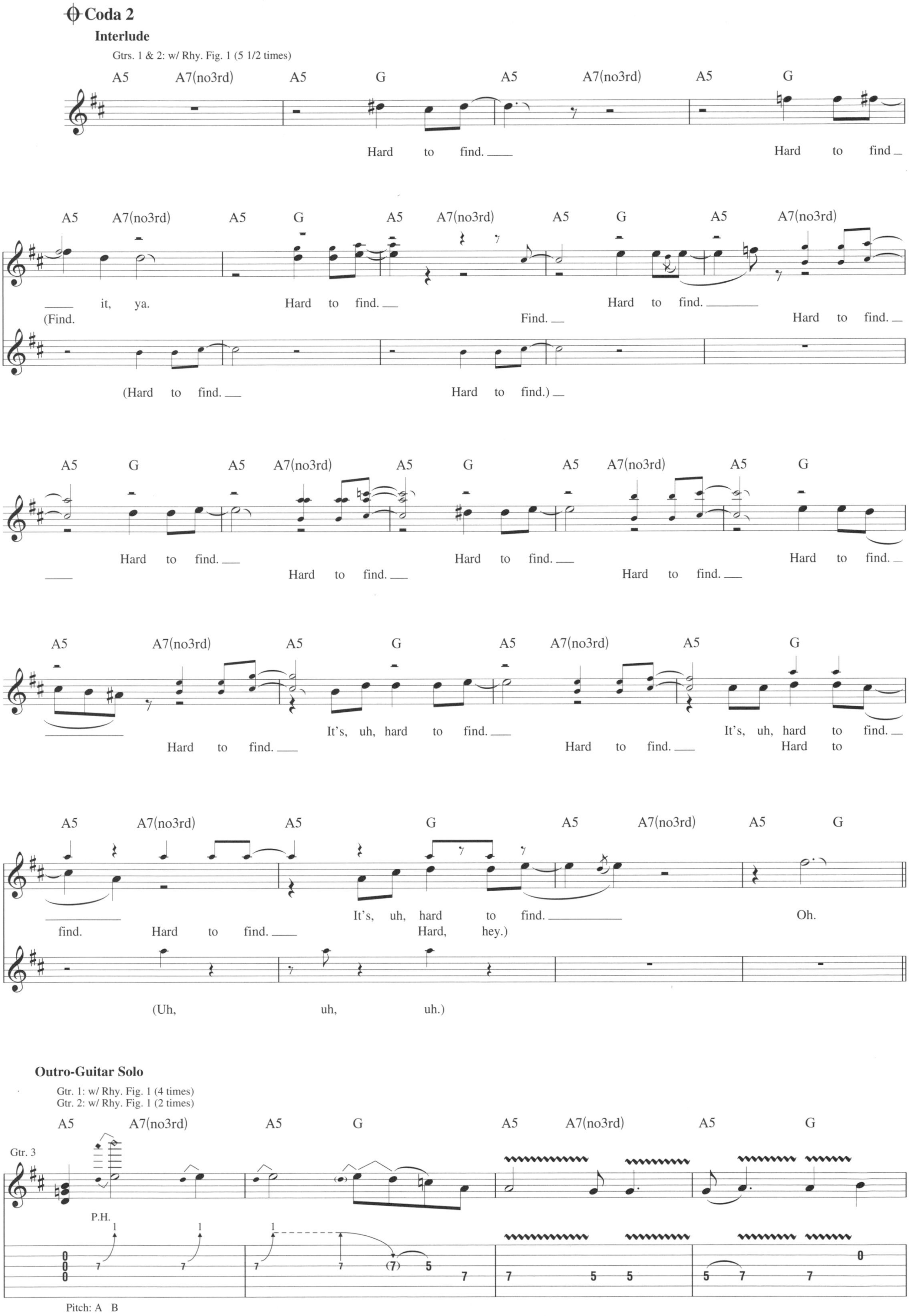
Coda 2
Interlude
Gtrs. 1 & 2: w/ Rhy. Fig. 1 (5 1/2 times)
A5 A7(no3rd) A5 G A5 A7(no3rd) A5 G
Hard to find. Hard to find
it, ya. Hard to find. Hard to find.
(Find. Find. Hard to find.
(Hard to find. Hard to find.)
Hard to find. Hard to find. Hard to find.
Hard to find. Hard to find.
It's, uh, hard to find. It's, uh, hard to find.
Hard to find. Hard to find. Hard to
It's, uh, hard to find. Oh.
find. Hard to find. Hard, hey.)
(Uh, uh, uh.)
Outro-Guitar Solo
Gtr. 1: w/ Rhy. Fig. 1 (4 times)
Gtr. 2: w/ Rhy. Fig. 1 (2 times)
Gtr. 3
P.H.
Pitch: A B

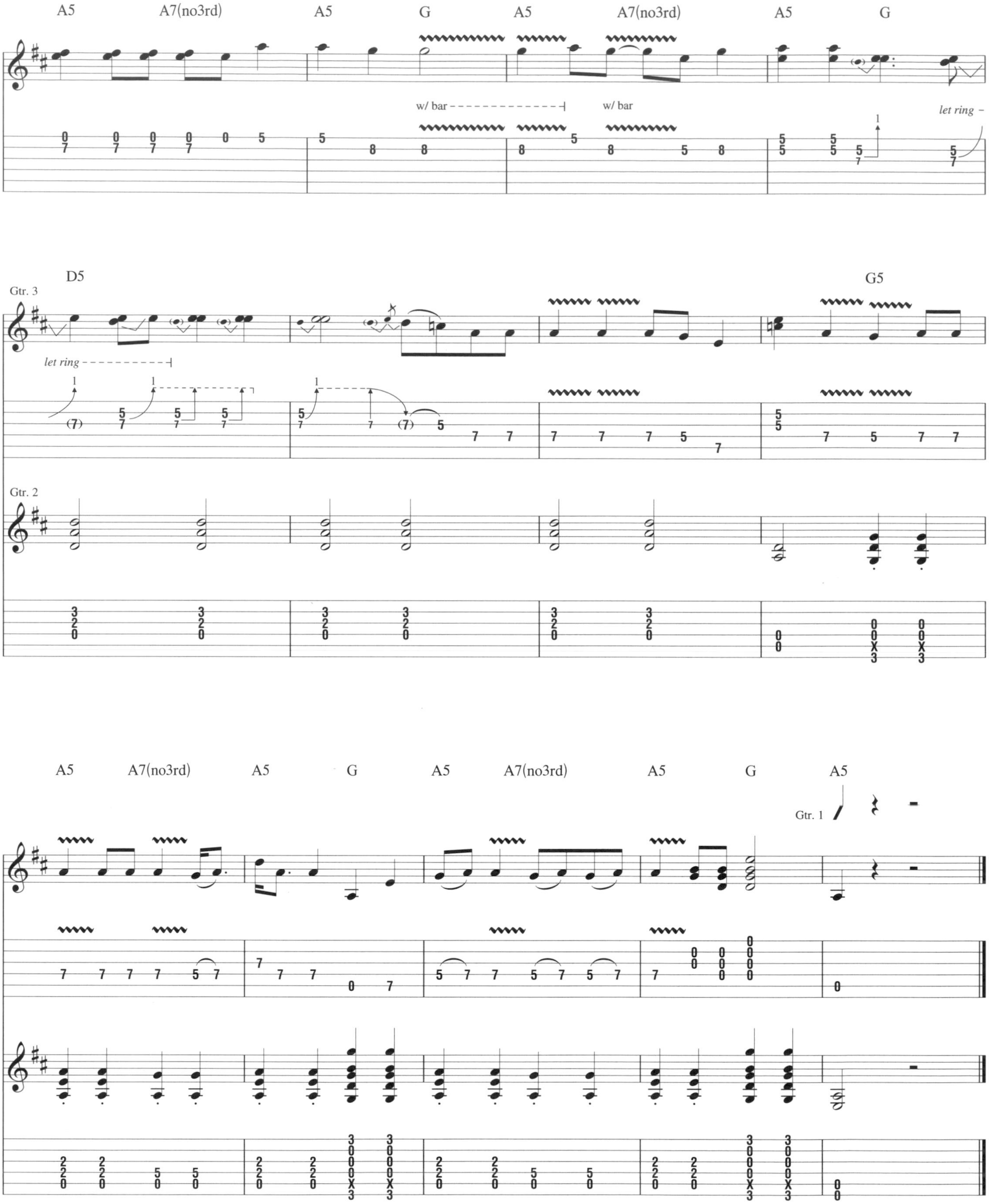

Additional Lyrics

5. I'm sleeping in every hallway.
   I just can't accept the stares.
   I'm using too many covers.
   I'm warm there, so I don't care.

Chorus I'm thinking of no one in my mind.
Sedan delivery is a job I know I'll keep.
It sure was hard to find.

HEY HEY, MY MY (INTO THE BLACK)

Words and Music by Neil Young

Hey hey, my my
Rock and roll can never die
There's more to the picture
Than meets the eye
Hey hey, my my

Out of the blue and into the black
You pay for this, but they give you that
And once you're gone, you can't come back
When you're out of the blue
And into the black

The king is gone but he's not forgotten
Is this the story of Johnny Rotten?
It's better to burn out 'cause rust never sleeps
The king is gone but he's not forgotten

Hey hey, my my
Rock and roll can never die
There's more to the picture
Than meets the eye

Hey Hey, My My
(Into the Black)

Words and Music by Neil Young

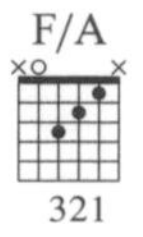

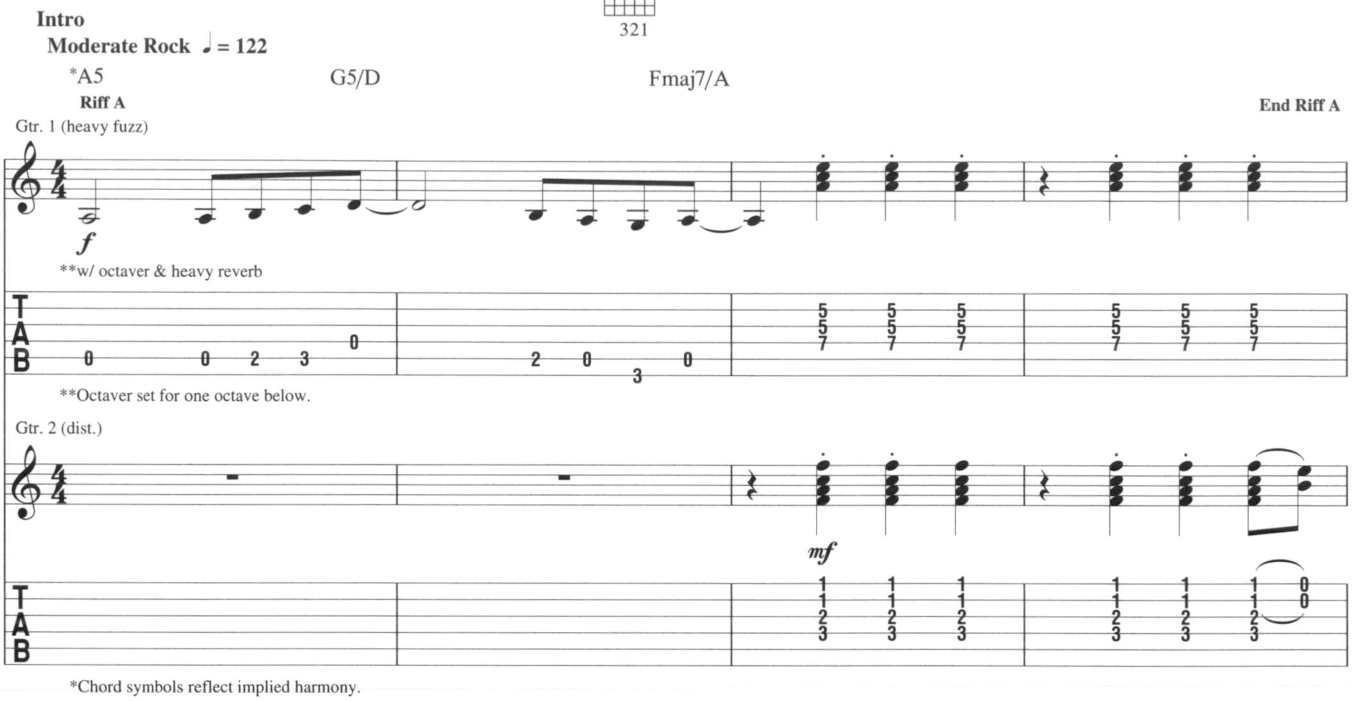

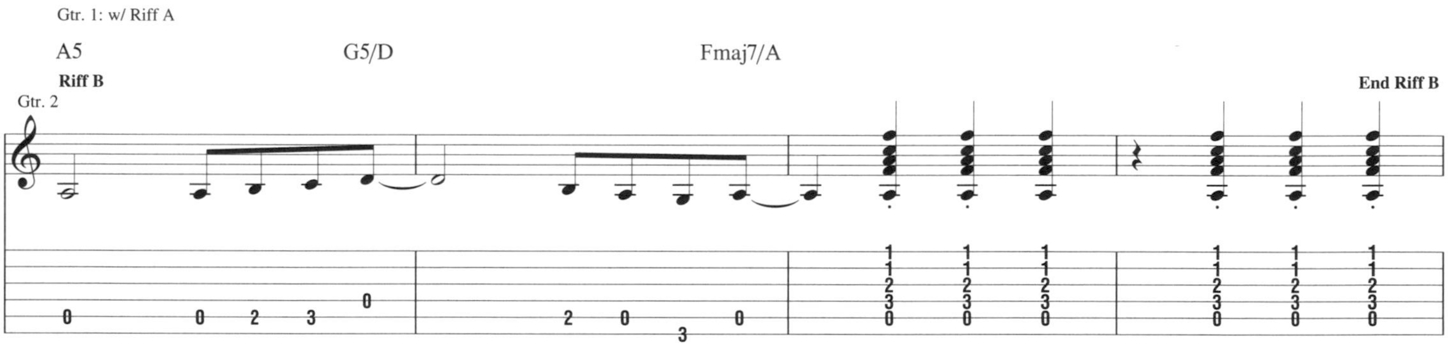

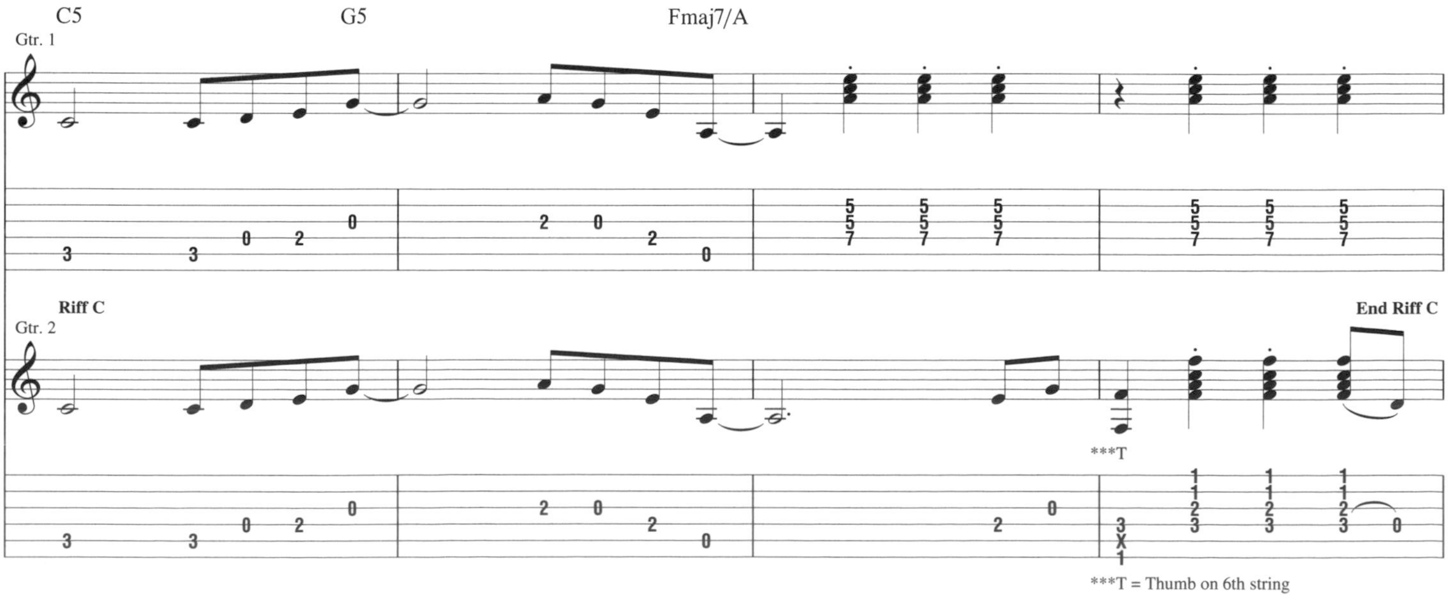

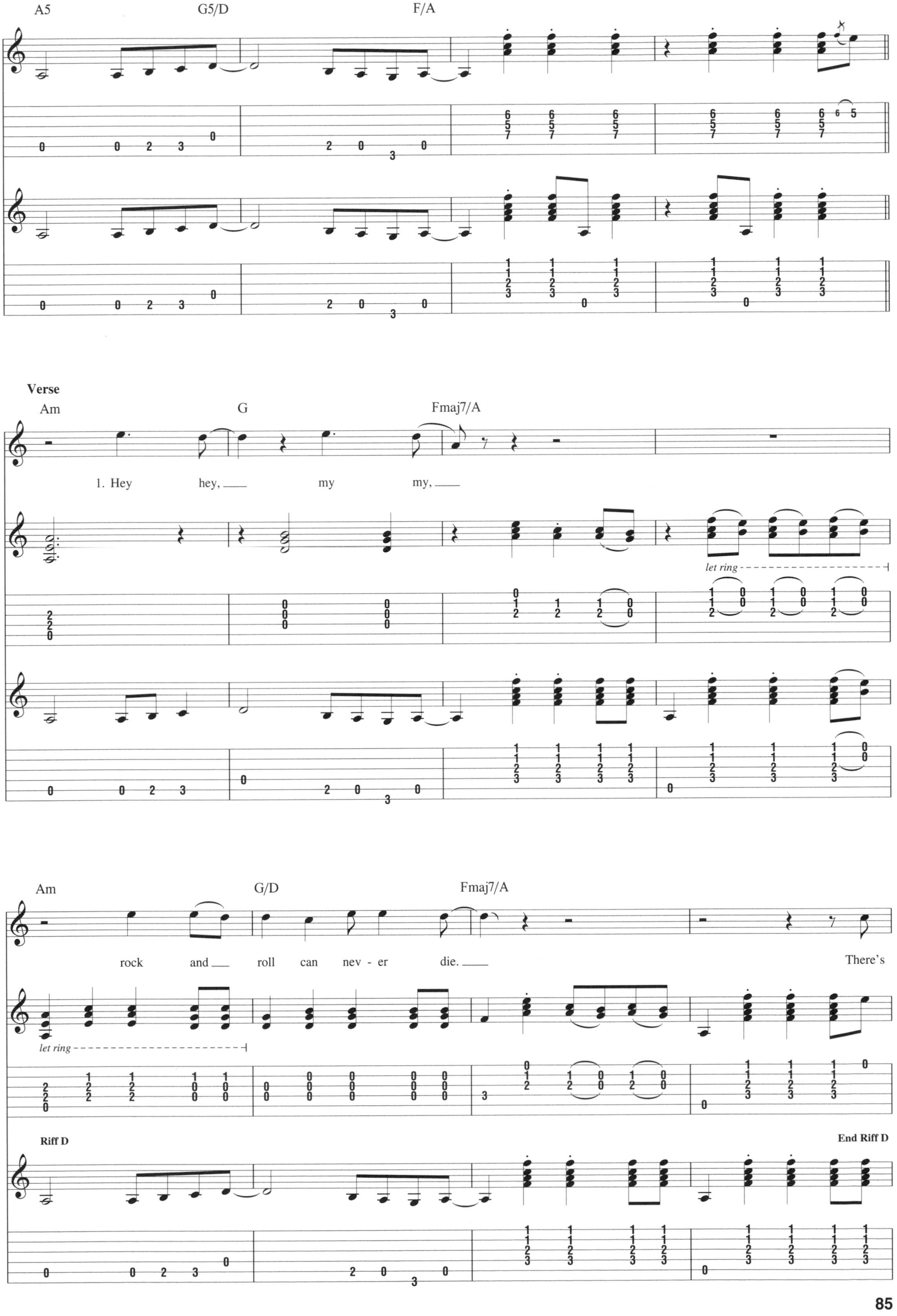
A5
G5/D
F/A
Verse
Am
G
Fmaj7/A
1. Hey hey, my my,
let ring
Am
G/D
Fmaj7/A
rock and roll can nev - er die.
There's
let ring
Riff D
End Riff D

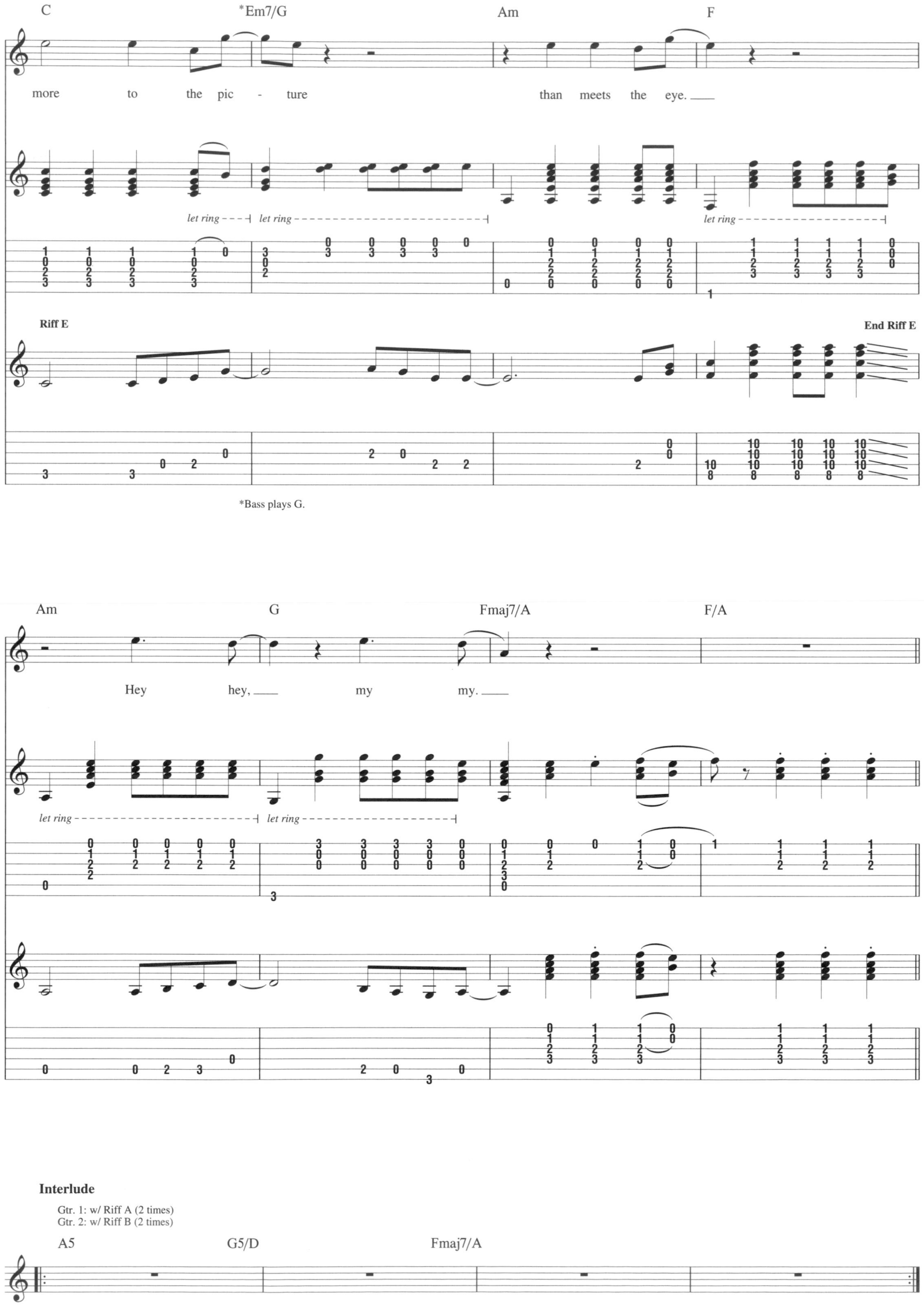
C
*Em7/G
Am
F
more to the pic - ture
than meets the eye.
let ring
Riff E
End Riff E
*Bass plays G.
Am
G
Fmaj7/A
F/A
Hey hey,
my my.
Interlude
Gtr. 1: w/ Riff A (2 times)
Gtr. 2: w/ Riff B (2 times)
A5
G5/D
Fmaj7/A

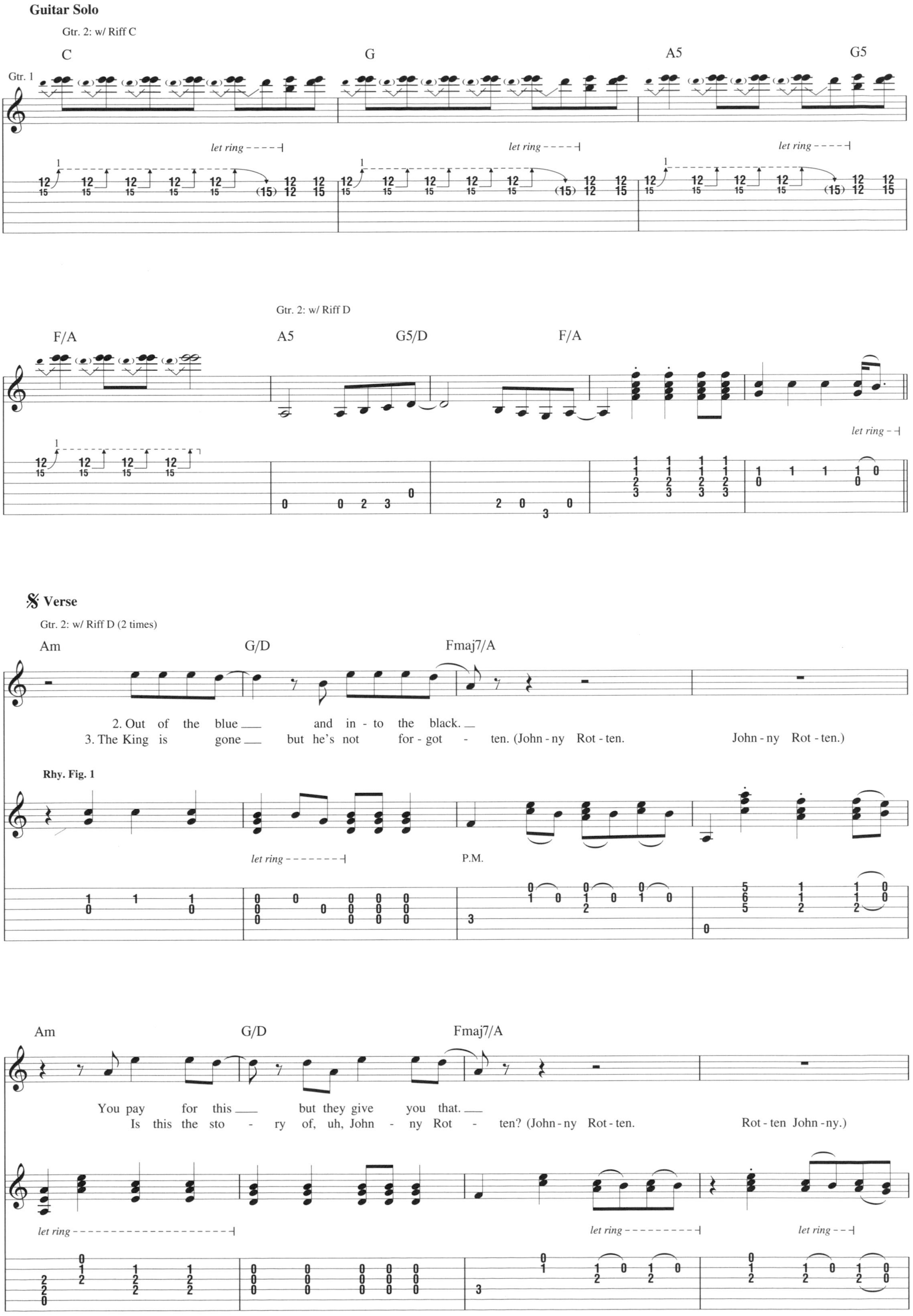
Guitar Solo
Gtr. 2: w/ Riff C
C
G
A5
G5
Gtr. 1
let ring
F/A
Gtr. 2: w/ Riff D
A5
G5/D
F/A
Verse
Gtr. 2: w/ Riff D (2 times)
Am
G/D
Fmaj7/A
2. Out of the blue and in - to the black.
3. The King is gone but he's not for - got - ten. (John - ny Rot - ten. John - ny Rot - ten.)
Rhy. Fig. 1
P.M.
You pay for this but they give you that.
Is this the sto - ry of, uh, John - ny Rot - ten? (John - ny Rot - ten. Rot - ten John - ny.)

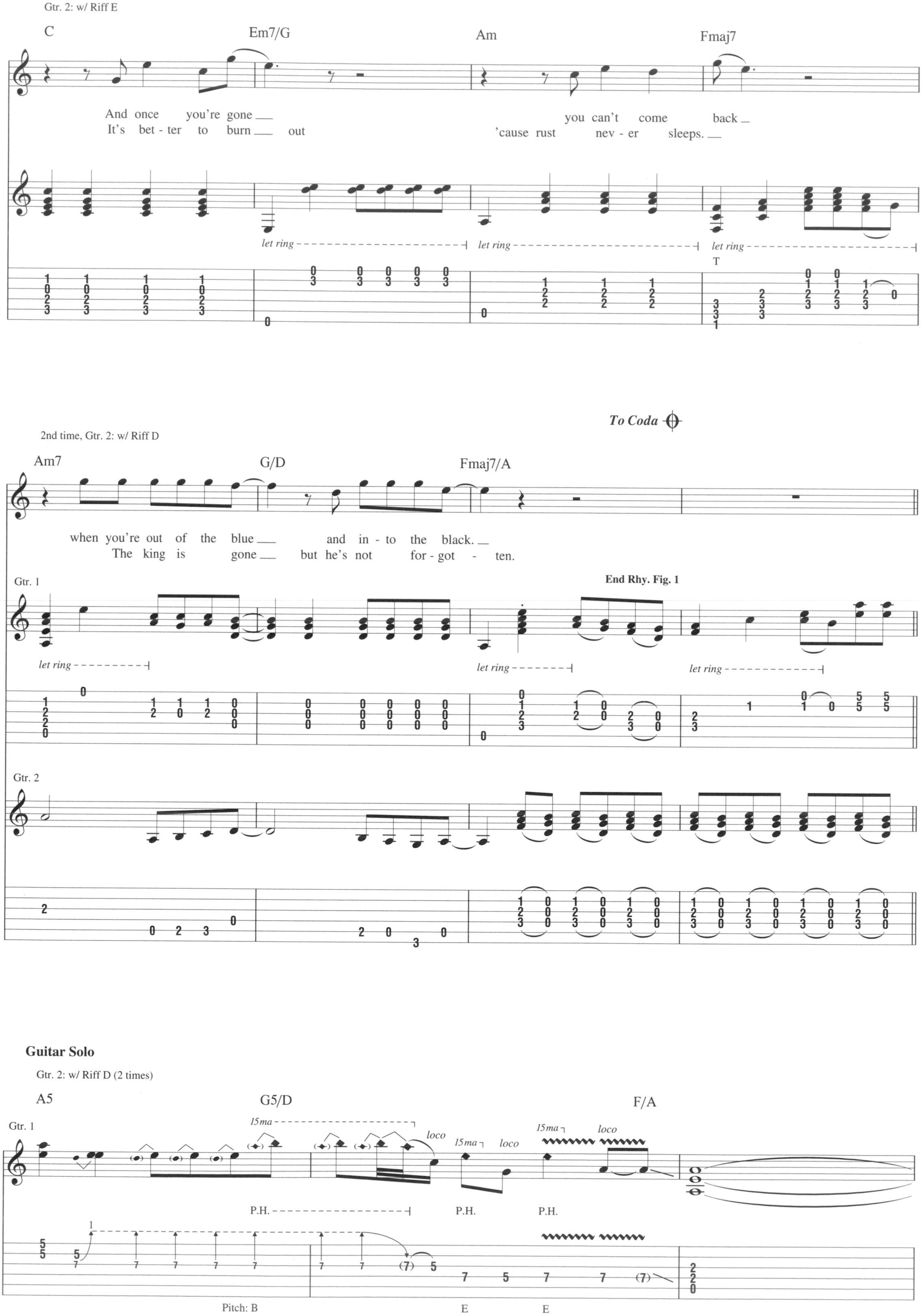
Gtr. 2: w/ Riff E
C
Em7/G
Am
Fmaj7
And once you're gone
you can't come back
It's bet - ter to burn out
'cause rust nev - er sleeps.
let ring
T
2nd time, Gtr. 2: w/ Riff D
To Coda
Am7
G/D
Fmaj7/A
when you're out of the blue
and in - to the black.
The king is gone
but he's not for - got - ten.
Gtr. 1
End Rhy. Fig. 1
Gtr. 2
Guitar Solo
Gtr. 2: w/ Riff D (2 times)
A5
G5/D
F/A
15ma
loco
P.H.
Pitch: B
E

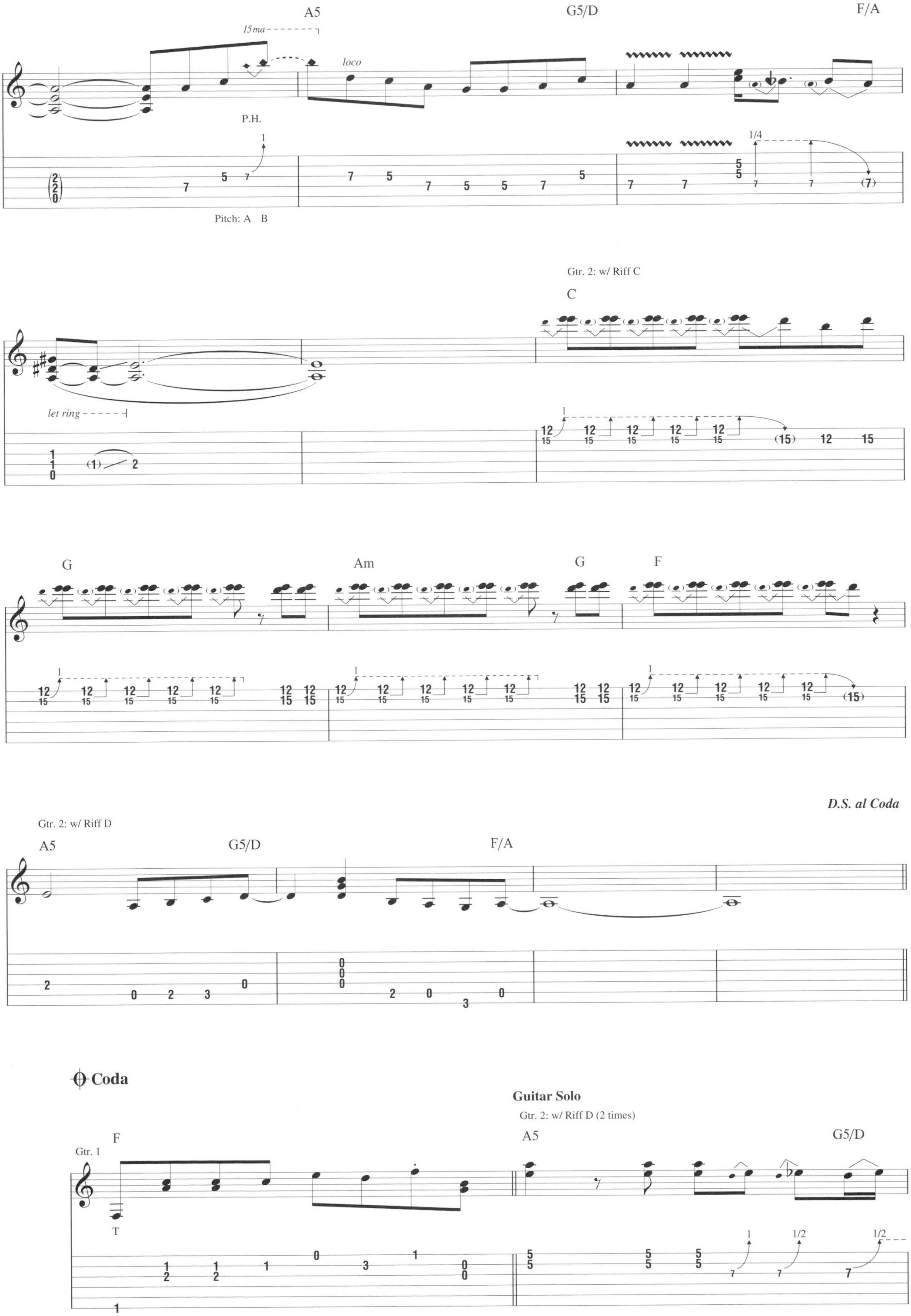
A5
G5/D
F/A
15ma
loco
P.H.
1
1/4
Pitch: A B
Gtr. 2: w/ Riff C
C
let ring
G
Am
G
F
D.S. al Coda
Gtr. 2: w/ Riff D
A5
G5/D
F/A
Coda
Guitar Solo
Gtr. 2: w/ Riff D (2 times)
F
Gtr. 1
A5
G5/D
T
1/2

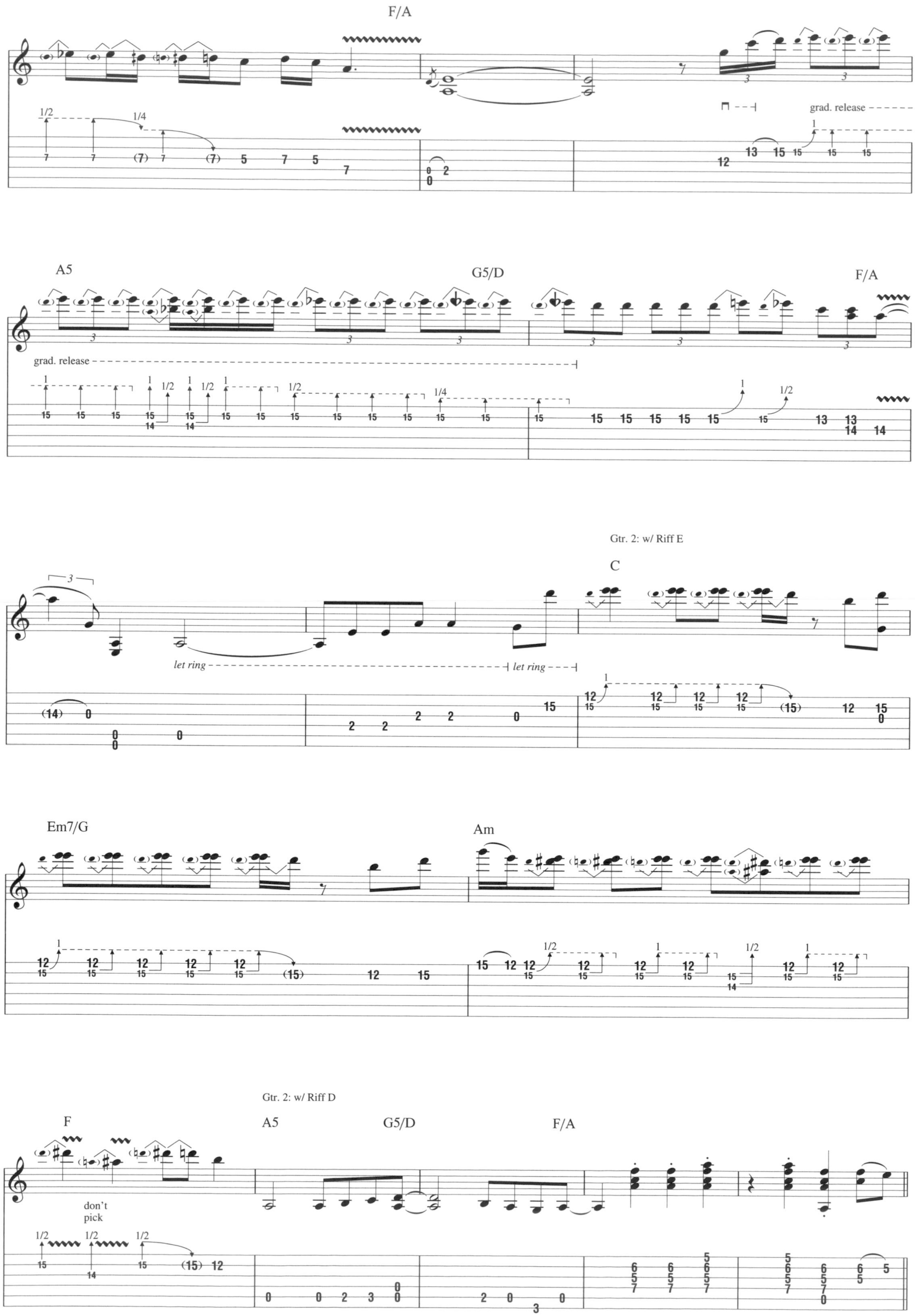
F/A
grad. release
A5
G5/D
F/A
grad. release
Gtr. 2: w/ Riff E
C
let ring
let ring
Em7/G
Am
Gtr. 2: w/ Riff D
F
A5
G5/D
F/A
don't pick

Verse

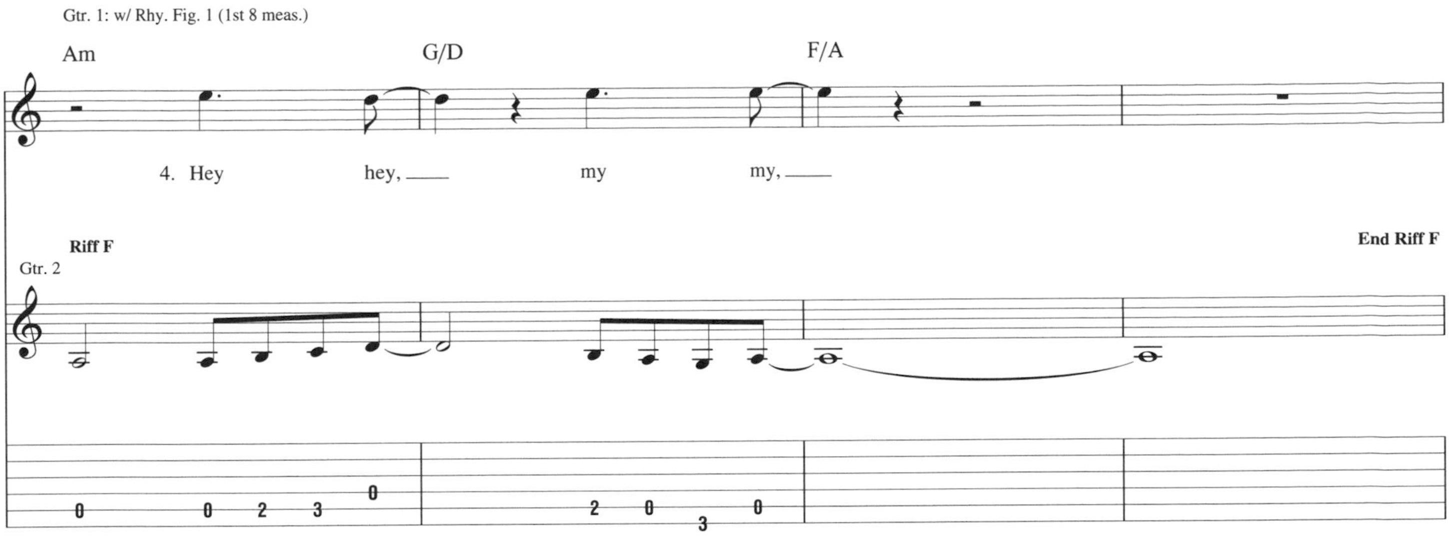

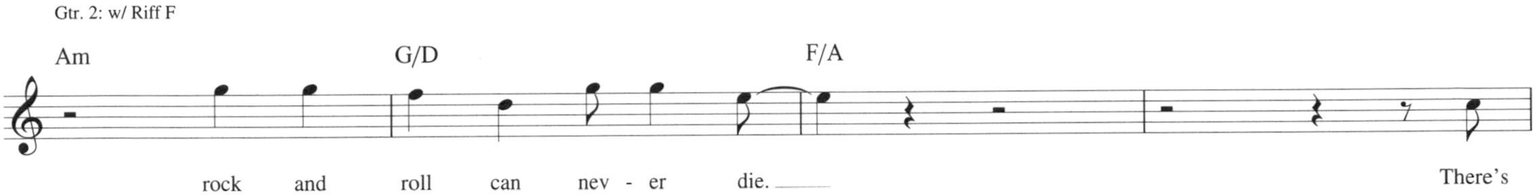

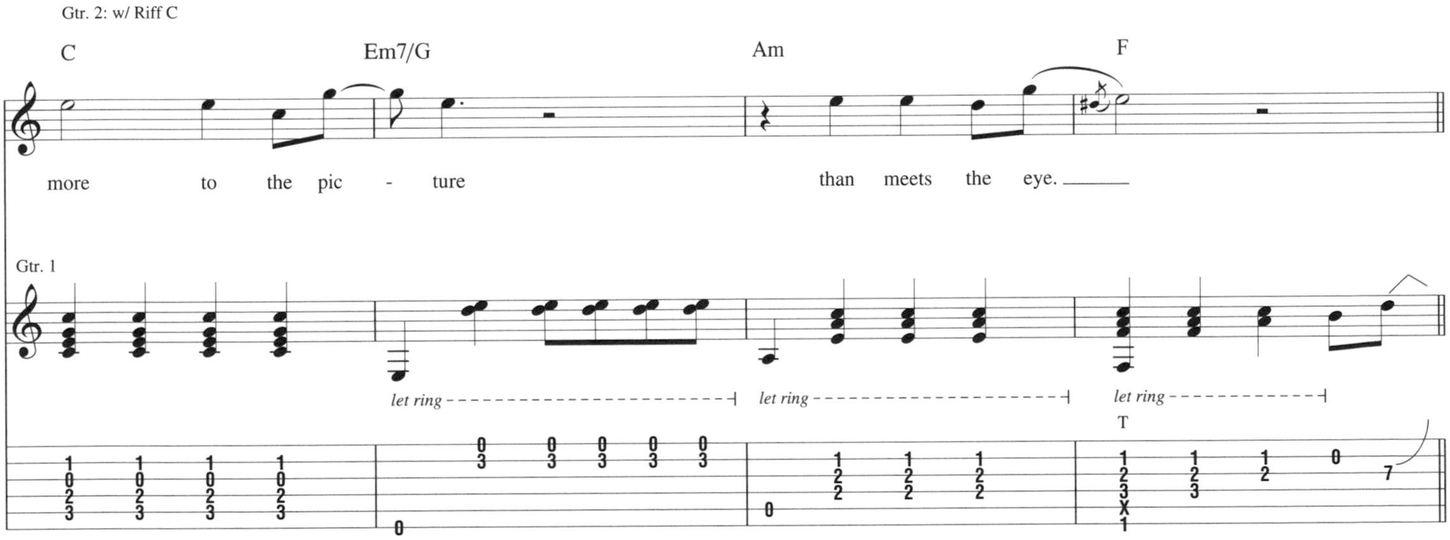

Guitar Solo

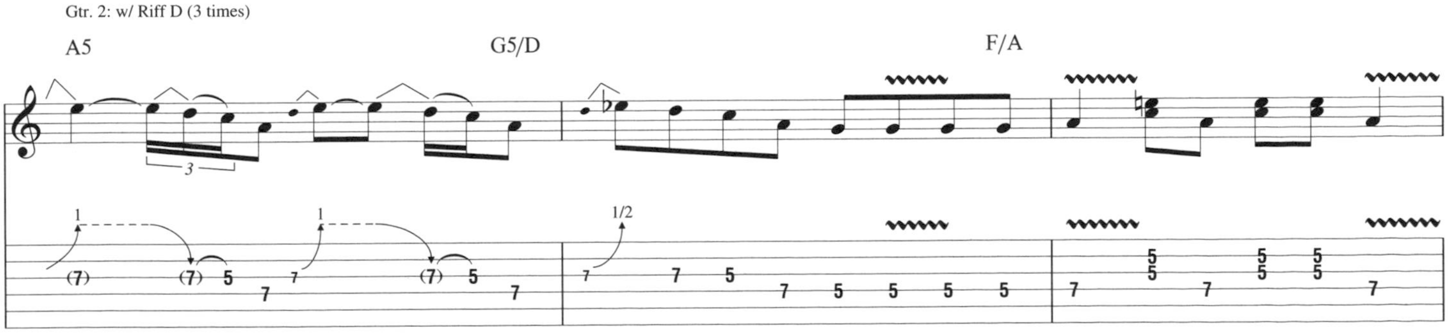

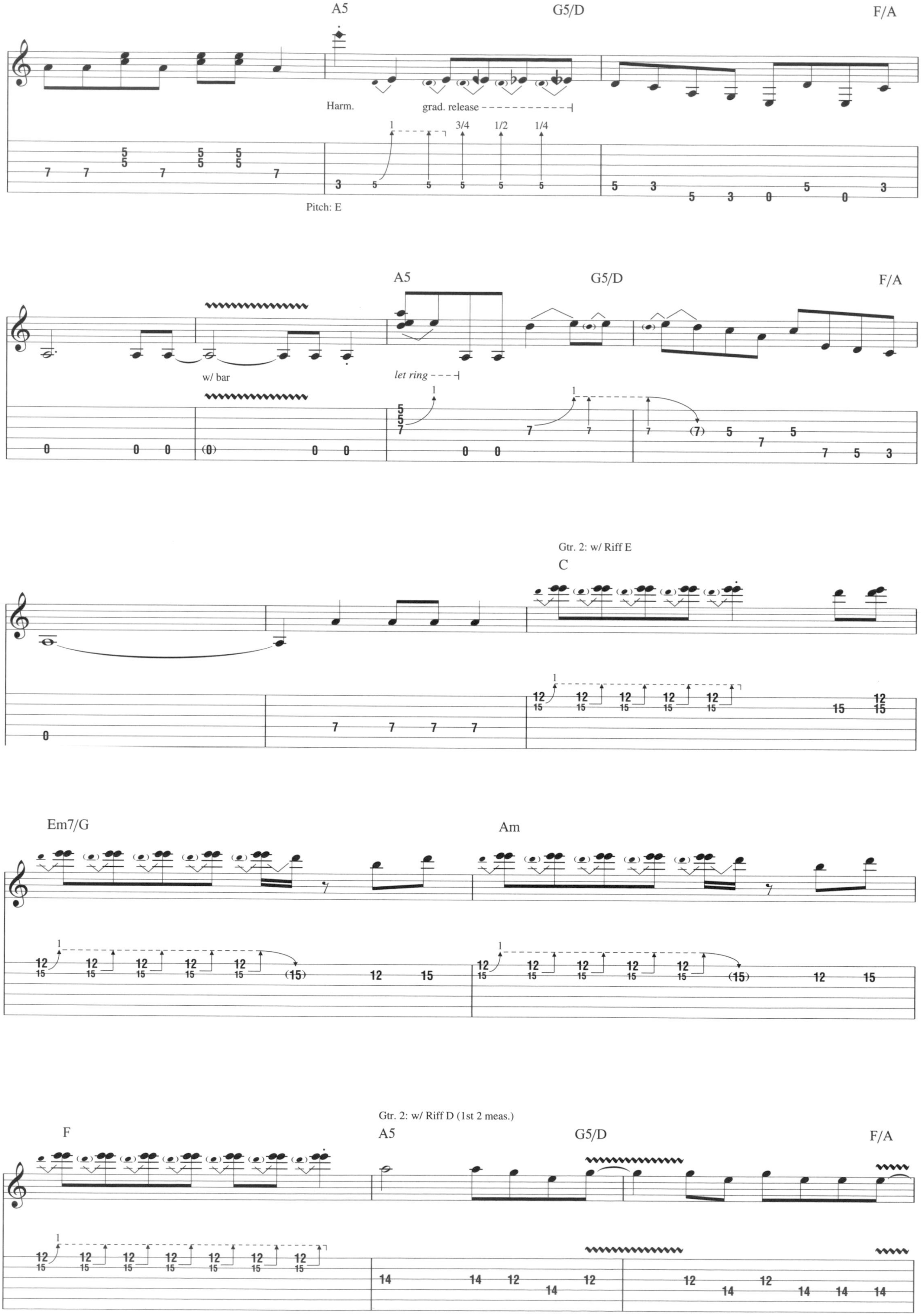
A5
G5/D
F/A
Harm.
grad. release
1
3/4
1/2
1/4
Pitch: E
A5
G5/D
F/A
w/ bar
let ring
Gtr. 2: w/ Riff E
C
Em7/G
Am
F
Gtr. 2: w/ Riff D (1st 2 meas.)
A5
G5/D
F/A

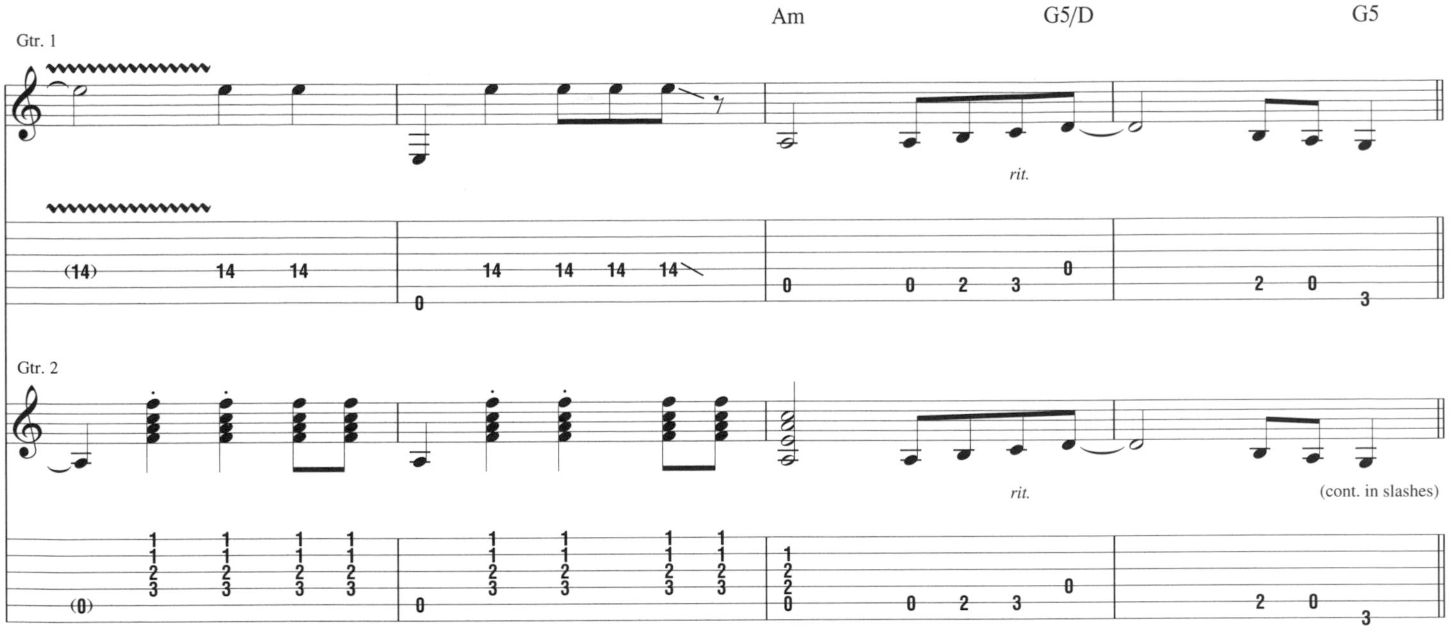

Outro

Free time

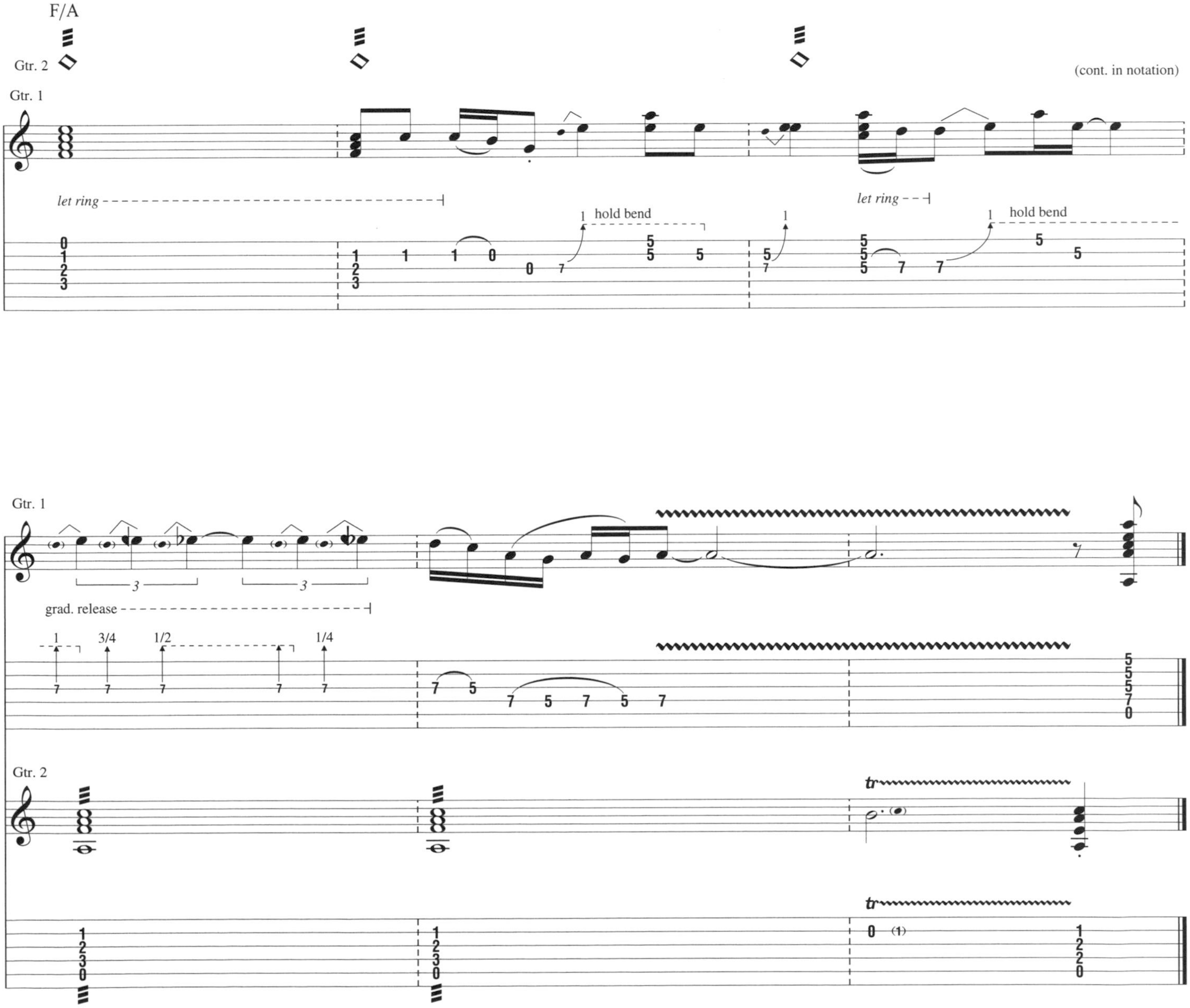

MY MY, HEY HEY (OUT OF THE BLUE)
THRASHER
RIDE MY LLAMA
POCAHONTAS
SAIL AWAY*
POWDERFINGER
WELFARE MOTHERS
SEDAN DELIVERY
HEY HEY, MY MY (INTO THE BLACK)

NEIL YOUNG & CRAZY HORSE:
NEIL YOUNG: GUITAR, VOCAL
FRANK SAMPEDRO: GUITAR, STRINGMAN, VOCAL
BILLY TALBOT: BASS, VOCAL
RALPH MOLINA: DRUMS, VOCAL

*NEIL YOUNG & THE GONE WITH THE WIND ORCHESTRA:
NEIL YOUNG: GUITAR, VOCAL
NICOLETTE LARSON: VOCAL
KARL T. HIMMEL: DRUMS
JOE OSBORNE: BASS
ET AL.

WORDS AND MUSIC BY NEIL YOUNG
PUBLISHED BY SILVER FIDDLE MUSIC (ASCAP)
EXCEPT - MY MY HEY HEY (OUT OF THE BLUE)
WORDS AND MUSIC BY NEIL YOUNG & JEFF BLACKBURN
PUBLISHED BY SILVER FIDDLE MUSIC (ASCAP)

PRODUCED BY NEIL YOUNG,
DAVID BRIGGS AND TIM MULLIGAN

PHOTOGRAPHY:
FRONT COVER BY PEGI YOUNG
BACK COVER BY LARRY CRAGG
ALL INSIDE PHOTOGRAPHY BY JOEL BERNSTEIN

SONGBOOK ART DIRECTION & DESIGN
BY GARY BURDEN AND JENICE HEO FOR R. TWERK & CO.

SONGBOOK DESIGN
BY JESSE BURDEN FOR R. TWERK & CO.

Guitar Notation Legend

THE MUSICAL STAFF shows pitches and rhythms and is divided by bar lines into measures. Pitches are named after the first seven letters of the alphabet.

TABLATURE graphically represents the guitar fingerboard. Each horizontal line represents a string, and each number represents a fret.

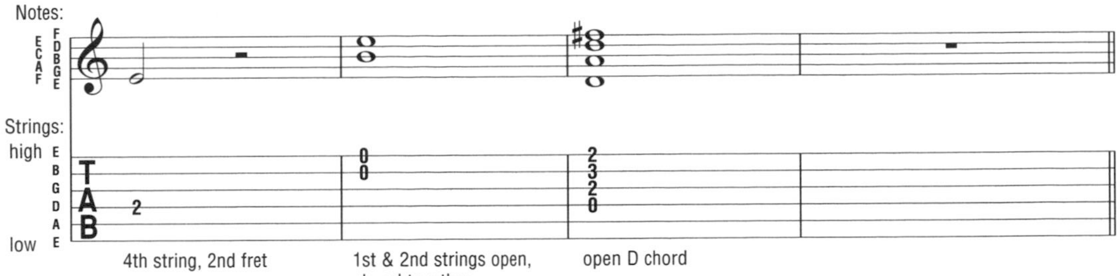

HALF-STEP BEND: Strike the note and bend up 1/2 step.

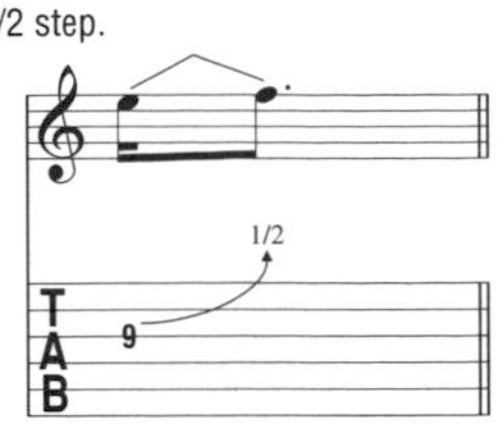

WHOLE-STEP BEND: Strike the note and bend up one step.

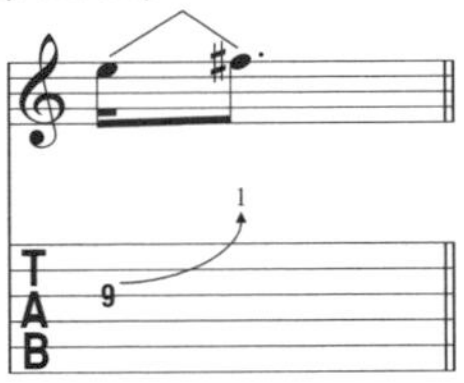

GRACE NOTE BEND: Strike the note and immediately bend up as indicated.

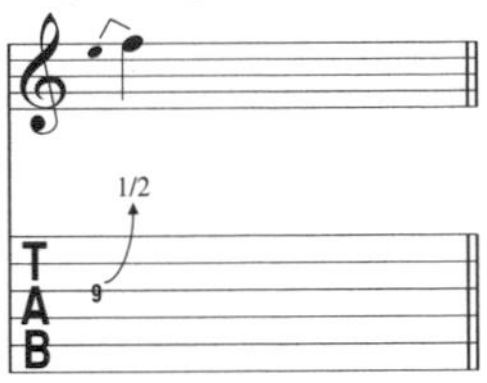

SLIGHT (MICROTONE) BEND: Strike the note and bend up 1/4 step.

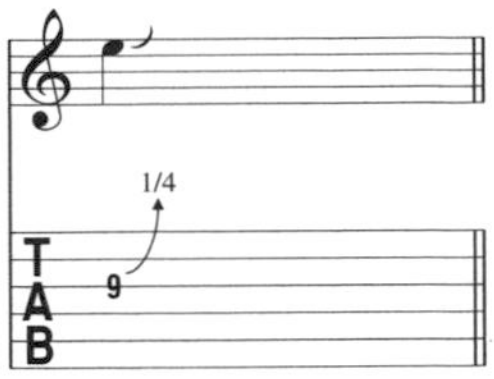

BEND AND RELEASE: Strike the note and bend up as indicated, then release back to the original note. Only the first note is struck.

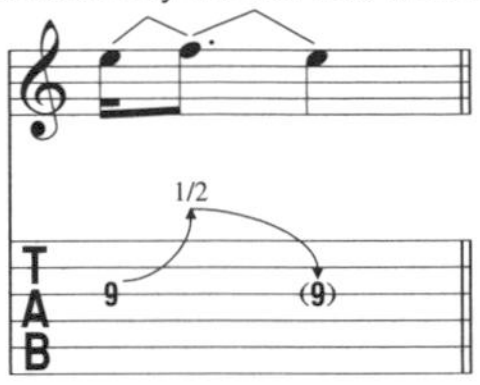

PRE-BEND: Bend the note as indicated, then strike it.

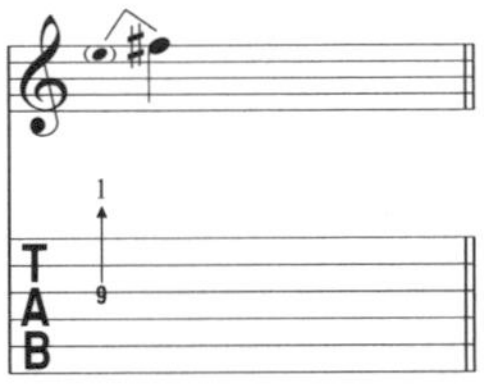

VIBRATO: The string is vibrated by rapidly bending and releasing the note with the fretting hand.

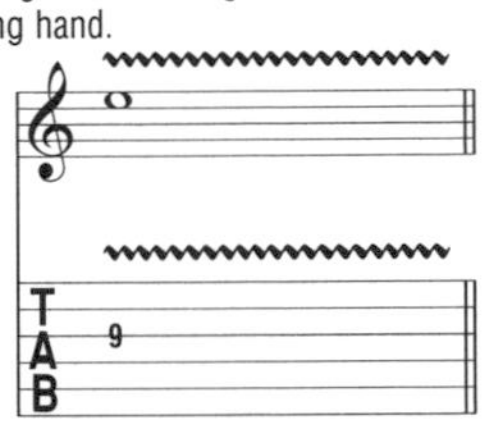

PALM MUTING: The note is partially muted by the pick hand lightly touching the string(s) just before the bridge.

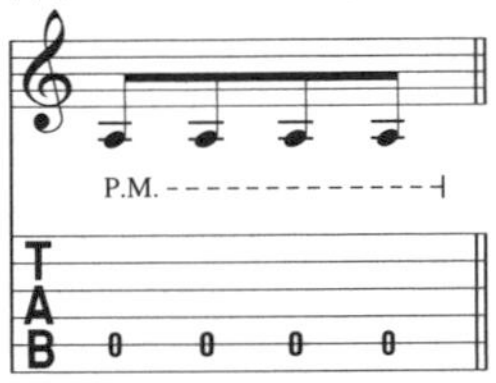

HAMMER-ON: Strike the first (lower) note with one finger, then sound the higher note (on the same string) with another finger by fretting it without picking.

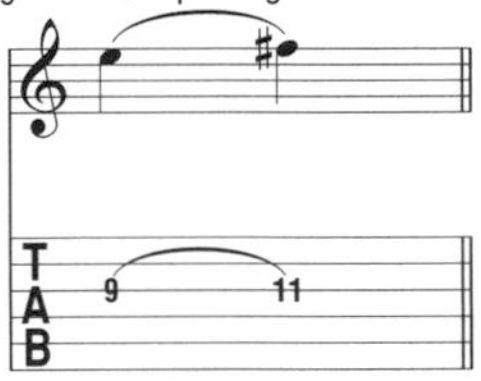

PULL-OFF: Place both fingers on the notes to be sounded. Strike the first note and without picking, pull the finger off to sound the second (lower) note.

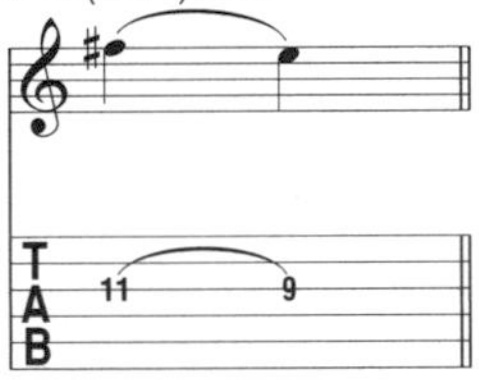

LEGATO SLIDE: Strike the first note and then slide the same fret-hand finger up or down to the second note. The second note is not struck.

SHIFT SLIDE: Same as legato slide, except the second note is struck.

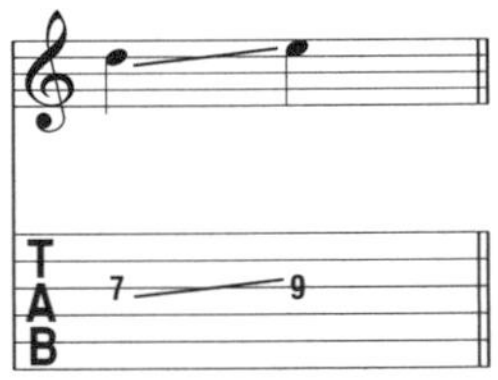

TRILL: Very rapidly alternate between the notes indicated by continuously hammering on and pulling off.

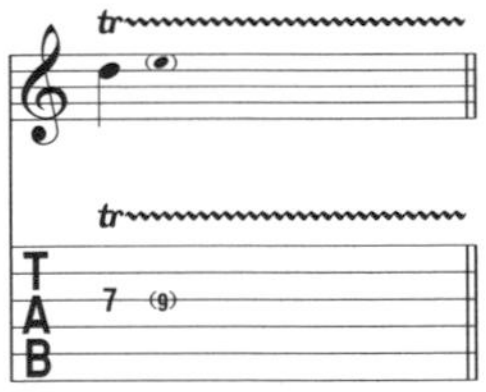

TAPPING: Hammer ("tap") the fret indicated with the pick-hand index or middle finger and pull off to the note fretted by the fret hand.

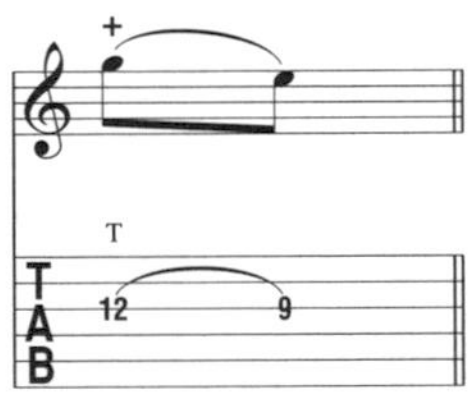

NATURAL HARMONIC: Strike the note while the fret-hand lightly touches the string directly over the fret indicated.

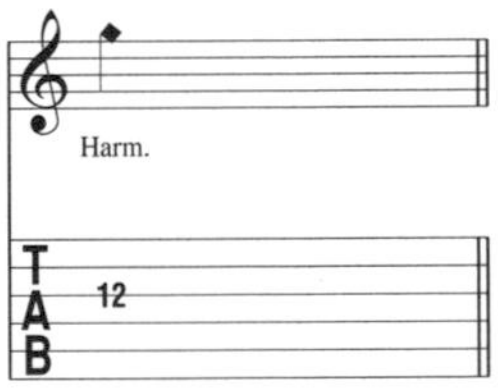

PINCH HARMONIC: The note is fretted normally and a harmonic is produced by adding the edge of the thumb or the tip of the index finger of the pick hand to the normal pick attack.

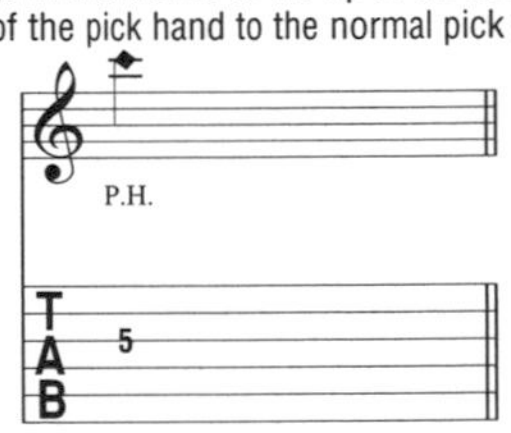

TREMOLO PICKING: The note is picked as rapidly and continuously as possible.

VIBRATO BAR DIVE AND RETURN: The pitch of the note or chord is dropped a specified number of steps (in rhythm), then returned to the original pitch.

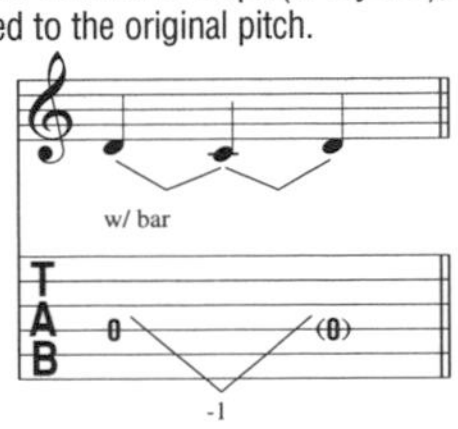

VIBRATO BAR SCOOP: Depress the bar just before striking the note, then quickly release the bar.

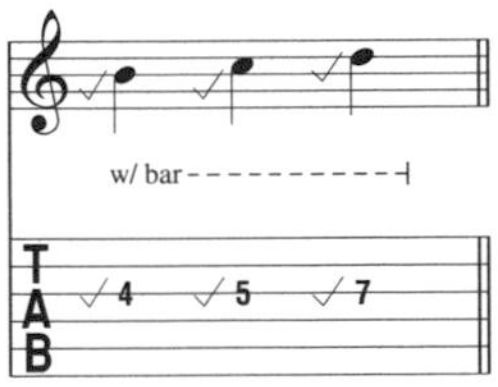

VIBRATO BAR DIP: Strike the note and then immediately drop a specified number of steps, then release back to the original pitch.

Additional Musical Definitions

 *(accent)* • Accentuate note (play it louder).

 *(staccato)* • Play the note short.

D.S. al Coda • Go back to the sign (𝄋), then play until the measure marked "***To Coda***," then skip to the section labelled "**Coda**."

D.C. al Fine • Go back to the beginning of the song and play until the measure marked "***Fine***" (end).

Fill • Label used to identify a brief melodic figure which is to be inserted into the arrangement.

N.C. • Harmony is implied.

 • Repeat measures between signs.

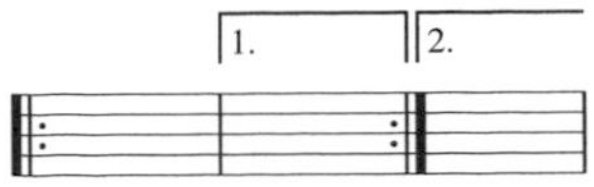

• When a repeated section has different endings, play the first ending only the first time and the second ending only the second time.

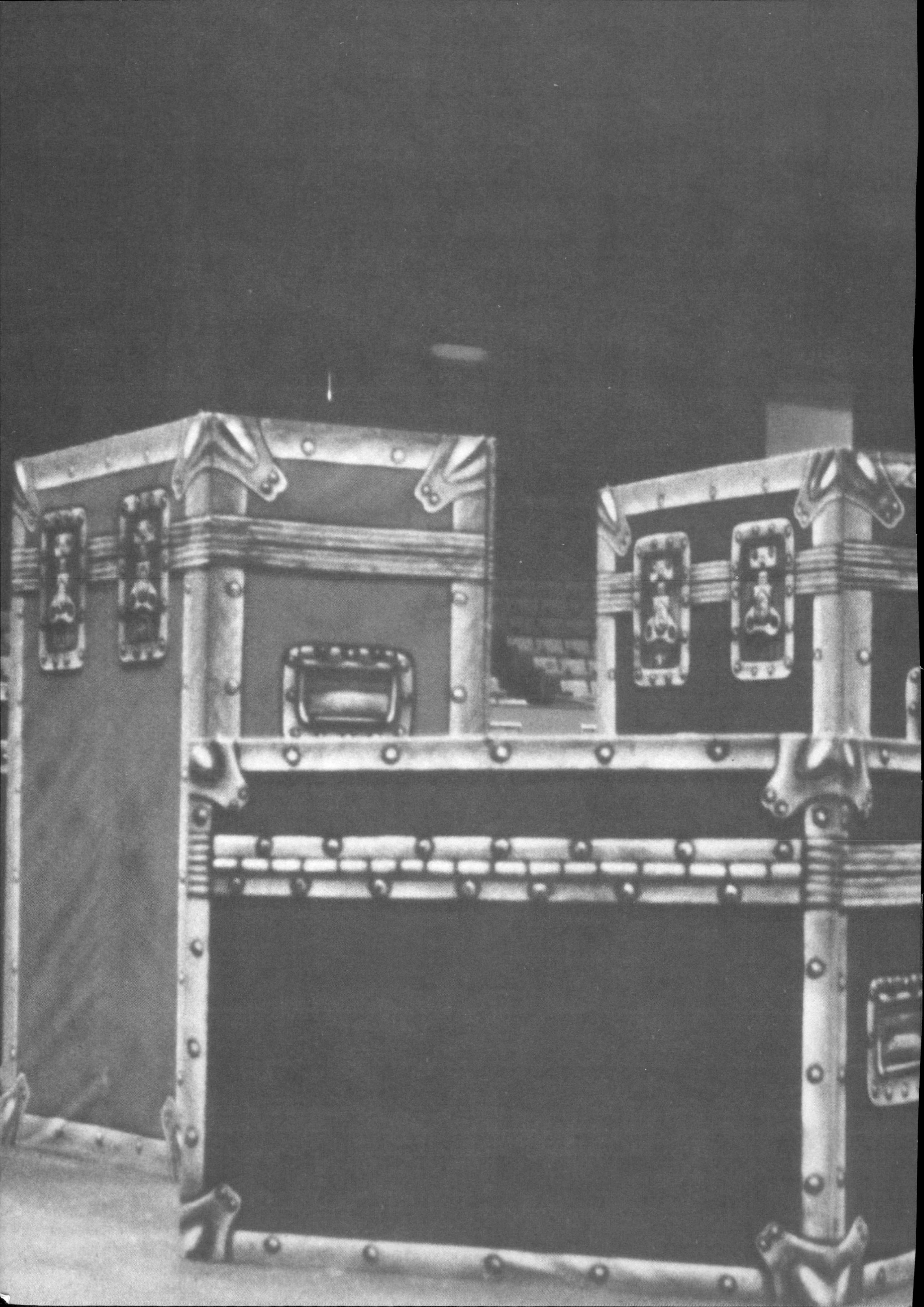